A Genesis Journal

A Fresh Reading of Genesis 1-12

Stanley V. Udd

WESTBOW
PRESS
A DIVISION OF THOMAS NELSON
& ZONDERVAN

WestBow Press books may be ordered through booksellers or by contacting:

WestBow Press
A Division of Thomas Nelson & Zondervan
1663 Liberty Drive
Bloomington, IN 47403
www.westbowpress.com
1 (866) 928-1240

Because of the dynamic nature of the Internet, any web addresses or
links contained in this book may have changed since publication and
may no longer be valid. The views expressed in this work are solely those
of the author and do not necessarily reflect the views of the publisher,
and the publisher hereby disclaims any responsibility for them.

Any people depicted in stock imagery provided by Thinkstock are models,
and such images are being used for illustrative purposes only.
Certain stock imagery © Thinkstock.

ISBN: 978-1-4908-6557-7 (sc)
ISBN: 978-1-4908-6558-4 (hc)
ISBN: 978-1-4908-6556-0 (e)

Library of Congress Control Number: 2015900260

Print information available on the last page.

WestBow Press rev. date: 3/4/2015

Contents

Preface vii

Foreword ix

Introduction xi

1   Presuppositions 1
2   Genesis 1: Day One 16
3   Genesis 1: Days Two and Three 37
4   Genesis 1: Day Four 52
5   Genesis 1: Days Five and Six 60
6   An Excursus on the Image of God 74
7   Genesis 2: Day Seven... 82
8   Genesis 2: The Early Earth 91
9   Genesis 2: God's Special Creation 100
10 Genesis 3: The Fall into Sin....................................109
11 A Note on the Fall of Satan....................................132
12 Genesis 4: Life on the Early Earth 136
13 Genesis 5 and 11:10-26: The Genealogies.................149
14 Genesis 6: God Changes His Mind...........................161
15 Genesis 7: The Mabbûl 177
16 Genesis 8: God Rescues Noah 188
17 Genesis 9: A New Dispensation............................... 202
18 Genesis 10 and 11: The Babel Dispersion 217
19 Genesis 12: The Master Plan 233

Appendix A: Alternative Views on Genesis 1:1 241
Appendix B: Chart of the Year in the Ark........................ 248
Index 249

Preface

The world that God created for us to enjoy has always been a source of wonder and amazement to me. My undergraduate and master's degrees were in the biological sciences. Then God drew me in another direction and I was introduced to the world of the Bible through the Hebrew and Greek languages. At the beginning of my teaching career in 1967 I began keeping notes on the intersection of science and the Bible.

I taught my first Hebrew grammar course on the graduate level in 1975 and have been privileged to teach this course most years since then. This year two grandsons are taking my introductory Hebrew grammar class.

Having used the book of Genesis as the reading assignment in the later stages of Hebrew grammar class, I began compiling notes on specific themes. My doctoral dissertation focused on the reality of that illusive character in the book of Job called leviathan.

This book is a collection of the notes that emerged from interaction between the original Hebrew and those students who wanted to keep the professor on "the straight and narrow." It is impressive to observe how often God intervened directly in those early years of earth history.

Unless indicated otherwise, the translation of various sections of both the Old and New Testaments are the author's personal work. These are based on the Hebrew and Greek texts. The sketches scattered throughout this work were drawn by my son Kris. I also wish to thank my son-in-law, Nathan Boeker, for his technical assistance, and Vi, my wife of fifty years, who supported this work with more than her heart.

It is my prayer that this book will stimulate the reader to pause and reflect on how great is our God!

Foreword

In a day of troubling news reports and downward trends in society, there is refreshment to be found in the Book of Genesis. Two millennia ago, the Apostle Paul recognized the significance of Genesis as he addressed the leading philosophers in Athens. These Greek scholars had considerable science knowledge but completely lacked wisdom concerning the Creator of the universe. Their city was filled with idols, even so far as an altar to an unknown god, just in case needed. How does Paul address these people? Before challenging them with the gospel of Christ, Paul lays the foundation of biblical creation. He declares God as the Creator and Author of life, including our first parents, Adam and Eve (Acts 17:24-26). What a novel idea Paul uses: To understand this world, he goes back to the beginning of time for instruction from the Author of heaven and earth. Genesis remains the foundational book for origins and society, including the importance of families and the value of life itself, including the young and the old.

In this volume my friend Dr. Stan Udd sets out to unfold the first twelve chapters of Genesis and he is in a good position to do so. Credentials include study under theologian John C. Whitcomb at Grace Theological Seminary where Stan earned M.Div., Th.M., and Th.D. degrees. His academic career includes leadership positions in the Bible Department at both Calvary Bible College in Kansas City, and Grace University in Omaha.

Unlike many modern commentaries on Genesis, Dr. Udd promotes a recent supernatural origin of the cosmos during literal days of creation. His careful translation of the Hebrew text provides abundant evidence to support this conservative approach to God's Word.

The book chapters are filled with topics of keen interest, including the following: The three heavens (1 Corinthians 12:2), the creation of angels, weaknesses of macro evolution, dinosaurs and Bible history, the Nephilim of Genesis 6:4, biblical genealogies, and more. There are fresh insights from the Hebrew text. For example, it is suggested that the roof of the ark of Noah may have been covered with sewn-together animal skins. This idea is illustrated by one of many simple figures included in the work. As another example, Dr. Udd suggests that during the Genesis 11 Babel episode, God physically scattered or transported the people to far off places.

Throughout this book Dr. Udd lets the Bible speak for itself. The result is a clear exposition of chapters 1-12 of Genesis. May the volume remind many readers of the riches of the Book of Genesis and also our responsibility before our Maker.

Don DeYoung
President, Creation Research Society

The Creation Research Society is comprised of 1700 scientists and friends worldwide who favor biblical creation. Dr. Stan Udd is a longtime member.

Introduction

The purpose of this book is to examine the words of the Hebrew text of Genesis 1-12 and, as clearly as possible, to restate in understandable terms what those words mean. In reality, the words mean what they say, but in many cases it is helpful to expand or explain in contemporary thought the sense of this profound section of God's Word.

This is a book about faith. God's Word can be trusted when it speaks on historical matters such as the creation of the world. This material cannot be checked or verified; it can only be accepted or rejected. I choose to accept it at face value.

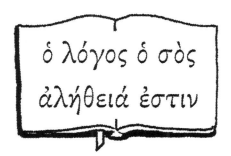

Figure 1: Your Word is Truth.

This does not mean, however, that I understand everything in God's record to mankind. There are many things that I cannot explain to my own satisfaction, but the fault lies with me, not with the revelation that God has so graciously extended to us. In spite of this lack on my part, the purpose of this book is to explore in detail the information the sovereign Lord has communicated to us in the first chapters of Genesis.

The plan is to incorporate the findings of science wherever they might be helpful. Science will not be used to *interpret* the Word of God because the findings of science, by their very nature, must be filtered through a human grid in order to make any meaningful contribution. Instead, the Bible will be used as a guide to interpreting scientific findings.

Understanding Genesis

Since the rise of evolutionary theory with its antisupernaturalistic bias, the book of Genesis has suffered much at the hands of biblical scholars. In fact, it is not uncommon today for authors to refer to the creation account as myth.[1] This current work is not an apologetic for the book of Genesis.[2] Many conservative works, readily available, provide such apology. This work will rather build on the foundation of these conservative scholars. Their works are assumed as the basis for the present book. The goal here lies beyond a defense of Genesis and toward the work of exegesis on the Hebrew text, exposing what the text of the first twelve chapters of the Bible actually means.

---

[1] Ada Feyerick, *Genesis: World of Myths and Patriarchs*, contributing authors: Cyrus H. Gordon and Nahum M. Sarna (New York: New York Univ. Press, 1996). The book of Exodus has been treated similarly (see Ernest S. Frerichs and Leonard H. Lesko, eds., *Exodus: The Egyptian Evidence* [Winona Lake, Ind.: Eisenbrauns, 1997], especially William G. Dever, "Is There Any Archaeological Evidence for the Exodus?" 67-86).

[2] An excellent survey of the history of how these early chapters of Genesis have been viewed by scholars may be found in the chapter by Richard S. Hess, "One Hundred Fifty Years of Comparative Studies on Genesis 1-11: An Overview" in *"I Studied Inscriptions from Before the Flood": Ancient Near Eastern, Literary, and Linguistic Approaches to Genesis 1-11*, eds. Richard S. Hess and David Toshio Tsumura in *Sources for Biblical and Theological Study*, ed. David W. Baker (Winona Lake, Ind.: Eisenbrauns, 1994): 3-26.

Authorship

Tradition claims that Moses was the author of Genesis. If it could be established that Moses did write Genesis, the truth being conveyed would not change appreciably. Had Jeremiah, for example, written Genesis, the account would still be true. Also, whether Moses composed the book from preexisting sources or whether he wrote down, for the first time, information that God revealed to him on Mount Sinai does not have a profound effect on how one interprets the book. But it *is* important that these words be treated with respect and understood as the inerrant Word of God.[3]

Figure 2: In the beginning

The better we understand God and his revelation to mankind, the better we will understand ourselves. The Bible teaches us about our origin—we were created by God. It instructs us about our nature—we are patterned after God. And it informs us of our destiny—believers will ultimately dwell with God.

---

3   This author currently holds that Moses, writing in the fifteenth century BC, may have had significant documents at his disposal. Even Noah may have preserved some of these. A strong case can be made for the composition of the book of Job in the early part of the second millennium BC, hundreds of years before Moses. If one such document survived, is it not possible that others also existed? Note also the use of the word *scroll* in Gen. 5:1 as a label for the story of Adam. "This is the scroll of the story of Adam."

Let not your hearts be troubled. Believe in God; believe also in me. In my Father's house are many rooms. If it were not so, would I have told you that I go to prepare a place for you? And if I go and prepare a place for you, I will come again and will take you to myself, that where I am you may be also.

—John 14:1-3 ESV

– 1 –

Presuppositions

Basis for Evolutionism

Those who believe in the evolutionary theory often claim that evolution is based on the assured results of science, while those who believe in creationism have only their faith in the Bible to support their belief system. This chapter is not designed to bolster the faith of those who adhere to the creationist viewpoint. It rather demonstrates that the evolutionary scheme is also based on certain articles of faith.

Various attempts have been made to increase the scientific acceptability of the idea of creation, but at the heart of the matter stands this verse: *"By faith we understand* that the worlds were prepared by the word of God, so that what is seen was not made out of things which are visible" (Heb. 11:3 NASB). Faith is unarguably an essential element in the framework of creationism. One cannot *understand* the concept of creation apart from faith. Such faith is directed toward God and accepts the revelation that he has given us concerning the creation of all things.

Evolutionists, on the other hand, contend that their scheme is grounded only in those tangible elements that can be seen and felt. Largely, the evolutionary system relies on an interpretation of the sedimentary rock strata found on every continent of the globe, together with the fossil evidence located within those strata.[1]

Some philosophical underpinnings, however, guide the evolutionist in his quest to understand earth history; he does not operate in a vacuum. These philosophical presuppositions have not been artificially imposed upon the evolutionary scheme by creationists. Instead, they are the result of the careful analysis of men—often theologians—who founded the evolutionary movement and gave to the theory its three major foundational tenets. These presuppositions are so vital to the evolutionary viewpoint that they have been given the moniker "laws of evolution." When this author took an introductory course in geology at a major university, these presuppositions were called the "laws of historical geology."

It is common for college textbooks to reference these laws and to recognize that they are the basis for much of the discussion of evolution.

We have already been using several of the basic assumptions geologists make as they study the earth:

Uniformitarianism: Processes that act to change the earth today are the same as the processes that have acted in the past. Hence the present is the key to understanding the past.

Horizontality and Superposition: Virtually all sediments are deposited in horizontal layers, and if undisturbed, we may assume that the older sedimentary rock lies beneath the younger layer.

---

[1] Seventy-five to eighty percent of the surface of the continents is currently covered by sedimentary rock. Areas that were once covered by large continental glaciers are often stripped of sedimentary layers.

Organic Succession: Based on our understanding of the changes that have occurred in plants and animals over millions of years, and particularly on our knowledge of when certain types of life became extinct, it is possible to use the fossil remains found in sedimentary rock to date that rock.[2]

A closer look at these assumptions follows.

Uniformitarianism

Uniformitarianism: Processes that act to change the earth today are the same as the processes that have acted in the past. Hence the present is the key to understanding the past.

The law of uniformitarianism was developed by James Hutton in the second half of the eighteenth century.[3] But it was Charles Lyell who popularized the concept in his three-volume work, *Principles of Geology* (1830-33). This work, in turn, had a profound effect on the thinking of Charles Darwin. "'I feel as if my books,' Charles Darwin once confessed, 'came half out of Sir Charles Lyell's brain.'"[4]

At first glance, the phrase "the present is the key to the past" seems quite innocuous. Who could disagree with such a simple

---

[2] Robert T. Dixon, *Physical Science: A Dynamic Approach*, 2d ed. (Englewood Cliffs, N. J.: Prentice-Hall, 1986): 325.

[3] Hutton wrote: "In examining things present, we have data from which to reason with regard to what has been; and, from what has actually been, we have data for concluding with regard to that which is to happen hereafter. Therefore, upon the supposition that the operations of nature are equable and steady, we find, in natural appearances, means for concluding a certain portion of time to have necessarily elapsed, in the production of those events of which we see the effects" (James Hutton, *Theory of the Earth with Proofs and Illustration*, in four parts [Edinburgh: William Creech, 1795]: 1:19, reprint edition [Leutershausen, Germany: Strauss & Cramer GmbH, 1972]).

[4] Loren C. Eiseley, "Charles Lyell," reprinted from *Scientific American,* August 1959 (San Francisco: W. H. Freemam, 1959): 3.

statement? Is it not important to know the history of an object in order to understand it better?

A personal illustration may demonstrate the significance of this phrase. While taking a course in historical geology, this author was required to write a book review. The assignment was to submit a critique of the book *Earth in Upheaval* by Immanuel Velikovsky. This work claimed to present physical evidence for a cataclysmic encounter of the earth with the planet Venus. My analysis centered on the cataclysmic nature of the evidence, for I thought that by emphasizing the irregular and non-constant nature of Velikovsky's evidence, I had somehow dealt a significant blow to uniformitarianism. But at the end of the critique, the professor scrawled these words: "If V.[elikovsky's] catastrophes could be proven, wouldn't this be uniformitarianism?"

My mind was awash in questions during the lecture of the day. For if uniformitarianism included everyday uniform happenings *and* if uniformitarianism included catastrophic events, *what was excluded?*

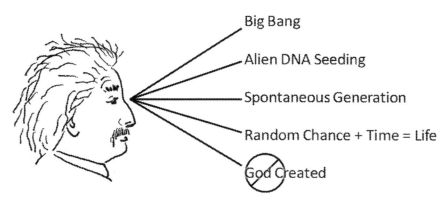

Figure 3: Available options

In response to this question, the professor gave a simple answer: "It [uniformitarianism] excludes the supernatural." To the evolutionist, any explanation is acceptable as long as it does not include God.[5] An adjustment to the age of the universe does not affect the essence of the evolutionary scheme. A major change in the sequence of stellar evolution does not upset the evolutionist. The discovery of a genuine "missing link" or the discrediting of the same has no effect on the belief system of the evolutionist—as long as God is kept out of the equation. The law of uniformitarianism is not a statement about scientific inquiry. It is rather a theological statement, a dogma, disavowing the activity of God in the realm of earth history. Therefore, one who holds to the doctrine of uniformitarianism is a practical atheist.[6]

---

[5] "'I shall adopt a different course,' the young Lyell had written when he was contending for the uniformitarianism view of geology. 'We are not authorized in the infancy of our science to recur to extraordinary agents.' The same point of view led him, in company with T. H. Huxley, Joseph Hooker, and later, Darwin, to reject the claims of progressionism. All of these men, Lyell foremost among them, were uniformitarians in geology. They believed in the play of purely natural forces upon the earth. They refused or were reluctant to accept the notion of divine interposition of creative power at various stages of the geological record. They felt in their bones that there must be a natural explanation for organic as well as geological change, but the method was not easily to be had. Since Lyell was the immediate parent of the new geology, and since he was committed to natural processes, he was continually embarrassed by those who said: 'you cannot show how nor why life has altered. Why then should we not believe that geological changes are equally the produce of mysterious and unknown forces?'" (Eiseley, *Charles Lyell*, 7).

[6] My geology professor said that if I wanted to believe that God had created the original blob of matter, that was fine with him. He said that he could explain everything since then in scientific terms. Near the end of the semester I asked him, "Why do you believe in evolution?" He replied, "If I didn't believe in evolution, I would have to believe in God."

More recently, a significant shift has occurred within the scientific community toward seeing "design" and toward considering the possibility that "an intelligent agent" is in fact responsible for the observable universe (see Tom Woodward, "Meeting Darwin's Wager," *Christianity Today* [April 28, 1997]:14-21). But to acknowledge that the intelligent agent might be the God of the Bible is not an automatic conclusion for most.

Predictability is a part of the makeup and composition of this natural world. Creationists do not *deny* the existence of laws of nature such as the laws of thermodynamics. But creationist teaching knows *more* than the law of conservation of matter and energy or the law of entropy. Creationists also understand that this natural world with its natural laws had a beginning. There was a time before these laws of thermodynamics came into existence. "For He commanded and they were created. He has also established them forever and ever; He has made a decree that will not pass away" (Ps. 148:5b-6 NASB).

Since the close of the creative week, this world has operated under the influence of the laws of nature that God established. A Christian researcher performs experiments in full confidence that the laws of the natural world will hold. In addition, creationists recognize that, at various points in history, God has intervened with supernatural acts, such as extended daylight when Joshua fought the Amorites (Josh. 10:12-14). Creationists also acknowledge that God will again intercept earth history at the close of this age (Joel 2:28-32).

The uniformitarianist has arbitrarily chosen to limit his field of inquiry, though this is not immediately apparent in the ebb and flow of the scientific enterprise. Uniformitarianism is, however, critically damaged when it comes to a study of the origin of the universe or the development of the fossiliferous stratigraphic rock layers. The correct solution to the question of origins has been categorically ruled out before the investigation has begun. God, acting by supernatural means, can never be a hypothesis in the uniformitarianist's quest for truth.

Sometimes uniformitarianism is seen as a debate about the rate at which natural processes occur. Was it slow? Or was it sudden? Did it happen "naturally" or catastrophically? Is time actually the evolutionist's friend? Does time increase the probability that an unlikely event will occur? Probability is independent of time. For example, a shuffled deck of nine cards dropped from a second-story window has a certain probability of falling in a row, spelling E-V-O-L-U-T-I-O-N. How does one increase the *time* in this example? Repeating the experiment does not increase the time. To increase the time, the cards must be dropped from, say, a tenth-floor window. Would that improve the chances of the cards falling in a row to read the word *evolution*? Obviously not. Uniformitarianism is not about the rate or the speed at which something occurs. It is about the cause that produced the result. For evolutionists, only natural causes are allowed: "We are not authorized in the infancy of our science to recur to extraordinary agents."[7]

Is God in the business of creating today? No. For the evolutionist this means that God never created because creation is not a process that we can observe today. Uniformitarianism unnecessarily limits the purview of the evolutionary scientist.

Horizontality and Superposition

Horizontality and Superposition: Virtually all sediments are deposited in horizontal layers, and if undisturbed, we may assume that the older sedimentary rock lies beneath the younger layer.

The second assumption of evolutionism derives from the pattern that James Hutton first observed in the fossiliferous strata.[8] The regularity in the sequencing of the layers and of the fossils imbedded in those layers led to the conclusion that this type of sequencing must occur worldwide. But what

[7] Eiseley, *Charles Lyell*, 7.
[8] See John Phillips, *Memoirs of William Smith* (New York: Arno, 1978), reprint of the 1844 ed. published by John Murry: London.

about the exceptions? In many places the exposed strata are layered contrary to the currently accepted "geologic column."[9] For example, Chief Mountain in Glacier National Park, Montana, has at its base a layer of Cretaceous gray shale. For the evolutionist, this layer is at the very top of the geologic column. At Chief Mountain, however, atop the Cretaceous layer lies a thick Precambrian layer, which for the evolutionist is just below the region where life begins. The geologic column of Chief Mountain is in exactly the reverse order from what is expected by the evolutionist. Would this evidence not disprove the conclusions of the evolutionary understanding of geology?

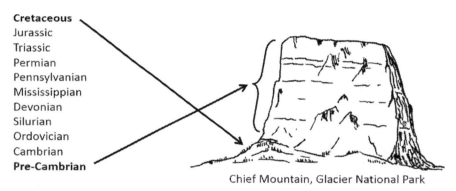

Cretaceous
Jurassic
Triassic
Permian
Pennsylvanian
Mississippian
Devonian
Silurian
Ordovician
Cambrian
Pre-Cambrian

Chief Mountain, Glacier National Park

Figure 4: Chief Mountain, Glacier National Park

Instead of dealing with the evidence, the evolutionist states that the crust is disturbed in this case. He posits that a huge overthrust folded the bottom layer up and over the top layer. The only component that this theory lacks is physical evidence.

---

9   Walter E. Lammerts, "Recorded Instances of Wrong-order Formations or Presumed Overthrusts in the United States: A Bibliography—Part I-VIII," *Creation Research Society Quarterly,* 21:2 (1984): 88; 21:3 (1984): 150; 21:4 (1984): 200; 22:3 (1985): 127; 22:4 (1986): 188-9; 23:1 (1986): 38; 23:3 (1986): 133; 24:1 (1987): 46.

No geologic evidence of overthrusting exists at the boundary of the two plates.[10]

The law of horizontality and superposition contains this exception clause that allows the evolutionist to reject certain pieces of physical evidence: if the "younger" layer does not lie atop the "older" strata, the evolutionist has the prerogative to declare that the sequence has been disturbed, even where no physical evidence exists for such a disturbance.

The law of horizontality and superposition gives the evolutionary geologist the authority to determine which layers are in the correct sequence. Even without physical evidence for a geologic displacement, the law of horizontality enables the practitioner to declare that evidence that is contrary to accepted theory is not, in fact, evidence at all. Instead, he contends that these layers had obviously been disturbed at one time.

By simply declaring that all sequencing to the contrary had been disturbed, apart from any physical evidence, the law of horizontality and superposition enabled evolutionary geologists to construct an airtight case for the sequencing of the geologic column. Suddenly, all the geologic evidence for the evolutionary scheme could be harmonized under one rubric, for only those data were admissible that agreed with the previous arrangement. The ability to select the evidence that can be used in any discussion of the geologic column is a formidable weapon indeed.

---

[10] An older work that has yet to be answered by evolutionists examines the 350 miles of the so-called Lewis Thrust and concludes that there is no physical geologic evidence for thrusting along the appropriate boundary (Clifford L Burdick, "The Lewis Overthrust," *Creation Research Society Quarterly,* 6:2 [Sept 1969]: 96-106).

Organic Succession

Organic Succession: Based on our understanding of the changes that have occurred in plants and animals over millions of years, and particularly on our knowledge of when certain types of life became extinct, it is possible to use the fossil remains found in sedimentary rock to date that rock.

The third law of evolutionism justifies the circular reasoning necessary to establish the broad outline of organic evolution, which moves from simple organisms to forms that are more complex. A general pattern in the fossiliferous strata from smaller, "simple" organisms to larger, more "complex" life forms does seem to exist. To the evolutionist, this means that simple organisms evolved into more complex forms with the passage of time. Other explanations are ignored.[11]

If one assumes that this pattern—from simple to complex—denotes evolution, even though no transition forms have been found, the life forms found at the bottom of the sequence are obviously older than those found near the top. In such a case, the rock strata are the determining factor in establishing the relative age of the fossils.

---

[11] Other theories that explain the evidence include the action of the floodwater in Noah's day in which objects were sorted and graded according to the hydrologic properties of those objects. Simple rounded objects, such as clams, would have been among the first objects to settle out of the floodwaters (see John C. Whitcomb and Henry M. Morris, *The Genesis Flood: The Biblical Record and Its Scientific Implications* [Philadelphia: P&R, 1961]: 273-77).

A second explanation relates to the relative locations of animals and plants in the biosphere. Aquatic life would have been buried before terrestrial life. Additionally, "higher" forms have greater mobility, which would have given them some advantage in a flood. Obviously, exceptions to this general rule would have occurred as well, which is exactly the situation found in the fossil record.

Figure 5: Land and seascape: animals tend to be buried in their habitat.

In those instances in which surface rocks contain fossils from the lower part of the geologic column but have no overburden of "younger" layers, the fossils found at the surface may be used to date those rocks. The "older" fossils on the surface could, in theory, be used as evidence that the "older" fossils are actually "younger" fossils. But here the evolutionist retreats to the law of organic succession. This law allows the evolutionist to assign an "old" date to the rock simply based on the fossils it contains.

Notice both components of this law and how they interrelate: "Based on our understanding of the changes that have occurred"—assuming organic evolution has happened—"it is possible to use the fossil remains found in sedimentary rock to date the rock." In the first instance, the rock dates the fossil; in the second, the fossil dates the rock. Circular reasoning is admittedly not valid scientific procedure, so to help legitimize the technique, the law of organic succession was developed to add credence to the procedure.

The basic tenet of organic evolution is based on the assumption that life forms have increased in complexity as time has passed. In fact, numerous experimental evidences point to a general pattern in nature that is exactly the opposite. All systems, both organic and inorganic, progress irreversibly from systems of higher complexity to systems of lesser order.[12] To date, no exception to this rule has been observed. The lack of evidence for naturally occurring increases in complexity demonstrates the necessity for the evolutionist to generate an assumption like the law of organic succession.

If the three presuppositions of uniformitarianism, horizontality and superposition, and organic succession are accepted, it is impossible to put forth *any* evidence that is contrary to the theory of evolution. The law of uniformitarianism disallows supernatural explanation and limits all theories to purely naturalistic or chance mechanistic operations. The law of horizontality and superposition gives the evolutionist the right to select only data that confirms the theory of evolution and the right to ignore any data that contradicts it. Finally, the law of organic succession legitimizes the circular reasoning necessary to establish the major outlines of the progression of organic evolution.

All three laws are necessary to justify the evolutionist's preconceived interpretation of earth history. They are not grounded in scientific principles. They cannot be proved or disproved. They can only be accepted or rejected. They are expressions of faith.

---

[12] Charles B. Thaxton, et al., *The Mystery of Life's Origin: Reassessing Current Theories* (Dallas: Lewis and Stanley, 1984). See especially ch. 7 ("Thermodynamics of Living Systems") and ch. 8 ("Thermodynamics and the Origin of Life"); A. E. Wilder-Smith, *The Scientific Alternative to Neo-Darwinian Evolutionary Theory: Information Sources and Structures*, (Costa Mesa, Calif.: TWFT, 1987); Henry M. Morris, *The Twilight of Evolution*, (Philadelphia: P&R, 1963).

Basis for Creationism

Creationism is also an expression of faith and rests upon certain presuppositions. These are three in number as well: (1) God exists, (2) he created, and (3) he gave us a reliable and accurate record of his activity.

While not intending to downplay the significance of philosophical inquiry, it must ultimately be understood that one's acceptance of God's existence is an exercise of faith. "And without faith it is impossible to please Him, for he who comes to God must believe that He is" (Heb. 11:6a NASB). Evidence for God's existence is available to everyone "because that which is known about God is evident within them [ungodly and unrighteous men]; for God made it evident to them" (Rom. 1:19 NASB). Even so, this evidence does not categorically compel mankind to believe in God's existence, "for they exchanged the truth of God for a lie" (Rom. 1:25a NASB). So to be a creationist, one must first accept the truth that God exists.

Secondly, creationism is based on the assumption that God created. This is first stated in Genesis 1:1—"In the beginning, God created. . . ." This statement is repeated in numerous other texts, but it always means the same: God, by supernatural means, called into existence material (or arrangements of previously created material) that was new.

Some would modify downward this concept of creation so that God's involvement over the eons of geologic history was nothing more than an imperceptible nudge here and there along the evolutionary chain of events. However, such a view does not satisfy the biblical concept of creation. "By the word of the Lord the heavens were made, / and by the breath of his mouth all their host / . . . For he spoke, and it was done / he commanded, and it stood firm" (Ps. 33:6, 9). Neither incrementalism nor vast eons of time resonate with this biblical presentation of God's creative activity.

A creationist is one who acknowledges that, before God created, there was only God. A creationist also maintains that by his powerful word God spoke material into existence.

Finally, creationism is based on the assumption that God has given us an accurate record of his creative activity. The Bible is the primary source of information for the creationist. Were it not for the inspired text, the order in which things were created could not be known. Were it not for the inspired text, one could not know the amount of time involved in the creation process. Were it not for the inspired text, one could not know the reason for God's creative activity. Once the Bible is accepted as the accurate record that it is, an abundance of additional data becomes available.

The creationist viewpoint supplies the researcher with an accurate lens through which to view the tangible world. It gives him insight that would otherwise be unavailable, and it prevents him from pursuing avenues of inquiry that are shown in the Bible to be futile.

Just as evolutionism cannot be proved wrong if its three foundational assumptions are adopted, so creationism cannot be proved wrong if its three foundational assumptions are accepted. In order for a creationist to have a valid dialogue with an evolutionist, one of them must be willing to set aside his assumptions.

It is fascinating to observe that even with these three valuable tools at their disposal, evolutionists are no closer to understanding the fundamental nature of our world than they were a hundred years ago. In a recent edition of *Science News*, ten pages were devoted to a discussion of the "Top 5 cosmic questions":[13]

---

[13] Tom Siegfried, "Suggesting risky answers to Top 5 cosmic questions," *Science News,* April 23, 2011, 2. For a conservative response, see Stan Udd, "Does the Bible have the Answers to Today's Pressing Questions?" *Creation Matters,* 17:2 (March 2012): 1, 4-5.

- What happened before the Big Bang?
- What is the universe made of?
- Is there a theory of everything?
- Are space and time fundamental?
- What is the universe's fate?

The conclusion of these experts was that evolutionists are today no closer to answering these fundamental questions than they were years ago. They have only slightly refined the questions. Perhaps the scientific community is using the wrong tools of inquiry.

This present volume is not addressed to the obvious impasse between evolutionary thinking and creationism. Instead, it is assumed that creationism is correct. The goal of this volume is to allow the Word of God to speak for itself.

— 2 —

Genesis 1: Day One

In the beginning God created the heavens and the earth. Now the earth was unfinished and unfilled, and darkness was over the surface of the deep, and the Spirit of God was hovering over the surface of the waters. And God said, "Let there be light." And there was light. And God saw the light that it was good, and God separated the light from the darkness. And God called the light day and the darkness he called night. And there was evening and there was morning, the first day.

> —Genesis 1:1-5
> author's translation
> based on the Hebrew text, here and hereafter

The opening verse of God's Word to mankind is given in clear, simple, and untrammeled language: "In the beginning God created the heavens and the earth." How is this verse to be understood? Does it simply mean what it says?

The most natural way of understanding Genesis 1:1, and the way in which it has traditionally been understood, is to see "in the beginning" as a chronological marker that opens Day One of creation. The initial phase of the creation week had begun.

Beginning of Time?

The phrase "in the beginning" speaks of the start of Day One. What are the implications of this for the concept of time? Does this phrase refer to the beginning of time? Was time created at this point, before which only timeless "eternity"[1] existed?

The concept of time is certainly larger than a definition that merely measures its passage (i.e., seconds, minutes, hours, days). Time is not defined by man's acknowledgment of its passage. The fundamental nature of time is linked to sequence. If two events can or do occur *one after the other,* time exists. If time does not exist, all events happen simultaneously.[2] In a timeless state, one could not *do, cause,* or *receive* anything; one could only *be.* The essence of existence relates to one's ability to express oneself and to manipulate events in time.

Figure 6: Timepiece versus sequence

---

[1] The concept of eternity has doubtless been affected by the church's hymnody, which on occasion refers to that period when "time shall be no more." The English language does know the concept of eternity defined by the *absence* of time. More commonly, however, *eternity* is defined as "time without end" (*The Oxford English Dictionary,* 2d ed., s. v. "eternity").

[2] This statement itself contains time-bound words: "happen," "events." What I mean to say is this: if time does not exist, then all is simultaneous.

In a timeless state, by definition, sequence cannot occur; cause and effect cannot exist. Furthermore, an action cannot follow a decision. Consequently, a righteous deed cannot occur in a timeless state. The reasoning is simple: a righteous act flows from a positive moral decision, which necessitates the existence of cause and effect. Cause and effect necessitate the existence of sequence. Hence, time must exist in order for *righteousness* or *unrighteousness* to be meaningful terms.

Does the biblical text indicate that sequential events occurred before Genesis 1:1? If so, "in the beginning" does not refer to the creation of time.[3] Consider the following texts from the English Standard Version:[4]

> And now, Father, glorify me in your own presence with the glory that I had with you before the world existed.
>
> —John 17:5

> Because you loved me before the foundation of the world
>
> —John 17:24b

> Even as he chose us in him before the foundation of the world.
>
> —Ephesians 1:4a

> But because of his own purpose and grace, which he gave us in Christ Jesus before the ages began [literally, "before times eternal;" see also Titus 1:2].
>
> —2 Timothy 1:9b

---

[3] Note that the object of the verb *to create* in the text of Gen. 1:1 is "the heavens and the earth," not "time" or "in the beginning."

[4] *The Holy Bible: English Standard Version* (Wheaton, Ill.: Crossway Bibles, 2001).

> He was foreknown before the foundation of the
> world.[5]
>
> —1 Peter 1:20a

Each of these verses uses verbs that describe activity and sequential events. Each of these activities and events necessitates the existence of time before the initial point of creation.

Scripture does not speak of the beginning or the cessation of time. In Revelation 10:6, the King James Version reads, "there should be time no longer." More recent translations, however, give the sense of the verse with a different understanding: "there will be no more delay" (NIV, ESV) and "there will be delay no longer" (NASB).[6]

If one ignores these scriptural indicators and relies instead on the "assured results" of modern science, a much different conclusion can be drawn. Instead of time being the inevitable forward progression of events, it suddenly becomes a plaything—something that can be expanded and contracted, warped or ignored.

The study of physics opines that mass, time, and space must all occur together. If there is no mass or energy, it is thought that there can be no space or time. That statement is irrational and contradicts biblical truth. But based on this type of logic, Albert Einstein, in 1955, said in a letter: "The distinction between past, present, and future is only an illusion, however persistent."[7]

---

[5] Other passages that contain similar terminology include Matt. 13:35; 25:34; Heb. 4:3; 9:26; Rev. 13:8; 17:8.

[6] ". . . the context within the Apocalypse as a whole . . . shows that the sense here is not an abolition of time and its replacement with timelessness, but 'no more time' from the words of the angel until the completion of the divine purpose. This certainly comes near to 'delay' in general effect" (James Barr, *Biblical Words for Time*, in *Studies in Biblical Theology*, no. 33 [London: SCM Press, 1962]: 76, n. 2).

[7] Letter to Michele Angelo Besso, March 21, 1955.

So much for our hope in the second coming of Christ or of an eternity with God![8] As one can see, the conclusions are significantly different, depending on one's starting point.[9]

A person's view of eternity past doubtless affects his view of eternity future. "Many theologians are taking a closer look at the nature of the eternal state. The concept of a timeless, non-historical eternity is giving way to the notion of a time-sequenced existence on the new earth, which is felt to be more consistent with biblical descriptions."[10] This certainly seems to be a step in the right direction.

How does God relate to time? Is God timeless? Is he above time or outside of time? He had no beginning and will have no end (Rev. 22:13). At the same time, God inhabits the present as we do. Unlike us, his memory is perfect so that nothing of the past is a mystery to him, and he can make plans for the future that he will carry out in unerring detail. However, it would

---

[8] Wayne Grudem, "God's Eternity: Timeless, Yet Timely," *Moody,* September 1988, 40.

[9] The theory of relativity does not seem to be a strong or adequate base upon which to build doctrine. According to Einstein's *Gedanken* [thought] experiments, time was thought to be in the same category as mass (and/or energy) and space. His mathematical manipulations then allowed him to suggest that time can be "diluted" or slowed down relative to the rest of the universe under the influence of acceleration. This suggestion has been repeatedly proved self-contradictory, hence scientifically invalid, though it is still widely accepted in the scientific community. The mention in biblical texts of God's involvement in necessarily sequential actions, before the creation of any aspect of the physical universe, suggests strongly that Einstein's connection of mass with time with space is artificial. Time warp and even black holes belong exclusively to the realm of science fiction (see Thomas G. Barnes, *Physics of the Future: A Classical Unification of Physics* [El Cajon, Calif.: Institute for Creation Research, 1983]. An abbreviated edition is also available in *Creation Research Society Quarterly,* 21 [1984]: 56-62). More recently, Stephen Hawking has called into question the validity of the event horizon (www.nature.com/news/stephen-hawking-there-are-no-black-holes-1.14583, accessed July 11, 2014).

[10] Craig A. Blaising, "Development of Dispensationalism by Contemporary Dispensationalists," *Bibliotheca Sacra,* 145 (July-September 1988): 268.

seem that in an ontological sense, God inhabits the present, as we do.

If God is now in the past, what can he *do* back there? The past cannot be changed in any meaningful sense. God cannot, for example, shorten the life of an individual who had children so that he now dies before he fathers children, can he? History would be meaningless if it suddenly became subject to such adjustment. Even our salvation through the death of Christ would not be secure if historical events could be altered. So if one feels compelled to argue that God inhabits the past just as he inhabits the present, it also follows that either God can do nothing while he is back there in history or that history has suddenly become an arbitrary idea that is unreliable.

A similar problem exists with the future. Can God actually do anything in the future? Is not God restricted to planning and preparing for the future? He can and will carry out his plan with precision, but the future is still the future even to God. Christ has not already come back a second time, has he?

The understanding that God inhabits time as we do can be illustrated with an example from the book of Hebrews (actually, this should be stated in the reverse: we who have been made in the image and likeness of God reflect God in the way that we inhabit time). Events of significance occurred *in heaven* at the death of Christ. Hebrews 9:15 states that "since a death has taken place for the redemption of the transgressions that were *committed* under the first covenant, those who have been called may receive the promise of the eternal inheritance" (NASB). For example, the salvation of King David was not apparently confirmed or verified until the actual historical event of Christ's death had been accomplished. However, this no more detracts from the certainty of David's salvation before the first coming of Christ than Christ's second coming detracts from our own personal salvation today (see Heb. 9:28). The point of the illustration is that the Bible makes the claim that something actually happened in heaven simultaneously with events here on earth, which argues that heaven also inhabits time.

Does this understanding confine our God or restrict his greatness? The answer is a resounding no. Time is not confining. It is instead that medium through which God expresses his essential greatness. Time does not limit God. It shows rather that he exists and allows him to be himself.

It would further seem reasonable to conclude that if time is an expression of God's existence, then the same could be said of space. If God exists, he must exist somewhere; he cannot be nowhere. Time and space are essential attributes of God's existence. Time and space are expressions of the fact that God exists.[11]

"In the beginning" does not refer to the creation of time and space. Significant events of sequence and reciprocal relationships were already in existence before "the beginning," according to the biblical text. What was it then that was being marked off as beginning? This phrase refers to the beginning of earth history. "In the beginning" refers to the start of Day One of the creation week. The phrase is a chronological marker, and one would expect the opening of this significant week to be noted by just such a phrase. Day One begins with verse 1.

Meaning of Creation

After the chronological marker is planted, the text is unequivocal about God's action: "God created." Creation is the

---

[11] The discussion of God's relationship to time is by no means a settled issue. For recent discussion, see Paul Helm, *Eternal God: A Study of God without Time*, 2d ed. (New York: Oxford, 2010). In this volume, Helm responds to an earlier critique by William Lane Craig (*Time and Eternity* [Wheaton, Ill.: Crossway], 2001).

exclusive domain of God.[12] It is difficult to explain how God created because a supernatural activity, by definition, is one that cannot be explained. The best we can do is to reflect on the activity as it is recorded in the Bible itself. The creative process has been described as possessing three characteristics: (1) supernaturalness, (2) suddenness, and (3) the superficial appearance of history.[13]

When God speaks regarding his unique, elevated position, he often cites his ability to create as the power that sets him apart.

> For thus says the Lord, creator of the heavens:
> (He is the God who formed the earth and made it.
> He established it and did not create it to be empty, but
> formed it to be inhabited.)
> "I am the Lord, and there is none else."[14]
>
> —Isaiah 45:18

This activity, referred to as creating, usually involved verbal articulation on the part of the Creator. The material that God had thus addressed then came into existence. "For he commanded and they were created" (Ps. 148:5b; see also Ps. 33:9). At least eight times in Genesis 1, the text records,

---

[12] In the Hebrew Scriptures, the verb meaning *to create* is "a specifically theological term, the subject of which is invariably God" (Ludwig Koehler and Walter Baumgartner, subsequently revised by Walter Baumgartner and Johann Jakob Stamm, with assistance from Benedikt Hartmann, Ze'ev Ben-Hayyim, Eduard Yechezkel Kutscher, and Philippe Reymond, *The Hebrew and Aramaic Lexicon of the Old Testament*, trans. and ed. under M. E. J. Richardson, study ed. in 2 vols. [Leiden: E. J. Brill, 2001]: 153. Hereafter HALOT).

[13] John C. Whitcomb, *The Early Earth*, rev. ed. (Grand Rapids, Mich.: Baker, 1986): 19-49.

[14] See also Isa. 40:18; 40:25-26.

"and God said. . . ."[15] In each case, a description of his creative activity follows. The text indicates that, without struggle or exertion, he simply brought new material into existence.

The concept of *ex nihilo* (meaning "out of nothing") creation could be concluded from a reading of the first chapter of the Bible, but the clear statement of the doctrine is not given until the New Testament book of Hebrews. "By faith we understand that the worlds were prepared by the word of God, so that what is seen was not made out of things which are visible" (Heb. 11:3 NASB). The created universe—"what is seen"—was not made of preexisting matter—"things which are visible." No, the universe was constituted out of nothing by the process called "creation."

However, not all of the Lord's creative activities in that initial week were *ex nihilo*. In Genesis 1:11, God commanded the earth to sprout vegetation. The sense of this verse suggests that the plant kingdom was, in fact, created *from* the pre-existing earth. The same can be said about the waters that produced fish and fowl (see v. 20). And, of course, Adam was created "of dust from the ground" (2:7), while Eve was fashioned from the "rib" that he had taken from the man (2:22). God did not therefore always create out of nothing; sometimes he used pre-existing material. Either method was equally difficult. It is not easier to make life from non-living material than to make it from nothing.

---

[15] Notice also the use of *word* in Heb. 11:3—"By faith we understand that the worlds were prepared by the word of God." Here the sense of *word* is on "command(ment), order, direction" (Walter Bauer, *A Greek-English Lexicon of the New Testament and other Early Christian Literature*, 3d ed., rev. and ed. by Frederick William Danker, on previous English editions by W. F. Arndt and F. W. Gingrich [Chicago: Univ. of Chicago Press, 2000] 753. Hereafter BDAG).

The God of Creation

Who is this Being who has the power to create? The Genesis account simply identifies him as "God" (*'elohîm*). The etymology of this word is neither obvious nor necessary.[16] *'Elohîm* is the only noun used in Genesis 1 to identify God. The word is plural in form, but the verb *created,* with which it is linked, is singular, thereby designating that only one person is under view. The use of a noun in the plural form to designate a singular concept is not unique to *'elohîm*[17] or to the Hebrew language.[18] This plurality bespeaks greatness, majesty, and splendor rather than number.[19] Perhaps one could see this use of the plural noun as an indicator of the trinitarian doctrine of the New Testament, but one certainly cannot see "three-ness" in this plural form.[20] Plural is not restricted to the number three.

The New Testament is quite specific regarding which person of the Godhead actually created. According to John 1:3, creation was the sole domain of the *Logos*—Christ. "All things came into being through him, and apart from him nothing came

---

[16] The root idea of this word is associated with power or greatness and when used as an adjective it is so translated—almost as a "superlative" (HALOT, 53) (1 Sam. 14:15; Gen. 23:6; Jonah 3:3). See *Theological Dictionary of the Old Testament*, eds. G. Johannas Botterweck and Helmer Ringgren, trans. John T. Willis (Grand Rapids, Mich.: Eerdmans, 1974): 1:273.

[17] The word for "master" *'adonîm* (Ex. 21:4) and the word for "owner" *b^{ec}lîm* (Isa. 1:3) also exhibit this same phenomenon. See Joshua Blau, *A Grammar of Biblical Hebrew* (Wiesbaden, Germany: Otto Harrassowitz, 1976): 66; Bruce K. Waltke and M. O'Connor, *An Introduction to Biblical Hebrew Syntax* (Winona Lake, Ind.: Eisenbrauns, 1990): 123.

[18] So Phoenician (Johannes Friedrich and Wolfgang Rollig, *Phonizich-Punische Grammatik* [Rome: Pontificum Institutum Biblicum, 1970]: 306, 1), as well as Ugaritic (Stanislav Segert, *A Basic Grammar of the Ugaritic Language* [Berkeley: Univ. of California Press, 1984]: 179).

[19] See *Gesenius' Hebrew Grammar,* ed. E. Kautzsch, rev. A. E. Cowley (Oxford: At the Clarendon, 1910): no. 124 g-o. Hereafter GKC.

[20] For a discussion on this question, see H. C. Leupold, *Exposition of Genesis* (Grand Rapids, Mich.: Baker, 1942): 43-44.

into being that has come into being." The role of the Father in creation is not as clear (see 1 Cor. 8:6). Instead, he seems to be the initiator or the planner of universal actions (Rev. 1:1-2). The Son, however, is repeatedly referred to as Creator throughout Scripture.

> He [Christ] is the image of the invisible God, the firstborn of all creation. For by Him all things were created, both in the heavens and on earth, visible and invisible, whether thrones or dominions or rulers or authorities—all things have been created through Him and for Him.
>
> —Colossians 1:15-16 NASB

> In these last days [God] has spoken to us in His son, whom He appointed heir of all things, through whom also He made the world.
>
> —Hebrews 1:2 NASB

God's First Creative Act

What, then, was the product of the creative action of God that started Day One? The verse indicates that the first thing God created was heaven. The Hebrew word for *heaven* can be translated as either a singular or plural word.[21] Thus, throughout the Bible, the same form of this word is translated *heaven* in some places and *heavens* in others.

---

[21] Grammarians know this form as a dual noun. It corresponds with the English word *pair*. Sometimes a pair consists of two items—a pair of earrings; sometimes a pair is one unit—a pair of scissors (Waltke and O'Connor, *Syntax,* 117).

According to the Hebrew lexicon, *heaven* may convey at least three distinct meanings:

- God's abode—"Heaven is my throne" (Isa. 66:1), "For God is in heaven and you are on earth" (Eccl. 5:2);
- The starry universe—"When I consider your heavens, the work of your fingers, The moon and the stars, which you have ordained" (Ps. 8:3); and
- The atmosphere—"Above them the birds of the heavens dwell" (Ps. 104:12).[22]

Which meaning should be applied to Genesis 1:1? The answer to this question comes from the greater context of Genesis 1. It is stated clearly and repeatedly that God created the atmosphere on the second day of creation (Gen. 1:6-7). This expanse or atmosphere is named *heaven* in verse 8. "So God named the atmosphere heaven" (1:8a). Because something cannot be created twice, the word *heaven* in Genesis 1:1 cannot refer to the atmosphere, which was created on Day Two.

The same process demonstrates that *heaven* is not a reference to the celestial bodies that populate the cosmic universe. Genesis 1:14-19 clearly describes the creation of the sun, moon, and stars on Day Four. So if the celestial universe was created on Day Four, the *heaven* created on Day One cannot refer to the cosmic entities that fill space. One must conclude, therefore, that *heaven* in this context must refer to the creation of the spiritual universe, complete with its myriad of angels.

Do other biblical notations indicate the creation of the angelic, invisible universe? A surprising number of passages do refer to the creation of angels. "The anointed cherub who covers"[23] of

---

[22] HALOT, 1559-62.
[23] The title "King of Tyre" should not be seen as a human being. Other biblical passages also refer to angelic beings as either a "prince" or "king" (see Dan. 10:13, 20).

Ezekiel 28:12-16 probably refers to Satan. His having been created is referred to twice in this pericope (vv. 13, 15). Colossians 1:15-16 speaks of the creation of the invisible world and describes the various ranks or classes of angels as "thrones or dominions or rulers or authorities" (NASB).[24] John 1:3 also seems to require the creation of angels. "All things came into being through him; and apart from him nothing came into being that has come into being" (NASB). God alone is self-existent. Angels are created beings.

The use of the word *hosts* in Genesis 2:1 could also be a reference to the angelic realm. "Thus the heavens and the earth were completed, and all their hosts." The term *hosts* is quite commonly used to refer to the invisible world. "And the heavenly hosts bow down before you" (Neh. 9:6).[25]

The first chapter of Genesis limits the creative activity of God to six days—from "in the beginning" (1:1) to "and he rested on the seventh day" (2:2). This is reaffirmed in Exodus 20:11—"For in six days the Lord made the heavens and the earth, the sea and all that is in them, and rested on the seventh day. Therefore the Lord blessed the Sabbath day and made it holy."[26] If God created the angelic realm and if God's creative work was limited to the first six days, then it follows that angels were created within that week.

One final passage that mentions angels in a creation context is Job 38:1-7. Here the Lord asked Job a series of unanswerable questions regarding the creation of planet earth. "On what were its bases sunk? Or who laid its cornerstone?" Then follows the affirmation that, while God was creating the earth, "the

---

[24] That these be understood as other than mortal beings can be seen by comparing this passage with Eph. 6:12.

[25] See also Deut. 17:3; 2 Kings 17:16; 21:3; 23:4,5; Isa. 34:4; Jer. 8:2.

[26] See also Ex. 31:17—"For in six days the Lord made heaven and earth, but on the seventh day he rested, and was refreshed." It is clear that God used the six plus one days to constitute the creation week as a grid for mankind to follow. He certainly could have shortened or lengthened the amount of time involved but used this framework for our benefit.

morning stars sang together, and all the sons of God shouted for joy" (Job 38:7 NASB). The parallel phrases *morning stars* and *sons of God* are used in Job to connote the spiritual world (Job 1:6; 2:1). The angels must have been created before the earth, if they sang at its birth. The creation sequences in Genesis 1:1 and Job 38:1-7 agree completely. First, God created his abode, replete and complete with all its spiritual beings. Then God created the earth.

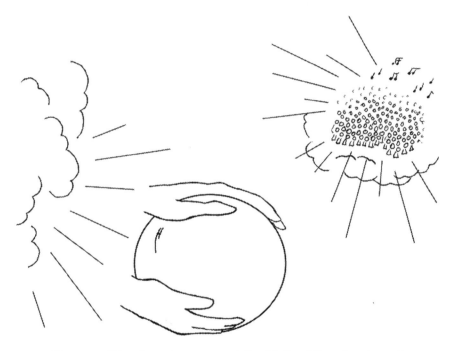

Figure 7: Morning stars sang at the birth of the planet earth.

The creation of light did not occur until after the concert performed by the heavenly host. Did they sing in darkness? One must remember that light has physical properties, whereas angels are spiritual beings. Light does not aid them in seeing. Of the one who inhabits the spiritual world, it is said, "darkness and light are alike" (Ps. 139:12b NASB).

The first verse in Genesis is therefore best understood to read as follows: "To begin the first day of earth history, God created, out of nothing, the spiritual universe, with all its angelic hosts. Then he created the earth." The creation of heaven was spiritual and invisible; the creation of earth was material and visible.

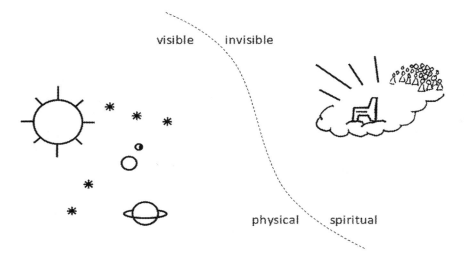

The physical is ever in the presence of the spiritual;
the spiritual rarely intersects the visible.

Figure 8: Comparison of the two universes

The first statement about the earth's creation is given in Genesis 1:1. The earth was the first speck of the material universe that God created. Here it was that God centered his attention. The Bible is very geocentric in its outlook. The focus of the text is not pointed toward some distant galaxy; instead, it concentrates on *terra firma*. "It is I who made the earth, and created man upon it. I stretched out the heavens with My hands" (Isa. 45:12 NASB).[27]

---

[27] In light of this verse, it is probably ill-advised to spend resources on the investigation of life on other planets.

The Earth at Its Creation

Genesis 1:1 opens the drama of earth history. To start Day One, God created, from nothing pre-existing, the heavenly, spiritual realm. Then the angelic host sang for joy as God created this globe on which so much was planned to happen.

Verse 1 simply states that the earth was a direct creation of God. It does not give a description of the earth as it came from God's hand. Verse 2 is devoted to that portrayal: "Now the earth was unfinished and unfilled ['without form and void' (KJV)], and darkness was over the surface of the deep, and the Spirit of God was hovering over the surface of the waters."

The form of the first verb used here ("Now the earth *was*") does not describe an action happening to the earth after its creation. Nor does that verb carry the sense of a sequential condition. The verb is simply used to describe the earth as it came from the hand of God.[28]

Since the days of Hermann Gunkel, it has been popular to describe the early earth as chaotic.[29] This has even become one of the definitions of the word *chaotic* in the modern English dictionary.[30] This concept certainly does not arise from the Hebrew text of Genesis 1:2 nor, for that matter, from the Greek translation of that verse.[31] Instead, it appears to have arisen

---

[28] Some other occurrences of this identical form include: "Now the serpent *was* crafty" (Gen. 3:1), "She *was* the mother of all living" (Gen. 3:20), "Rachel *was* beautiful of form and face" (Gen. 29:17), "Timna *was* a concubine" (Gen. 36:12), "Now Nineveh *was* an exceeding great city" (Jonah 3:3).

[29] Hermann Gunkel, *Schophung und Chaos in Urzeit und Endzeit* (Gottingen, Germany: Vandenhoeck und Ruprecht, 1895).

[30] ". . . the disorder of formless matter and infinite space, supposed to have existed before the ordered universe" (*Webster's New World Dictionary*, 1979, s. v. "chaos").

[31] The Greek translation of Gen. 1:2 approximates this: "Now the earth was invisible and not working. . . ." The English word *chaos* is merely a transliteration of the Greek word *chaos*. *Chaos* is not used in Gen. 1:2 in the Greek Old Testament, commonly referred to as the LXX. The Greek

from the early Greek philosophers[32] or perhaps from later Aramaic translations.[33] So it seems best to understand the phrase "without form and void"[34] as simply meaning that the earth was unfinished. "At this stage the earth was perfect but incomplete."[35]

One can further conclude that the earth was not a smoldering accretion of cosmic debris because twice reference is made to oceanic waters that covered the earth's surface. Verse 2 states, first, that darkness was over the surface of the "deep" and, secondly, that the Spirit of God was hovering over "the surface of the waters." Since water exists in the liquid phase only between $0°C$ ($32°F$) and $100°C$ ($212°F$), the surface of the earth was of moderate temperature at the moment of its creation. Any reconstruction of Genesis 1 must start from the premise that both the earth and its layer of water were created by God near the start of Day One. Both Exodus 20:11 and Nehemiah 9:6 refer to the creation of the seas separate from the earth. This is done with the use of the conjunction and a separate direct object marker. This confirms that water on the earth did not

---

word *chaos* occurs only twice in the LXX (Mic. 1:6 and Zech. 14:4). In both instances it translates the Hebrew concept of "valley" or "chasm" (Edwin Hatch and Henry A. Redpath, *A Concordance to the Septuagint and the Other Greek Versions of the Old Testament* [*including the Apocryphal books*] [Graz, Austria: Akademische Druck- u. Verlagsanstalt, 1975]: 2:1454).

32 Henry George Liddell and Robert Scott, *A Greek-English Lexicon*, revised and augmented by Sir Henry Stuart Jones and Roderick McKenzie (New York: Oxford Univ. Press, 1996): 1976. Hereafter L & S.

33 The Targum rendering of Genesis 1:2 is "be waste" and "chaotic" (Marcus Jastrow, *A Dictionary of the Targumim, the Talmud Babli and Yerushalmi, and the Midrashic Literature*, 2 vols. [New York, 1903]: 1648, 142). The *Targum Neophyti* of Genesis 1:2 is translated "the land was desolate and void" (Michael Sokoloff, *A Dictionary of Jewish Palestinian Aramaic of the Byzantine Period* [Ramat-Gan, Israel: Bar Ilan Univ., 1990]: 576).

34 See the excellent word study on this phrase in the work by Weston W. Fields, *Unformed and Unfilled* (Nutley, N. J.: P&R, 1976): especially 113-30.

35 Whitcomb, *The Early Earth*, 38.

accumulate via some kind of earth degassing or the capture from nearby snowy meteorites. The water was instead a direct, initial creation by God.

The surface of the water would have been perfectly smooth. Celestial bodies had not yet been created to cause the surge of tides. The atmosphere had not yet been created, so no wind currents generated waves. The surface of the water was not even broken by the occasional breach of an aquatic animal. Instead, the surface of the water lay peaceful and unruffled— completely still.

Liberal commentators have suggested for some time that the phrase *Spirit of God* should be understood as "the wind of God" and be translated as "an awesome wind."[36] *The New English Bible* renders verse 2 in this way: "the earth was without form and void, with darkness over the face of the abyss, and a mighty wind that swept over the surface of the waters." However, since the atmosphere was not created until the following day, it does not seem likely that a huge storm is intended with the phrase *Spirit of God.*

The pristine sphere called earth would have been physically impossible to see because no light, however small, had yet been created. But angelic beings—"the sons of God"—were there and sang together at the birth of the earth (Job 38:7). The Spirit of God[37] was there as well, hovering attentively.[38] The earth was

---

[36] E. A. Speiser, *Genesis* in *The Anchor Bible* (Garden City, N. Y.: Doubleday, 1964): 3.

[37] There seems to be no basis for seeing this reference to the *Spirit of God* as anything but a reference to the Holy Spirit. Note that he was not creating; he was simply in attendance and expressing great interest in the creative process.

[38] So the Syriac translation (*The Old Testament in Syriac: According to the Peshiṭta Version* [Leiden: E. J. Brill, 1977]: I: 1, 1). The Syriac participle used for *hovering* (*mrḥp'*) is elsewhere used to describe "a hen brooding over her young" (J. Payne Smith, *A Compendious Syriac Dictionary* [Oxford: At the Clarendon, 1903]: 538).

probably rotating slowly on its axis, much as it does today. This motion would have been very hard to detect because nothing yet existed in the physical universe to serve as a fixed point against which such movement could be observed. It would also seem reasonable to suggest that the earth's magnetic field was in place at this time as well, but this suggestion is not based on biblical evidence.

Creation of Light

Suddenly, after the magnificent creation of heaven and earth, God spoke: "Let there be light," and the entire universe was instantly filled with electromagnetic radiation. The only place at which this radiation was physically visible, however, was at or on the earth. Light needs an object to reflect from in order to become visible to the human eye. So had man been there to observe this amazing moment in history, the entire surface of the earth would have been suddenly illuminated before him. Suspended in space against a completely black background, the planet earth, in an instant, would have been "turned on." A spectacular blue, pristine sphere would have appeared in man's view.

It is probably not wise to suggest that, instead of creating new light in Genesis 1:3, God simply let his glory show forth. It is now known that light has *physical* properties. Electromagnetic radiation (energy) can be changed into ordinary physical material (mass), and vice versa. The essential nature of God is spiritual, not physical. We can measure light. We can manipulate light. We can make more light. None of these statements are true of God.

God's evaluation of the created light was that it was "good." He was pleased with what he had created. One would not have expected otherwise, but it does seem a bit curious that the statement "and God saw that it was good" keeps recurring. The only place in which God's evaluation of his creative activity is negative is in the context of Eve's creation. "Then the Lord God said, 'It is *not good* for the man to be alone'" (2:18). It should be concluded from this passage that the lack of "goodness" actually relates to the incompleteness of God's creation rather than to a statement regarding morality.

After creating light, God separated the light from the darkness, thereby making the day-night cycle on the earth. "God separated the light from the darkness. And God called the light day, and the darkness he called night" (1:4b-5a). It is impossible to know how this division of light from darkness was accomplished. In the first place, a supernatural event[39] is being described; in the second, this condition only existed for the first three days of earth history. Nevertheless, two possibilities can be posited. First, it could be that some type of barrier or light filter intersected the universe, and God placed all of the "packets" of electromagnetic radiation on one side of this filter. The earth would have then rotated in the plane of this barrier so that day and night would have occurred on a 24-hour cycle.

A second possibility is that God collected the light that he had just created and placed it in a temporary "vessel" situated so that it would emanate light on the earth. The sun would then have replaced this vessel on the fourth day. In either case, approximately half of the globe was cast in light. The other half lay in darkness, with periods of transition, morning and evening, between the two.

---

[39] Though Kline differs on the length of the days of creation and on God's use of "providence" as opposed to a "flurry of stupendous events," he agrees that the view presented in this work must posit "something extraordinary or even supernatural, to account for the effects of light and the day-night cycle mentioned in day one" (Meredith G. Kline, "Space and Time in the Genesis Cosmogony," *Perspectives on Science and Christian Faith,* 48:1 [March 1996]: 13).

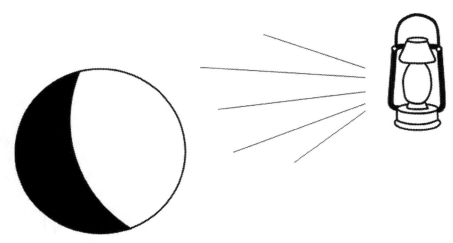

Figure 9: Light shining on the earth to produce the day-night cycle

Verse 5 suggests that the close of the first day was approaching. "And there was evening and there was morning, day one" (1:5b). It is also quite clear that this unit of time, called a "day," was the first of its kind. The Hebrew text uses the absolute form of the numerical adjective *one* to describe this, the first of days. Day One of earth history was now complete. The rest of the days in this chapter are noted by means of the construct form of the numerical adjective—"a second day," "a third day," "a fourth day,"—but the first day is marked off as unique. There had never been one before.

– 3 –

Genesis 1: Days Two and Three

Day Two

Then God said, "Let there be an expanse in the midst of the waters, and let it separate the waters from the waters." So God made the atmosphere and separated the waters that were below the atmosphere from the waters that were above the atmosphere, and it was so. And God called the atmosphere heaven. And there was evening and there was morning, a second day.

—Genesis 1:6-8

God's creative work on Day Two is probably the least understood of all his creative acts. This was the day on which he made the atmosphere. One reason this creative work is misunderstood is that the Hebrew word for *atmosphere* (*raqîaᶜ*) was translated "firmament" in the King James Version.

The word *firmament* is obviously cognate to the English word *firm*. This understanding of "hardness" is reflected even in the major Hebrew lexicons.[1] But this definition does

---

[1] "... the beaten metal plate, or bowl; firmament, the firm vault of heaven ... the gigantic heavenly dome which was the source of the light that brooded over the heavenly ocean and of which the dome arched above the earthly globe" (HALOT, 1290); "extended surface, (solid) expanse (as if *beaten out;*

not arise from the Hebrew root word *raqîaᶜ,* which simply means *expanse.*[2] Instead, the translation "firmament" comes directly from the fourth-century AD Latin Vulgate translation *firmamentum.* The Vulgate, in turn, was influenced by the "scientists" or philosophers of classical Greek culture who thought that the sky was made up of a series of crystal balls, one inside the other.[3] The various celestial bodies were "plastered" on the inner surface of each rotating ball. To the outermost sphere were fastened all the stars. This is certainly *not* the Hebrew concept of the universe.

The Greek translation of the Old Testament uses the Greek word *stereoma* to translate the concept of *raqîaᶜ* or *atmosphere* in Genesis 1:6-8. While it does have overtones of firmness,[4] it is also a fitting word to depict the sky, as in Deuteronomy 33:26. "There is none like the God of the loved one, who mounts up to heaven to help you, even the majestic one of *the skies.*"

In the narrative of Day Two, the concept that waters overlay the atmosphere is repeated three times.

- "Let there be an atmosphere *in the midst of the waters.*"
- "Let it separate *the waters from the waters.*"
- "So God made the atmosphere and divided the waters that were under the atmosphere from *the waters that were above the atmosphere.*"

---

cf. Job 37[18])" (Francis Brown, S. R. Driver, Charles A. Briggs, *A Hebrew and English Lexicon of the Old Testament* [Oxford: Clarendon, 1907] 956).

[2] For an examination of both the noun and its cognate verb, see Stanley V. Udd, "The Canopy and Genesis 1:6-8," *Creation Research Society Quarterly,* 12 (September 1975): 90-3.

[3] See G. J. Toomer, trans., *Ptolemy's Almagest* (New York: Springer-Verlag, 1984): 38-47. Ptolemy apparently assumed the concept of a solid crystalline sphere, though he does not define his understanding of "spheres" in this work.

[4] BDAG, 943.

The words are really quite simple, but the idea of water lying atop the atmosphere stretches the limits of credulity. Obviously, no layer of water rests atop our atmosphere today. Does the Bible actually mean what it appears to say? Does water lie atop the atmosphere, or not? The two positions seem mutually exclusive.

First, it should be pointed out that *both* are true: God did raise a layer of water above the atmosphere on Day Two, and there is no such layer of water above the atmosphere today. The solution to this seeming incongruity is found in the record of the great flood of Noah's day. "In the six hundredth year of Noah's life, in the second month on the seventeenth day of the month— this very day—the entire fountain of the great deep was broken up and the windows of heaven were opened and a torrent of water fell upon the earth for forty days and forty nights" (Gen. 7:11-12). The reason no layer of water exists above our atmosphere today is *not* that God did not initially place water there. It is that God subsequently caused that layer of water to descend upon the earth in judgment of the generation in Noah's day.

Locus of Creation

The text indicates that God created the atmosphere "in the midst of the waters" (1:6). The waters mentioned here must be the same waters as those mentioned in Genesis 1:2—the primeval ocean that covered the early earth. The term translated "in the midst" does not require that the atmosphere be created in the exact medial plane because this term often simply means "midst."[5] So, somewhere below the surface of the primeval ocean, God created the atmosphere, and, as the atmosphere was being created, it separated the single body of water into two bodies of

---

[5] HALOT, 1697. The word is translated *among* 135 times in the NASB (Robert L. Thomas, gen. ed., *New American Standard Exhaustive Concordance of the Bible* [Nashville: Holman, 1981]: 1614, no. 8432).

water. Consequently, at the end of Day Two, the earth was still covered with a layer of water. This lower ocean then interfaced with the newly created atmosphere at its surface. Then, atop the atmosphere rested an additional layer of water.

How high did the atmosphere lift the water? The answer is simple: high enough to allow the atmosphere to exist below it. Beyond that, it is difficult to speculate. Curiously enough, with the advent of space exploration, materials have been discovered that may serve as evidence for the location of that early blanket of water. A joint European venture sent up a Nike Cajun rocket in 1971 to sample the ion composition of the high latitude summer mesopause. One result was an unexpected collection of water cluster ions. Groupings of up to six molecules of water were found clustered around an electric charge at about eighty-five kilometers (51 mi.) above the surface of the ocean. The band of these water cluster ions was quite narrow and quite well defined at the D layer of the mesosphere about fifty miles above the surface of the earth. "It is striking that such large clusters are present and that there is a rapid change in ion composition around 85 km."[6] In other words, below this boundary lays the atmosphere created on Day Two and above these water cluster ions is located the more typical interstellar atmosphere of magnesium and iron ions. Today this anomaly is still the subject of rather intense investigation.[7] The question for present-day scientists is how this water got there. An interesting theory put forth by Louis A. Frank of the University of Iowa was that "the Earth is bombarded

---

[6] A. Johannessen, et al., "Detection of Water Cluster Ions at the High Latitude Summer Mesopause," *Nature,* 235 (January 28, 1972): 215.

[7] H. S. S. Sinha, et al., "Detection of long-living neutral hydrated clusters in laboratory simulation of ionospheric D region plasma," *Journal of Geophysical Research Space Physics,* 118 (2013) 583–589; Robert R. Conway, et al., "Satellite Measurements of Hydroxyl in the Mesosphere," *Geophysical Research Letters,* 23:16 (August 1, 1996): 2093-6.

every day by thousands of house-sized snowballs, a previously unknown type of interplanetary object."[8] A suggestion more in keeping with the biblical text is that the layer of water cluster ions is residue from the former canopy of liquid water that once enclosed the atmosphere. Perhaps these water cluster ions should be treated as "fossil" evidence for the water canopy.

A second unanswerable question is this: how much water once lay above the atmosphere? Or, how thick was this canopy of water? The only clue is the biblical statement that it took forty days and nights for the layer of water to empty. If it rained at the rate of one-half inch per hour, twelve inches would have fallen per day. Thus, the canopy of water must have been at least forty feet thick.[9]

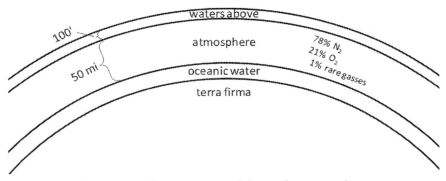

Figure 10: The structure of the early atmosphere

---

8   R. Monastersky, "Is Earth Pelted by Space Snowballs?" *Science News,* 151 (May 31, 1997): 331. "Shuttle Boosts 'Snowball' Idea," *Omaha World Herald,* August 12, 1997, 6. Devastating argumentation against this proposal has also been advanced (R. Monastersky, "Small comet theory melts under scrutiny," *Science News,* 153 [June 6, 1998]: 356-7). But to date, the scientific community has put forth no other theory regarding their formation 50 miles above sea level.

9   The canopy was probably less than 100 feet thick, though this figure is certainly not worth quibbling over. For a discussion of some of the more technical aspects of this problem, see Stanley V. Udd, "The Early Atmosphere," ThM thesis, Grace Theological Seminary, Winona Lake, Ind., 1974, especially 59-66.

Stanley V. Udd

The author of Genesis must have anticipated that the concept of water bounding both the upper and lower extremes of the atmosphere would be difficult to grasp. Three times he states that the atmosphere was created in the midst of the water and that it functioned as a divider between the two bodies of water. So the layering would have consisted first of water, then atmosphere, and finally water, with no intervening gaps. The atmosphere was to form an interface with water at both of its extremities.

The concept of water overspreading the atmosphere is not limited to Genesis 1. Other passages in the Bible also point to the canopy of water above the atmosphere, and these verses consistently refer to it as being in the liquid phase.

"He lays the beams of His upper chambers in the waters / He makes the clouds His chariot / He walks upon the wings of the wind" (Ps. 104:3). The New American Standard translation has rendered the verse as well as anyone might, but the meaning is still not clear. The phrase *to place the beams*[10] *of His roof-chamber*[11] *in the waters* is not easy to understand, but it is clear that this verse speaks of water being upward from the earth.[12]

"For when they maintain this, it escapes their notice that by the word of God the heavens existed long ago and the earth was formed out of water and by water, through which the world at that time was destroyed, being flooded with water (2 Peter 3:5-6 NASB). Though the meanings of the prepositions *out of* and *by* are not patently clear (various translations use an assortment of English prepositions to represent them), two separate bodies of water are clearly indicated. In this passage Peter adds that the combining of these two bodies of water later destroyed the world.

---

[10] HALOT, 1138.
[11] Ibid., 832.
[12] A similar passage, found in the setting of an earthquake, mentions the Lord as "the One who builds His upper chambers in the heavens" (Amos 9:6a).

"Praise Him, highest heaven / and the waters that are above the heavens. / Let them praise the name of the Lord! / For he commanded and they were created (Ps. 148:4-5). The entire psalm offers a poetic description of God's marvelous creation. Verse 4 refers specifically to "the waters that are above the heavens." They are to be a source of praise to the Lord. Two conclusions that can be drawn from this reference are that God created this condition (v. 5) and that liquid water was at one time located above the atmosphere.

Was the Canopy Vaporous?

It was at one time common for creationists to espouse the view that the waters that were above the atmosphere were in the gaseous or vapor phase.[13] The biblical text, however, consistently refers to these waters with the Hebrew word *māyim*, and in every occurrence of this word, the translation is, without exception, *water*—not *vapor*. The Hebrew language knows the word *vapor*[14] and uses it in the following passages, where it is associated with the hydrologic cycle:

> When he utters his voice, there is a tumult of waters in the heavens,
> And he causes the *vapors* to ascend from the ends of the earth;

---

[13] "The earth was surrounded by a vapor blanket. This is based on the evidences suggested in the previous chapters. In particular we focus on the statement of Genesis 1:6-7 of the celestial ocean. It is 'inferred' that this ocean turned to vapor by the fourth creative day due to lower pressure and higher temperatures. We admit that the text does not explicitly say this, but that has little effect on either the model or the predictions" (Joseph C. Dillow, *The Waters Above: Earth's Pre-flood Vapor Canopy* [Chicago: Moody Press, 1981]: 137).

[14] The Hebrew word for *vapor* comes from the root that means "to ascend or go up" (*nāsā'*).

He makes lightning for the rain,
And brings out the wind from his storerooms.
—Jeremiah 10:13

When He utters His voice, there is a tumult of waters
in the heavens.
And He causes *clouds* to ascend from the ends of the
earth;
He makes lightning for the rain, and brings forth the
wind from His storehouses.
—Jeremiah 51:16 NASB

He causes the *vapors* to ascend from the ends of the
earth;
Who makes lightnings for the rain.
Who brings forth the wind from His treasuries.
—Psalm 135:7 NASB

Like *vapors*[15] and wind without rain
Is the man who boasts falsely of his gifts.
—Proverbs 25:14

That the creation narrative uses the word *water* instead of a form of the word *vapor* strongly suggests that the meaning intended by the author was that the canopy was in the liquid state. This liquid canopy lay atop the atmosphere. The canopy was like a bubble of water, inside of which were the atmosphere and the earth.

How this canopy of water was held in place is beyond the pale of inquiry. Its descent at the time of the flood of Noah was not due to a flaw in the design of the canopy, for God takes the credit for causing the descent of the waters upon the inhabited

---

[15] "Billowing clouds" (HALOT, 728).

earth. "And behold, I, even I myself am bringing the flood of water upon the earth, to destroy all flesh in which is the breath of life, from under heaven. Everything that is on the earth shall perish" (Gen. 6:17; see also 7:4, 11, 23).

The canopy may have been held in place by a combination of the upward/outward pressure of the atmosphere, the surface tension of the water itself, and the rotational (circumpolar?) motion supplied by creative fiat on Day Two.[16] The physics required to maintain the water shield cannot be analyzed because the canopy is no longer there, but the Bible repeatedly states without apology that such a body of water was once there, and we must accept that witness.

"And God called the atmosphere heaven. And there was evening and there was morning, a second day" (Gen. 1:8). This verse establishes that the atmosphere can correctly be termed *heaven*. It also validates the previous conclusion that the creative work of God on Day One did not include the atmosphere.

On Day Two God created the atmosphere, using it to divide the water that was on the surface of the earth into two separate bodies. When the work of the second day of creation was completed, the newly created atmosphere was encapsulated in a canopy of water that would help provide a uniform, warm, moist climate around the earth. This bubble of water provided a significant protective covering. Ultra-violet radiation would have been measurably reduced, compared to today. The presence of this layer above the atmosphere doubtless raised the barometric pressure above current levels. The uniform conditions resulting from the insulating effect of this canopy would have significantly reduced the differential heating.

---

[16] It does not seem necessary to suggest that some supernatural mechanism was present to support the water canopy. This layer was simply a part of the natural created order and, as such, did not require the continual input of divine energy to maintain itself.

Weather forecasting would have been monotonous: "Tomorrow is projected to be another fine day." No hurricane, no tornado, no polar vortex, no monsoon, no drought . . . just one beautiful day after another. This creative act further prepared the earth for human habitation.

Day Three

> Then God said, "Let the waters below the heavens be gathered into one place, and let the dry land appear," and it was so. And God called the dry land earth, and the gathered waters he called seas, and God saw that it was good.
>
> —Genesis 1:9-10

The command of God at this point was very specific. He directed his statements to the waters that were under the atmosphere. Had he not done so, he would have undone considerably the work of the preceding day. Instead, he now began to shape and form the planet. The gathering of the waters and the appearance of the dry land were simultaneous events.

The water was gathered into one place.[17] This strongly suggests that the continent was also a single unit. Geologists have been collecting evidence for the past one hundred years that points in the same direction, namely, that all the major

---

[17] The *Biblia Hebraica Stuttgartensia* (BHS) is pointed to read *one place*. It has been suggested that the word *place* be re-vocalized into a form that is based on the previous jussive *let be gathered*. The translation would then read, "Let the waters under the heavens be gathered into a single collection of them" (David Noel Freedman, "Notes on Genesis" in *Divine Commitment and Human Obligation: Selected Writings of David Noel Freedman,* ed. John R. Huddlestun [Grand Rapids, Mich.: Eerdmans, 1997]: 1:4). The present author does not view this adjustment as an improvement.

landmasses were once connected.[18] More will be said about continental drift in the commentary on Genesis 8, but for now, the working hypothesis is this: the earth—from creation to the flood—consisted of only one continent. It is further assumed that the size of that original continent approximated the size[19] of the combined continents today.[20]

Apparently more happened on Day Three than is mentioned in these verses because, at the time of the flood, mention is made of "the fountain of the great deep," which was broken up (see Gen. 7:11). Exactly what this fountain was or where it was located is not clear, and it cannot be viewed today because it has been destroyed ("burst open," NASB). But the great deep must have been an integral part of the continent, for its destruction played a significant role in the horrendous devastation of the earth (cf. Gen. 6:17; 7:11; and 7:23).

Genesis 2:5 indicates that today's hydrologic cycle (evaporation, transpiration, and precipitation) was not in operation between the creation of the earth and its destruction in the days of Noah. "God had not caused it to rain upon the earth." Instead, the watering system of the early earth consisted of a huge spring (*'edh*) that "came up from the earth and watered the whole surface of the ground" (v. 6).

Two items should be noted about this spring. First, the Hebrew verb *came up* is directional. The upward motion expressed by this verb is an invariable component of the action. The concepts of *mist* or *rain*[21] do not satisfy that directional

---

[18] This immense solitary continent is referred to by geologists as *Pangaea* (Charles A. Payne, et al., *Physical Science: Principles and Applications,* 5th ed. [Dubuque, Ia.: Wm. C. Brown, 1989]: 439).

[19] Landmasses cover about thirty per cent of the surface of the planet today.

[20] Actually, inclusion of the continental shelf to about the 1000-isobath level produces the best fit.

[21] The suggestion has been set forth that the Eblaite *i-du* (*rain cloud*) is cognate to Hebrew *'edh*. This etymology seems correct for Job 36:27 where NASB has *mist*, but it does not fit in Genesis 2:6. If *'edh* has a more

component. Secondly, the outflow of water from this spring was "from the earth." Water would well up from the earth, not condense from the sky. The source for this watering system lay necessarily beneath the surface of the earth. Large amounts of water gushed up and watered the entire surface of the continent.

The proposal is this: on Day Three God encapsulated a huge amount of fresh water beneath the continent and allowed it to vent to the surface at some central or high point on the land mass. No mention of this type of activity, however, is made in the first chapter of Genesis.

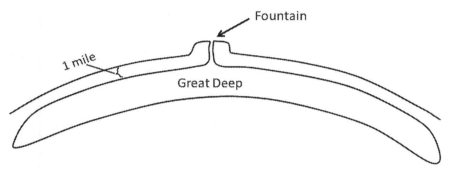

Figure 11: Cross-section of the early earth, showing the great deep

Two psalms, however, mention creative activities that might be linked to the construction of "the fountain of the great deep" on Day Three. Psalm 33:6 recounts the creation of the heavens by the word of the Lord. Verse 7 continues: "gathering in[22]

---

general meaning of "water source," then the fountain of the great deep would have correctly been identified as *'edh* prior to the flood, and rain clouds after the flood would have largely taken over the function of *'edh* (Mitchell DaHood, "Eblaite *i-du* and Hebrew *'ed,* 'Rain Cloud,'" *Catholic Biblical Quarterly,* 43 [1981]: 534-8; Meredith G. Kline, "Space and Time in the Genesis Cosmology," *Perspectives on Science and Christian Faith,* 48 [March 1996]: 12).

[22] No preposition is found in the text at this point, but "in poetic parallelism the governing power of a preposition is sometimes extended to the

a vessel[23] the waters of the sea / Placing in storehouses the deeps." Perhaps this is only a reference to the gathering of the waters under the heavens into the sea, but ancient versions like the LXX and Symmachus[24] translated the word *vessel* as "wineskin."[25]

A less troublesome passage is found in Psalm 136:6. This psalm of thanksgiving for God's faithfulness recites a number of supernatural acts recorded in the Old Testament. Verses 5-7 relate to the week of creation.

> To him who made the heavens with skill,
>   [Perhaps referring to Day Two]
> To him who spread out the earth above the water,
>   [Referring to Day Three]
> To him who made the great lights,
>   [Referring to Day Four]

How is the phrase "who spread out the earth above the water" to be understood? The preposition *above* could also be read as *upon*. In either case, the earth is superior to the water. If God did in fact capture the waters of "the great deep" at the time that he built the continent, this verse could be evidence of that activity.[26] This body of water would have vented then at a

---

corresponding substantive of the second member" (GKC, 384, no. 119, hh; also Waltke and O'Connor, no. 11.4.2).

[23] The NASB sees a different Hebrew root here and achieves the translation "heap." DaHood uses "jar." See the extended discussion at n. 7 (Mitchell DaHood, *Psalm I:1-50* in *The Anchor Bible* [Garden City, N. Y.: Doubleday, 1966]: 201-2).

[24] Fridericus Field, *Origenis Hexaplorum*, 2 vols. (Hildesheim: Georg Olms, 1964): 2:137.

[25] L & S, 258, s.v. "*askos.*"

[26] Harris disagrees and maintains "as waters below the earth refer to waters below shore line, so the earth above the waters refers to landmasses above the shore line. That surely is all" (R. Laird Harris, "The Bible and Cosmology," *Bulletin of the Evangelical Theological Society*, 5:1 [1962]: 15).

central point on the continent so that the whole surface of the ground could be irrigated by the runoff. The terrestrial ocean that remained would have been quite diminished because of the actions on Day Two and Day Three. On Day Three, as God gathered the waters of the sea into one place, he also raised a continent over a large body of fresh water known as the great deep.

> Then God said, "Let the earth sprout sprouts,[27] plants seeding seeds, and[28] fruit trees bearing fruit after its kind that has its seed in it, upon the earth," and it was so. So the earth brought forth vegetation, plants seeding seed after their kind, and trees producing fruit that had its seed inside it, after their kind, and God saw that it was good. And there was evening and there was morning, a third day.
>
> —Genesis 1:11-13

The Lord then overspread the newly created continent with vegetation. The text is not taxonomically sophisticated. It simply divides the plant kingdom into plants that produce edible seeds and plants that produce an edible peel or cortex surrounding an inedible pit. The first group of plants includes corn, wheat, beans, and such, whereas the second group includes plums, apples, cherries, grapes. It is hard to catalogue plant types such as tomatoes, melons, and walnuts. They do not fit neatly into the two biblical categories, but it must be maintained that they were also created on Day Three.

---

[27] This translation is admittedly a bit awkward, but it is an attempt to preserve the play on words that is found in the Hebrew text.

[28] A few Hebrew manuscripts contain the conjunction "and," as do copies of the Samaritan Pentateuch, the Greek Septuagint, the Syriac Peshitta, the Aramaic translation, and the Latin Vulgate. This seems to be a rare instance when Codex Leningradensis has dropped a letter.

A careful reading of the text suggests that God created the plant life utilizing preexisting materials—the earth. God addressed the earth, "Let the earth . . ." instead of the more usual "Let there be. . . ." Then, in the restatement of this creative activity, the author says, "So the earth brought forth vegetation" (v. 12). The use of preexisting material in no way detracts from the supernatural quality of the fiat creation that characterized this week. To create a plant from sterile soil is as difficult as creating a plant from nothing. Neither is humanly possible.

Aquatic plants are not mentioned in the brief text of Day Three. It seems reasonable to conclude that they were also created on this day. The presence of aquatic plant life is critical to the well-being of aquatic animals in that plants are an important source for food and oxygen in the water.

− 4 −

Genesis 1: Day Four

Then God said, "Let there be lights in the expanse of the heavens to separate the day from the night, and let them be for signs, and for months, and for days and years, and let them be for lights in the expanse of the heavens to give light upon the earth," and it was so. So God made the two great lights, the greater light to rule the day, and the lesser light to rule the night. He made the stars also. And God placed them in the expanse of the heavens to give light upon the earth, to govern the day and the night, and to separate the light from the darkness, and God saw that it was good. And there was evening and there was morning, a fourth day.

—Genesis 1:14-19

Even conservative theologians often misrepresent Day Four in commentaries. It is seemingly difficult for many to acknowledge that the earth was the only speck of matter in the physical universe before the fourth day. To them it apparently seems more credible if the sun, moon, and stars were created earlier, and on the fourth day God merely made them visible— or something of that sort.[1] In reality, to create a single star on

---

[1] C. F. Keil, "Genesis," in *Commentary on the Old Testament* in 10 vols., trans. James Martin (Grand Rapids, Mich.: Eerdmans, n. d.): 59. *New Scofield*

the fourth day was not more or less stupendous than to create a star on Day One.

The exegetical comments of John Sailhamer are especially curious. He posits that because a preposition (*to*) follows the jussive (*let there be*) in verse 14, the text is transformed so that the "narrative assumes that the heavenly lights already were created 'in the beginning.'"[2] He then achieves this translation for verse 14: "Let the lights in the expanse be for separating the day and night. . . ."[3] Against this suggestion, it should be noted that the authority Sailhamer cites in arguing his case is not referring to the use of the preposition with the jussive.[4]

Secondly, Sailhamer fails to interact with verses 15 and 16, which continue the *creative* thought: "So God *made* the two great lights and the stars. . . . And God *placed* them in the expanse of heaven." The time aspects of these two verbs *made* and *placed* are not at variance with their verbal counterparts on any other day in the creation narrative. It seems better, therefore, to understand the preposition to be describing the

---

Reference Bible (New York: Oxford, 1967): 1, n. 6. John H. Sailhamer, "Genesis," in *The Expositor's Bible Commentary* in 12 vols. (Grand Rapids, Mich.: Zondervan, 1990): 33-34. Others cite Day Four as the reason for rejecting that the creation narrative says anything scientific whatever. "The fact that God made the sun, moon, and stars on the fourth day, not on the first, ought to tell us that this is not a scientific statement (Gen. 1:14-19). This one detail in the narrative suggests that concordism [harmony between current evolutionary theory and the account of creation contained in Genesis] is not going to work well and that the agenda of the writer must have been something other than one of describing actual physical processes" (Clark H. Pinnock, "Climbing out of a Swamp: The Evangelical Struggle to Understand the Creation Texts," *Interpretation,* 43:2 [April 1989]: 148).

2   John H. Sailhamer, *Genesis Unbound: A Provocative New Look at the Creation Account* (Sisters, Ore.: Multnomah, 1996): 132.

3   Ibid.

4   GKC, 348h.

function that these celestial bodies were to perform at their creation on Day Four.[5]

Statement of Creation

Five times during the course of the narrative of Day Four, creative terminologies are used:

- Let there be lights (v. 14),
- Let them be for signs (v. 14),
- Let them be for lights (v. 15),
- So God made the two great lights (v.16),
- And God placed them (v. 17).

There can be no question but that the text is indicating both God's fiat creation of the celestial bodies and his secondary assignment of their functions from earth's perspective. In other passages this creative activity is seen as an indication of the greatness of God. [6]

> Lift up your eyes on high
> And see who has created these,
> The one who leads forth their host by number,
> He calls them all by name;
> Because of the greatness of his might and the strength
> of power,
> Not one is missing.
>
> —Isaiah 40:26

---

[5] HALOT, 508ff. Note also the use of *hoste* in vv. 15 and 17 in LXX.
[6] So Job 38:33; Isa. 42:5; Ps. 147:4; 148:3.

Figure 12: He made the stars as well.

Purpose for the Creation of the Sun, Moon, and Stars

The first stated purpose for the creation of the celestial bodies was to divide the day from the night. This so-called governing would be achieved by means of the light that shone on the earth from the sun, moon, and stars (vv. 17-18). The sun was to be the dominant light during the day, and the moon was to be the dominant light during the night (v. 16).[7]

The secondary purpose for the creation of the sun, moon, and stars is expressed in a fourfold manner. "And let them be for signs, and for months, and for days and years." The four purposes or functions will each be considered separately.

---

[7] Ps. 136:9a adds the stars to this ruling of the night: "The moon and stars to rule by night."

Signs

The word *sign* in this verse has generated considerable interest over the years. It has been fashionable for some time to read theological significance into the names of the signs of the Zodiac, based on the word *sign* in Genesis 1:14.[8] But because the names of the constellations are only the product of human imagination, "reading" the constellations seems a useless venture. Natural revelation cannot provide information about the salvific work of Christ. It can only put the stargazer in the position of being "without excuse" (Rom. 1:20). So the word *sign* does not refer to communication through natural occurrences.

The biblical text often uses the word *sign* to describe supernatural events.[9] One of the most obvious examples is the sign that occurred at Hezekiah's healing. "In those days Hezekiah became mortally ill, and he prayed to the Lord, and the Lord spoke to him and gave him a *sign*" (2 Chron. 32:24; Isa. 38:7-8). The sign was that the shadow caused by the sun moved backward. Other supernatural celestial occurrences that doubtless fall into this same category include the lengthening of the day during the conquest of Canaan (Josh. 10:12-14), the star that guided the magi from the east (Matt. 2), and the future wonders that will occur around the great and glorious day of the Lord (Acts 2:19-20).

One of the stated purposes for which God created the celestial bodies was that he might use them to show to mankind his blessing or direction in particular instances. This is the type of demonstration that God offered to Ahaz in

---

[8] Joseph A. Seiss, *The Gospel in the Stars; or, Primeval Astronomy* (Philadelphia: E. Claxton & Company, 1882). This 452-page book includes a sky chart.

[9] "Most of the eighty occurrences of *'ot* refer to 'miraculous signs'" (Robert L. Alden, *Theological Wordbook of the Old Testament,* eds. Harris, Archer, and Waltke [Chicago: Moody Press, 1980]: 18-19).

Isaiah 7 to strengthen his faith. But Ahaz refused the sign and thereby angered God. Only a very powerful God is capable of manipulating the sun, moon, and stars.[10]

Months

This word should be placed in quotation marks because our English understanding of the word *month* is not currently dependent upon the phases of the moon. Historical etymology connects the concept of *month* with the lunar cycle. Today, however, we change from one month to the next without regard to the phase or position of the moon in the night sky.

It is common for translators to use the word *seasons* for this word, but prior to the adjustments resulting from the flood of Noah's day, seasons, as we now know them, did not exist. The phenomenon of seasons began after the flood. "While the earth remains, *seedtime and harvest, and cold and heat, and summer and winter,* and day and night shall not cease" (Gen. 8:22). Before the flood, the canopy blanketing the atmosphere would have produced a moist, uniform, mild climate year round.

The translation of this word as *months* is made clear in Psalm 104:19—"He made the moon for *months*; he knows the sun's path."[11] The English language falters in capturing the precise meaning here, but if one understands *month* to refer to the cycle of the moon, then the meaning is clear.

---

[10] The NIV has downgraded this aspect of the purpose for celestial bodies by subordinating the concept of *signs* to the other three purposes that follow: "and let them serve as signs to mark seasons and days and years" (v. 14b). It could be that the editors were following the lead of *The Jerusalem Bible* or *The New English Bible*. The Hebrew text clearly does not allow for this subordination.

[11] An alternate translation might read: "The moon makes months, and the sun knows his going." In either case, the association of the moon with the concept of *month* stands.

So the second purpose for the celestial bodies was that the moon might mark off the twice fortnightly period estimated by the English word *month*. The Jewish calendar, begun in Exodus 12, employs the lunar cycle.

Days

Days are marked off by the apparent motion[12] of the sun across the sky, producing the 24-hour light and darkness cycle. This period is the shortest of the group and well understood.

Years

Years are marked off by the rotation of the "fixed" stars in the night sky. If, for example, one observes the Big Dipper at the same time each night, that constellation will appear to rotate 360 degrees around Polaris, the North Star, over the course of approximately 365 nights. This period defines the concept of *year*, and reflects the revolution of the earth around the sun.

For the purpose of marking years, starlight must be visible on the surface of the earth. The model that one chooses to construct for the creative action of Day Two—the creation of the atmosphere and the elevation of the water above the atmosphere—must allow for the penetration of light from distant stars. Since liquid water and water vapor are equally transparent to the visible spectrum of light waves, either model would have worked. Before the flood, years could still have been measured by the rotation of the constellations.

---

[12] In reality, the apparent path of the sun through the sky is a result of the rotational motion of the earth on its axis.

Locus of Creation

Because the texts of both Day Two and Day Four employ the same Hebrew word *raqîaᶜ*, translated *expanse* or *atmosphere*, it is commonly held that in both instances this word refers to the same object or area.[13] This, however, leads to rather foolish presentations of the creation narrative.[14] The Hebrew text consistently distinguishes between the two locations. When speaking of the atmosphere created on Day Two, the text uses only the word *expanse* (1:6-8). When speaking of the cosmic universe on Day Four, the text consistently uses the phrase *expanse of heaven* (1:14-18). Because the Hebrew text differentiates between these two areas of space—*expanse* versus *expanse of heaven*—it seems good exegetical practice to also note these obvious distinctions. The *expanse* and the *expanse of heaven* are not the same either grammatically or scientifically.

On the second day, God created the atmosphere. On the fourth day, he filled the starry universe with luminous bodies. These celestial objects provide convenient ways to measure the passage of time. They also give the Lord a large backdrop on which to make manifest his will.

Currently, NASA (the National Aeronautics and Space Administration) provides a website that features the "Astronomy Picture of the Day."[15] The magnificent photographic images exhibited there can quite often be neither understood nor explained. The viewer is driven back to David's exclamation: "The heavens display the glory of God" (Ps. 19:1).

---

[13] Sailhamer, for example, states that the word *sky* can handle both texts well (Sailhamer, "Genesis," 28-9).

[14] See the "graphic representation" in *The New American Bible* (1970): 5; Donald England, *A Christian View of Origins* (Grand Rapids, Mich.: Baker, 1972): 122.

[15] www.apod.nasa.gov/apod

– 5 –

Genesis 1: Days Five and Six

Day Five

Then God said, "Let the waters swarm with swarms of living creatures, and flyers let them fly over the earth before the expanse of the heavens." So God created the great sea creatures and every living creature that moves with which the waters swarmed after their kind, and all the winged birds after its kind, and God saw that it was good. And God blessed them, saying, "Be fruitful and multiply and fill the waters of the sea, and the birds, let them multiply on the land." And there was evening and there was morning, a fifth day.

—Genesis 1:20-23

The fifth day involved the creation of part of the animal kingdom. As in the case of the creation of the plants on Day Three, when God spoke to the *earth*, so here on Day Five, God spoke to the waters: "Let the waters swarm. . . ." The implication is that these creatures were not created *ex nihilo* but were instead created by God from the water itself. Just as God formed Adam's body from the dust of the ground (2:7), so here he used preexisting material to create these fabulous creatures.[1]

Three distinct categories of animals were created. First, God created creatures characterized by largeness, whose habitat is associated with water. This group would have included whales, large fish, and dinosaurs. Today's taxonomist would not see these three categories as "related," but it should be remembered that taxonomists were not consulted when God created these creatures. Furthermore, one should *not* look for relationships among various species and groups of animals, for the text is clear that the animals were each created after their own kind. Whales did not evolve from fish, nor did fish evolve from whales. Instead, the Bible indicates that all of these large sea creatures were created essentially simultaneously. Any similarity that may exist between the various species is due to a common Creator, not to a common ancestry.

The association of large reptiles, better known as dinosaurs, with a watery habitat is further confirmed in Psalm 104:

> O, Lord, how many are your works!
> In wisdom you have made them all.
> The earth is full of your creations.
> There is the sea, vast and wide,
> In which are swarms beyond counting,
> Animals both great and small.
> There the ships move along,
> And leviathan, this one you formed[2] to sport in it.[3]
>
> —Psalm 104:24-26

---

[1] When the Genesis account speaks of God creating something from nothing, it generally uses the phrase "and God said, 'Let there be . . . '" (e.g., 1:3—light; 1:6—atmosphere; 1:14—sun, moon, and stars). The exception is 1:1, when heaven and earth were created. Being the first created entities, neither heaven nor earth could have been created out of preexisting material.

[2] This verb of creation is first used in Gen. 2:7—"Then the Lord God formed man of dust from the ground." See also vv. 8 and 19 and Isa. 45:18.

[3] Leviathan is also associated with the sea in Job 41:1, 31-32.

So it seems that the general category of dinosaurs was created on Day Five. But what was this leviathan that God created to sport in the sea? Leviathan was a dinosaur. God himself gave a fuller description of this creature:

> I will not be silent about his anatomy or the fact of the greatness of his frame. Who of you can strip off his skin? Who can penetrate his folded coat of mail?[4] Who can open his mouth? His teeth are like rows of terror. His strong scales are his pride, closed up tightly and sealed. One fits closely against another. Even air cannot come between them. Each scale sticks to his brother. They are compact and inseparable. His sneezes sparkle with light and his eyes are like the gleam of dawn. From his mouth flame shoots out; streams of fire leap forth. From his nostrils goes forth billowing smoke, like a cooking pot that boils. His breath scorches live coals and flame goes forth from his mouth. In his neck resides strength. At his presence the languid leap. The muscle of his flesh clings firmly, molded firmly in place. His heart is as hard as a stone, as hard as a lower millstone. The mighty are afraid when he stirs. From the crashing they withdraw. The sword reaching him does no harm, nor does spear, dart, or javelin. He considers iron like straw; bronze, like rotten wood. He is not chased away by the bow. Sling-stones are like stubble to him, clubs are like stubble. He laughs at the whistle of the sword.
>
> His belly is rough as broken potsherds. He thrashes around like a sledge upon mud. He makes the deep boil like a cooking pot. He makes the sea

---

4   So the LXX (L & S, 814).

like a boiling kettle. Light follows in his wake. You would think the ocean had silver hair. There is no one upon the earth that is his equal—one without fear. He looks down upon all that is high. He is king over all the proud.[5]

—Job 41:12-34

As will later be seen, this description of leviathan comes from a time when animals were not subject to the human will (see commentary on Gen. 9). Before the flood—from Adam to Noah—the animals were subject to mankind (1:28). That was the "age of the dinosaur." Fortunately, this fire-breathing reptile is extinct. It is furthermore not possible to identify exactly which species is under view. The words of this passage are not species specific; they speak only in very general terms.

Whales and large fish were also created on Day Five. The KJV is not incorrect in using "whales" in the translation of verse 21, but the term *whales* is more limiting than the Hebrew word that it translates.[6]

The second category of animal created on the fifth day was "every living creature that moves [in the sea]." The ability to move is a general characteristic that distinguishes animals from plants. So the sea was suddenly filled with swarms or schools of zooplankton, small fish, shellfish of every description, anemones, eels, dolphins.

The third category of animal that God created on this day was "winged creatures." Again, the general characteristics of this category of animal are being feathered and able to fly. Were bats—mammals that fly but have no feathers—and flightless

---

[5] Based upon Stanley V. Udd, "An Evaluation of the Mythological Hermeneutic in Light of the Old Testament Usage of the Leviathan Motif," ThD dissertation, Grace Theological Seminary, Winona Lake, Ind., 1980.

[6] This Hebrew word *tannîm* is translated variously in NASB as "dragon," "sea monster," and "serpent."

birds like ostriches also created on this day? Probably, though a decision here is not especially significant.

Though the winged creatures were supernaturally created out of the water, they were not limited to a watery habitat. First, they were to fly about over the earth. These creatures are referred to as "birds of the heaven" in numerous passages.[7] The birds were also commanded to reproduce "on the earth" (v. 22). So the source of their substance (i.e., "the waters") did not determine their habitat. This same argument also applies to the category dinosaur. Though dinosaurs were created out of the water, their habitat was not restricted to that medium. They could certainly have lumbered around on the surface of the continent.

The so-called age of the dinosaurs, then, would have run from Day Five to the time of Noah's flood. All of the dinosaur fossils that have been recovered were creatures living at the time that Noah and his family entered the ark.

Day Five ended with a blessing: "And God blessed them, saying, 'Be fruitful and multiply, and fill the waters of the sea, and the birds, let them multiply on the land'" (Gen. 1:22). Here God was not simply wishing his creation a good day. No, this too was a creative statement. He was not merely speaking; he was working, and this work was expressed in the form of a *blessing*. Here the Creator endowed his creatures with those intricate responses that resulted in the propagation of the various species. God now blessed the fish and fowl with reproductive instinct. The amazing migratory patterns, homing instincts, nest-building abilities, and courtship displays that we observe are not products of "Mother Nature." They are the specific gifts of God to his creatures.

---

[7] At least 38 times in Scripture they are called "birds of the heaven," three times in Gen. 1 (vv. 26, 28, and 30). Once they are also referred to as "birds of the mountains" (Ps. 50:11).

Finally, the verb used to describe God's creative activity (i.e., "let them *swarm*") suggests that more than a single pair of each species was created. An adequate population of each of the species was produced, resulting in precise ecological balance. These animals were created "not only in a rich variety of genera and species, but in large numbers of individuals."[8] The sea and air were now populated with an appropriate balance of specific animals.

Day Six

> And God said, "Let the earth bring forth living creatures after its kind: cattle and creepers and beasts of the earth after its kind," and it was so. So God made the beasts of the earth after its kind and the cattle after its kind and all that creeps on the ground after its kind. And God saw that it was good.
>
> —Genesis 1:24-25

To start Day Six, God commanded the earth to bring forth three general categories of creatures. First, "cattle" were created. This category included more than Herefords, Angus, and Holsteins, for the Hebrew word is a general word used to describe any type of domesticated animal. Sheep, camels, and lamas—animals that respond to domestication—were created at this time.

"Creepers" or creeping things included insects, protozoa, worms, land snakes, toads—all sorts of creepy-crawlies. The class of animals called amphibians may have been created on either Day Five or Six.[9]

---

8 Keil, "Genesis," 61.

9 Even this sentence illustrates the tremendous hold that the theory of evolution has on one's thinking. The underlying assumption of the sentence is this: since all amphibians fall in one class of related animals, it follows

Finally, God created the "beasts of the earth." These included all creatures that are typically considered wild. However, these animals were not carnivorous before the flood. All animals— "every beast of the earth, every bird of the sky, and every moving, living thing"—were herbivorous (1:30).

As mentioned in the discussion on Day Five, God did not limit his creation to a single pair of each species. Ecological balance existed from the beginning. Had God created only two sheep, for example, God may have brought extinction to that species had he chosen a sheep when he fashioned the "garments of skin" for Adam and his wife.

The earth was now ready for man. God had finished creating the beautiful, ecologically balanced environment in which he now intended to place the crown of his creation—man.

Creation of Mankind

> Then God said, "Let us make man in our image, according to our likeness, and let them rule over the fish of the sea and over the birds of the heavens and over the domesticated animals and over all the earth, and over everything that creeps on the earth." So God created man in his own image, in the image of God he created him; male and female he created them.
>
> —Genesis 1:26-27

The "us" and "our" of verse 26 are obviously plural in form and could easily be understood as indicative of conversation

---

that if God created one species of amphibians on a certain day, he must have created all species of amphibians on that day. The option surely exists that some of what we call amphibians were created on Day Five and some on Day Six.

between the various persons of the Godhead.[10] While plurality is a legitimate conclusion from the text, trinitarian doctrine is not being explicitly taught here. This divine plurality may anticipate the very nature of mankind that God was about to create. Just as the Godhead can be seen as three and one at the same time, so Adam and Eve could be seen as two and one at the same time.

> He created him [sing.], male and female he created them.
> —Genesis 1:27

> This is the scroll of the story of Adam. At the time God created Adam (*'ādām* [sing.]), he made him in the likeness of God. He created them male and female and blessed them and called their name Man (*'ādām* [sing.]).
> —Genesis 5:1-2a[11]

These numbers—one, two, or three—are used to describe relationships[12] in these settings more than they are meant to count noses. (For a discussion of the term *image of God*, see ch. 6.)

---

[10] It might be argued from this passage that v. 26 reflects conversation between God and the angels. This, however, would suggest some cooperation or involvement on the part of the angels in the creation process. Neh. 9:6 argues effectively against such a position: "You alone are the Lord. You have made the heaven and the heaven of heavens with all their hosts, the earth and all that is on it, the sea and all that is in it. You give life to all of them and the heavenly host bows down before you."

[11] See also 2:24—"they shall become one."

[12] See Christ's prayer in John 17:20-22—"I do not ask in behalf of these alone, but for those also who believe in Me through their word; that they may all be one; even as You, Father, are in Me, and I in You, that they also may be in Us; so that the world may believe that You sent Me. The glory which You have given Me I have given to them, that they may be one, just as We are one" (NASB).

It is also observable from this passage that God is the inventor of and source for the differences between the genders. Sexuality is the product of the mind of God. Because of our sinful nature, it is easy to think of the attractions between men and women as originating in our sinful flesh. While it is true that these desires need to be carefully monitored, nonetheless, at the heart of the issue lies the fact that sexuality is a significant part of God's *good* creation.

Christ himself underscored this when he spoke to sinful men. "And He answered and said, 'Have you not read, that He who created them from the beginning made them male and female?'" (Matt. 19:4 NASB). We must conclude from this that Jesus still considered his creative ideas to be very good.

The Blessing of God

> And God blessed them; and God said to them, "Be fruitful, and multiply, and fill the earth, and subdue it and rule over the fish of the sea and over the birds of the heavens and over every living thing that creeps on the earth."
>
> —Genesis 1:28

God now blessed Adam and Eve with a twofold blessing. The first portion had to do with procreation. As seen in verse 22, this blessing was creative. God now implanted in the minds and bodies of Adam and Eve those instinctive drives and desires that guarantee the continuation of the human race. When "a young man's fancy turns to love," he is in fact responding to this creative endowment or blessing from God.

The Lord used three imperatives to describe the creative action he bestowed upon mankind: "be fruitful," "multiply," and "fill the earth." This certainly sounds as though the Lord intended that mankind should propagate and become numerous on the earth. Did God not know that overpopulation would become a significant problem in the twenty-first century? Perhaps the question might rather be: is overpopulation, in fact, a serious issue?[13]

If overpopulation were a function of the number of people per square mile, it follows that the countries with the greatest density of people would be the countries most plagued with overpopulation. According to *The World Almanac and Book of Facts: 2013*,[14] the most densely populated country is an island near Hong Kong named Macao, with a population of 73,350 per square mile, yet starvation is not an urgent problem on Macao.

Compare the situations between North and South Korea. North Korea often faces major famine. One would assume that this situation was at least partly influenced by the overburden of too many people. South Korea, however, has over two and a half times as many people per square mile ($1,288/mi.^2$ vs. $497/mi.^2$). It can, therefore, be concluded that North Korea's struggle is not a result of population density.

Why is it that India's people struggle for daily food, while the Netherlands enjoys a more prosperous economy (India = $945/mi^2$; the Netherlands = $1,259/mi^2$)? Can the prosperity of Taiwan, when compared to the austerity of mainland China, be linked to population density? Taiwan has a population density of $1,849/mi^2$, while China has only $365/mi^2$.

The matter of overpopulation is a function of economic theory, not population density. A free economy is able to handle very high densities—perhaps there is no upper limit. Socialistic

---

[13] The advocates for population control are often also advocates of abortion rights. Their agendas are usually couched in humanitarian terms, but population control is more a tenet of socialism than a matter of human density.

[14] Sarah Janssen, ed., *The World Almanac and Book of Facts: 2013* (New York: World Almanac, 2012).

or communistic economies, on the other hand, face problems of insufficient resources.[15] So the creative command by God to be fruitful, to multiply, and to fill the earth is not unreasonable, even in the twenty-first century.

These facts do not mean that the only biblical response for a couple is to have as many children as possible, though that could perhaps be argued. Instead, God was placing the choice of reproduction into human hands with this blessing. We have the privilege and responsibility of making reasoned choices regarding family size. The guiding principle seems to be that "children are a gift[16] of the Lord" (Ps. 127:3a). This principle is a remarkable contrast to the shrill hysteria of the population control advocates.

After creating Adam and Eve, God put them in charge of the fish, the birds, and the living things that move on the earth.[17] Two words describe this control—*to subdue* and *to dominate* (also used in v. 26). These words speak of substantial control. The Hebrew verb for *subdue* can also be used to describe rape. When King Ahasuerus saw Haman pleading for his life on Esther's couch, he asked: "Will he even assault [subdue, rape] the queen with me in the house?" (Est. 7:8 NASB). This usage suggests that the control that Adam and Eve had over the animal kingdom was much more extensive than our control today. Adam apparently had simply to speak to an animal, and

---

[15] See Rousas J. Rushdoony, *The Myth of Overpopulation* (Nutley, N. J.: The Craig Press, 1971): 10. Wayne Grudem and Barry Asmus, *The Poverty of Nations: A Sustainable Solution* (Wheaton Ill: Crossway Books, 2013).

[16] "Gift" is understood as meaning "given by" the Lord (HALOT, 688).

[17] Verse 26 lists:

Verse 26 lists:	Verse 28 lists:
(1) the fish of the sea,	(1) the fish of the sea,
(2) the birds of the heaven,	(2) the birds of the heaven,
(3) the domesticated animals,	(3) all the living creatures that creep on the earth.
(4) the creepers who creep on the earth.	

The division of the earthbound animals into two groups in v. 26 does not seem different than the grouping in v. 28. It is to be understood that man was in charge of *all*.

it obeyed.[18] Fishing would have been substantially easier with this arrangement. Even the insects would have done Adam's bidding. He and Eve likely used animals to help in the care and management of the garden of Eden.

Today we do not enjoy the same control of the animal world as Adam did. This control was taken from mankind after the flood (Gen. 9:1-2). As a result, it is difficult to imagine the types of things that Adam and his descendants could have done with the animals between the creation and the flood. It is fascinating to consider the implications of enjoying leviathan as an obedient pet.

The initial control that man enjoyed before the flood will again be reinstated, according to Psalm 8. Hebrews 2:5-8, which quotes Psalm 8, indicates that this reinstatement will occur when Christ finally has all things subjected to himself. It seems reasonable to conclude that this readjustment will be made at the beginning of the millennium (see Isa. 11:3-9). Thus, the dominion of man declined from dominant control to limited control, but dominant control will again one day characterize man's relationship to the animals.

The Provision of God

And God said, "Behold, I have given you every plant yielding seed that is on the surface of all the earth, and every tree that has fruit yielding seed; it shall be food for you. But to every beast of the earth and to every bird of the heavens and to everything that creeps on the earth that has the breath of life, every green plant shall be food," and it was so.

—Genesis 1:29-30

---

[18] The suggestion is that Adam used the spoken word, rather than a sort of mental telepathy.

God created Adam as a vegetarian. He was to eat seeds and fruit. The remainder of the living animals—every beast of the earth, every fowl of the air, and every creeping thing— were to live on the green, leafy parts of the plants. Obviously, carnivorousness did not exist in the original world. Many of the fossils recovered by evolutionary paleontologists are classified today as carnivores, based on their physical appearance.[19] But according to the biblical text, animals did not eat meat until God brought about notable changes at the close of the flood.

Some commentators believe that carnivorousness is a result of the entrance of sin, but the curse of Genesis 3 does not contain a statement to that effect, nor does it even allude to such a change.[20] Rather, the change occurred in Genesis 9:3—"Every moving thing that lives shall be food for you." That was the introduction of carnivorousness.

The preying of one species of animal on another will also be done away with in the millennium. "The cow and the bear will graze, their young will lie down together, and the lion will eat straw like the ox" (Isa. 11:7 NASB). The bear and the lion will still be recognizable morphologically, but their internal structures will be adjusted so that they will again eat "straw."

> And God saw all that he had made, and behold, it was very good. And there was evening and there was morning, a day, the sixth day.
>
> —Genesis 1:31

---

[19] The morphology of skeletal remains is not always determinative in ascertaining the eating habits of a species. For example, the skull of a giant panda would not lead to the conclusion that the animal is a strict herbivore. Considerable disagreement currently exists over the eating habits of the famous *Tyrannosaurus rex*.

[20] Henry M. Morris, *The Genesis Record*, (Grand Rapids, Mich.: Baker, 1976): 125.

Here is the statement of completion. Everything that God had made was functioning. Everything was fulfilling its designed responsibility, set in place by the Master Builder of the universe. The term *good* may be intended to exclude "the existence of anything evil in the creation of God."[21] However, its uniform application to all parts of the material universe suggests that the intended meaning is more in line with the concept of *perfect*. Everything that God had made was perfect in every detail.

The numerical adjective *sixth* has the article *the* attached to it. This is unique among the six days of creation and emphasizes the definite and conclusive nature of this day. The creation week started with "in the beginning" and ended with completion (*kalah*) (Gen. 2:1). God only created for six days. "For in six days the LORD made the heavens and the earth, the sea and all that is in them, and rested on the seventh day" (Ex. 20:11a NASB).

---

[21] Keil, "Genesis," 67.

– 6 –

An Excursus on the Image of God

"So God created man in his own image" (Gen. 1:27a). That sounds like a good thing, but what does it mean?

The "image of God" is the phrase used in the creation narrative to describe man's relationship to his Creator. Man was created to reflect and mirror God. This thought is expanded in the book of Isaiah, where it is stated:

> Bring My sons from afar
> And My daughters from the ends of the earth,
> Everyone who is called by My name,
> And whom I have created for My glory,
> Whom I have formed, even whom I have made.
> —Isaiah 43:6b-7 NASB

The Hebrew word for *glory* is often a relational word.[1] It is used to describe how God relates to mankind. When Moses requested to see God's glory in Exodus 33:18-23, he

---

[1] The same is true of the Greek word used to translate the Hebrew word *glory* in the LXX. Koiné Greek *doxa* also uses the nuance of *relationship* in numerous passages. See John 17 (8 times); Rom. 3:23; the phrase "Christ in you the hope of *glory*" in Col. 1:27; Heb. 2:10; etc.

encountered no visual images of splendor or radiance but rather proclamations of God's essential character: "compassionate and gracious, slow to anger and abounding in faithfulness and truth" (Ex. 34:6). These traits speak of God's relationship with man. These relational terms describe the fundamental nature of God's glory. Man actually shares in the characteristics that define God, in the qualities that make God relational. This, then, is the concept tied up in the phrase "image of God."

In the New Testament, *glory* and *image* are used together. "For a man ought not to have his head covered, since he is the image and glory of God; but the woman is the glory of man" (1 Cor. 11:7 NASB). The image of God and the glory of God are parallel concepts; both speak of the way in which man is related to God.

Two words are used to describe the relationship between God and man in the creation account—*image* and *likeness*. No essential difference exists between these two terms. This is evident because no necessary order is associated with these words (cf. 1:26 with 5:3). They share the same prepositions and modifiers (cf. 1:27 and 5:1).

In 1979, a statue unearthed in northern Syria contained a rather lengthy Aramaic and Assyrian inscription dated to the ninth century BC.[2] Twice the Aramaic text refers to the statue itself. Once the statue is called a likeness (*dmut*) of *Hadad-yis^c ī* (line 1), and once the statue is called the *image* (*tzlm*) of *Hadad-yis^c ī* (line 12).[3] It is clear that this language, a close cousin to the Hebrew, does not distinguish between the meanings of these two words. They are synonyms in Aramaic. The same is true in the Hebrew language.

---

[2] A. R. Millard and P. Bordreuil, "A Statue from Syria with Assyrian and Aramaic Inscriptions," *Biblical Archaeologist,* 45 (Summer 1982): 135-41.

[3] Ibid., 137-8.

The LXX does not translate these words rigidly as though they were separate concepts. Instead, these two words convey but one concept; they are true synonyms.[4]

The word *image* is usually translated just that way—"*image*." It can be used to describe a statue (2 Kings 11:18), a copy of something (1 Sam. 6:5), a drawing (Ezek. 23:14), a temporary apparition (Ps. 38:6), or the way in which Adam reflected God (Gen. 1:26).

It is grammatically possible that *image* could refer to the shape of the body that God formed from the dust of the ground. If, however, *image* has to do with mankind's particular shape, then primates, who share the same body contour, could also be said to be made in the image of God. Such is certainly not the case; mankind is unique. "God's image obviously does not consist in man's body, which was formed from earthly matter, but in his spiritual, intellectual, moral likeness to God from whom his animating breath came."[5]

Furthermore, the "image of God" does not connote a particular moral state, either righteous or wicked. Adam did not lose his likeness to God at the fall. He became sinful, but he did not lose his likeness in God's image. If Adam's likeness to God refers to Adam's righteous nature, then Adam would have lost his ability to reflect God after the fall. But the New Testament refers to men in the first century AD, and, by extension, to us today, as still made in the image of God. "With it [the tongue] we bless our Lord and Father; and with it we curse men, who have been made in the likeness of God" (James 3:9 NASB; see also 1 Cor. 11:7).

---

[4] *Dictionary of Classical Hebrew*, 2:449. J. Maxwell Miller has written a contrasting opinion ("In the 'image' and 'likeness' of God," *Journal of Biblical Literature*, 91:3 [Sept 1972]: 293).

[5] John E. Hartley, "*tzelem*," *Theological Wordbook of the Old Testament*, 2 vols., eds. Harris, Archer, and Waltke (Chicago: Moody Press, 1980): 762, no. 1923a.

Christ came in "the image of the invisible God" (Col. 1:15; see also 2 Cor. 4:4). "He is the radiance of the glory of God and the exact imprint of his nature" (Heb. 1:3a ESV). How can a person be made in the image of someone who is invisible? This is only possible if *image* refers to an intangible quality.

Furthermore, Christ argued that his oneness with the Father was a characteristic that all men in some way share with God. When Christ was accused of blasphemy because he claimed to be one with the Father, he cited Psalm 82:6 in his defense.

> Jesus answered them, "Has it not been written in your Law, 'I said, you are gods'? If He called them gods, to whom the word of God came (and the Scripture cannot be broken), do you say of Him, whom the Father sanctified and sent into the world, 'You are blaspheming'; because I said, 'I am the Son of God'?"
> —John 10:34-36 NASB

So man's creation in the image of God has nothing to do with his similarity to or reflection of God's bodily form or, for that matter, to a particular moral state. Instead, it is a reference to mankind's basic nature, to the immaterial portion of his makeup. Adam was created with the capacity for moral choice. He was given the ability to make decisions based on whether a choice was *morally* right or wrong. He was created with the ability to discern and choose between good and evil. This is what singularly and conspicuously distinguished Adam from the rest of God's creation. This is specifically what it means to be created in the image of God. Adam reflected God in his ability to be like God, to make moral choices.

With the capacity to make positive decisions based on a moral standard came also the capacity to make negative or evil decisions based on that same standard. With the capacity for righteousness came the capacity for evil. To be created in the image of God did not predetermine that mankind would be righteous or evil; it simply gave Adam and Eve the capacity, the ability to choose to become one or the other.

It should not be deduced from this that God is capable of evil or that the incarnate Christ was capable of sinning while he was on earth. Jesus had a righteous nature,[6] and his righteous nature affected each choice in moral matters so that he has never and will never make an evil decision.[7] God does make moral choices—and they are genuine decisions—but his righteous nature guarantees the outcome every time.

The ability to choose between options that are morally opposite lies at the heart of the concept of faith. To "have faith" is to exercise one's will in a moral decision by making a choice that pleases God. To be unfaithful means making a choice that displeases God or refraining from making choices that please God. Moral decisions of this sort can only be made when God has given command of rightness or wrongness. The book of Romans argues that everyone, by some divine means, receives enough revelation to be condemned. In the most elementary case, this revelation by God is linked to the depraved human conscience and the witness of the natural world.

> Because that which is known about God is evident within them; for God made it evident to them. For since the creation of the world His invisible attributes, His eternal power and divine nature, have been clearly seen, being understood through what has been made, so that they are without excuse.
>
> —Romans 1:19-20 NASB

---

6 A helpful discussion of "person," "nature," and "will" may be found in J. O. Buswell, *A Systematic Theology of the Christian Religion*, 2 vols. in 1 (Grand Rapids: Zondervan, 1962) 2:52ff.

7 See Heb. 4:15; 2:17-18.

Not every decision that a person makes is moral. Many, perhaps most, of life's decisions are either intellectual or arbitrary. Which shirt shall I wear today? Which bunch of bananas goes into the shopping cart? Shall I take an umbrella to work today? Whom will I see to repair the car? But sprinkled throughout each day are significant moral choices that are usually related to interactions with others who are also made in God's image.

The image of God in man should not be restricted to man's ability to make moral choices. Secondary characteristics flow from this concept. For example, man's ability to appreciate beauty is doubtless grounded in his reflection of God. His ability for invention, for creativity streams from the nature of his being, whether through works of literature, music, or art. His emotional persona somehow mirrors God as well. These secondary characteristics do not *define* the image of God, but they seem to tangentially relate to the moral fiber of our being.

The image of God in man gives every individual great worth. It is an intrinsic worth, based on his composition, not on his actions or choices. The reason for capital punishment, as given in Genesis 9, is based in God's creation of man in his image. "Whoever sheds the blood of a man, by mankind his blood shall be shed because in the image of God that man was made" (Gen. 9:6). If the victim was a righteous man, the punishment was death for the murderer. If the victim was an evil man, the punishment was death for the murderer as well. Death was prescribed because every individual is made in God's image and has great intrinsic value. God deemed death the appropriate penalty for the willful destruction of the only creatures he designed to mirror himself.

Genesis 5 makes it very clear that the image of God is propagated in the procreation process. "When Adam had lived 130 years, he begat [a son] in his likeness, according to his image, and he named him Seth" (Gen. 5:3). The same Hebrew words for *image* and *likeness* are used here as are used to describe the creation of man in God's image (Gen. 1:26). Seth was made in Adam's image and Adam was made in God's image; therefore, Seth was also made in God's image.

This link is likely the reason God is included in Christ's genealogy—". . . the son of Enosh, the son of Seth, the son of Adam, the son of God" (Luke 3:38). Notice also Jesus' willingness to refer to saints as *brothers*. "For which reason He is not ashamed to call them brethren" (Heb. 2:11b NASB).

The term *image* is used to describe five relationships in the Bible:

- Mankind in the image of God (Gen. 1:26-27),
- Christ in the image of the Father (2 Cor. 4:4; Heb. 1:3),
- Seth in the image of Adam (Gen. 5:3),
- Woman in the image of man (1 Cor. 11:7),[8] and
- Believers in the image of Christ (Rom. 8:29).

Each relationship shows the close and near perfect resemblance of one to the other.

Finally, the creation of the immaterial part of man— Adam in God's image—makes the incarnation possible. The body that God formed from the dust of the ground was appropriately designed to house a person made in his image. It was simultaneously a fitting vessel for God himself. God could have inhabited that first vessel of clay had he chosen to do so. Instead, he created a person like himself, a person in his own image—Adam—and placed him in that body.

The creative work that produced the first Adam is similar to the supernatural work that produced the second Adam,

---

[8] The actual word used in the phrase is *glory*, but the relationship being described could use the term *image* equally well, as in the preceding phrase ("[man] is the image and glory of God"). See also Gen. 2:23—"this is now bone of my bone."

Christ. In the case of the second Adam, the Holy Spirit[9] took of Mary's body and prepared a suitable and fitting body[10] for the emptied[11] Christ to inhabit so that he might be "made like His brethren in all things" (Heb. 2:17a NASB). In the incarnation, Christ became a man. "If it were not for the fact of the image of God in man, the incarnation would be a contradiction. But since man is created in the image of God, to hold that God has come in human flesh involves no contradiction whatsoever, but is entirely credible."[12]

Our creation in the image of God also makes possible the great eschatological promises.

> Beloved, now we are children of God, and it has not appeared as yet what we shall be. We know that when He appears, we shall be like Him, because we shall see Him just as He is.
>
> —1 John 3:2 NASB

This promise of future glorification is reserved for those made in God's image who have also chosen to accept his redemptive offer.

---

9   See Matt. 1:20; Luke 1:35.
10   See Heb. 10:5.
11   See Phil. 2:6-7.
12   Buswell, *Systematic Theology*, 1:233.

– 7 –

Genesis 2: Day Seven

> Thus completed were the heavens and the earth and all their hosts. So by the seventh day God ceased from his work that he had done, and rested on day seven from all his work that he had done. And God blessed the seventh day and dedicated it because on it he rested from all his work that God had created to make.
>
> –Genesis 2:1-3

The Lord had completed his work of creation. The seventh day was then the day on which God rested from all his work. The only activity mentioned on this day is that God blessed and sanctified the seventh day. This day was special. It was a day of rest for God. The Lord later referred to his rest as a pattern for his people to follow (Ex. 20:8-11).

What was God's relationship to his creation after he had finished his work? Was it necessary that he continually put energy into the universe in order to sustain it? Or did God create the world to run on its own?

Two major views are generally held regarding the doctrine of preservation. One view maintains that Christ is currently sustaining the universe. If he were, in fact, to suddenly stop energizing the world, it would immediately spin into oblivion.[1] This view is often called the continuous creation view. Two exegetical considerations form the heart of the evidence for the continuous creation view. The first is Hebrews 1:3. Speaking of the Son, the verse states that he "upholds all things by the word of His power" (NASB). The second verse is Colossians 1:17—"He is before all things, and in Him all things hold together" (NASB). The conclusion sometimes drawn from these two passages is that Christ is today actively holding the universe together.[2]

The second view, commonly called the completed creation view, maintains that the nature of the creative process of that first week was of such a quality that the universe operates on its own, apart from a constant input of energy on God's part.

Several arguments lead to the conclusion that the completed creation view is correct. First, the attitude expressed at the close of the creation week argues that God is no longer putting energy into the system. In Genesis 1:31-2:3, the author states approximately eight times that God's work of creation was finished at the close of the sixth day.[3] This repetition is a significant argument for the completed creation view. Would the text be accurate when it states that God "rested" and "ceased" from all his work if he were still actively maintaining the universe that he had just created?

---

[1] "Everything in the universe is sustained right now by Jesus Christ" (John F. MacArthur, *Hebrews* in *The MacArthur New Testament Commentary* [Chicago: Moody Press, 1983]: 16-17).

[2] This energizing input is often thought to intercept the natural world at the atomic level. The ubiquitous "nuclear glue" is seen as the evidence for such input. Or, the power of Christ is seen in natural laws such as gravity.

[3] "God saw all that he had made" (1:31); "Thus the heavens and the earth were completed" (2:1); "By the seventh day God completed his work" (2:2); ". . . that he had done" (2:2); "He rested on the seventh day from all his work" (2:2); ". . . that he had done" (2:2); "Because in it he rested from all his work" (2:3); ". . . that God had created and made" (2:3).

Secondly, if the continuous creation view is correct, then God is the direct and active cause of all events, including evil (cf. John 8:46). If, on the other hand, the completed creation view is correct, then God is not causing all events to happen by his sustaining power. Instead, he is free to be actively and personally involved in men's lives as he chooses, without directly involving himself in their sin.

A third argument contends that if Christ is actively sustaining the universe, one must also concede that the amount of energy Christ is putting into the universe is inadequate, for the entire observable universe is running down. This phenomenon is referred to as entropy, the second law of thermodynamics.

Fourthly, if divine energy is being infused into the universe at the atomic level, then it is curious that man is able to split atoms. Is man able to override the power of God?

A fifth argument against the continuous creation view revolves around the question of Adam's responsibility. Was not Adam put in charge of the biosphere? "And God blessed them, and God said to them, 'Be fruitful and multiply, and fill the earth, and subdue it, and rule over the fish of the sea and over the birds of the sky, and over every living thing that moves on the earth'" (1:28). This blessing and command was at best superficial if Christ is actually the one responsible for all activities, the one causing all events. The completed creation view, on the other hand, allows Genesis 1:28 to be a genuine bestowal of responsibility, which mankind abused and which authority Christ himself will one day inherit (Heb. 2:6-8).

Two final arguments deal with the exegetical support that is supposedly found in Colossians 1:17 and Hebrews 1:3. Regarding Colossians 1:17, the lexicon[4] indicates that the word sometimes rendered "held together" is found in only two passages, where it shares the same meaning: Colossians 1:17 and 2 Peter 3:5. Both are found in a creation context, not one of preservation. "By the

---

4   BDAG, 972-73.

Word of God the heavens existed long ago and the earth *was formed* (*sunestosa*) out of water and by water" (2 Peter 3:5b). The NASB translation of "hold together" (Col. 1:17) is based primarily on etymology[5] (the study of breaking apart words to extract their meaning), rather than on the way the word is used in the language. The word under consideration is a perfect, active, indicative form in the Greek language. This perfect form better fits a historical creation context than a present preservation context.

Finally, the salient portion found in Hebrews 1:3 reads as follows: "and upholds (*pheron*) all things by the word of his power." The Greek word used here is also found in the Septuagint. The lexicon puts together three passages: Hebrews 1:3, Numbers 11:14, and Deuteronomy 1:9, 12.[6] The nuance shared by all three passages is that of administration, not preservation. "I alone am not *able to carry* all this people, because it is too burdensome for me" (Num. 11:14), "I am not *able to bear* the burden of you alone" (Deut. 1:9b), and "How can I alone *bear* the load and burden of you and your strife?" (Deut. 1:12). These definitions seem to best capture the sense of Hebrews 1:3—"He is the radiance of His glory and the exact representation of His nature, and *administrates* all things by His powerful word."

If the universe can continue to exist only by the continual input of energy by Christ himself, what is to be said about the three days in which Christ was dead and buried? It seems much better to understand that the work of Christ in creation was of superior quality and that it is capable of continuing in its existence apart from any necessary input. "And God saw all that he had made and behold it was very good."

---

5   *Sunistami* is a compound word composed of two parts: *sun* (the preposition "with") and the verb *istami* (meaning "to stand"). But its meaning is "to come to be in a condition of coherence" (BDAG, 973). Even in English, breaking apart a word can be misleading. For example, the etymology of a word like *abundance* could lead to the meaning of "a dancing bun."

6   BDAG, 855.

Highlights from the Creation Week

This is the story[7] of the heavens and the earth when
they were created, in the day that the Lord God made
earth and heaven. Now no shrub of the field was yet
in the earth and no grass of the field had yet sprouted,
for the Lord God had not sent rain upon the earth,
and there was no one to work the ground. Instead, a
huge spring came up from the earth and watered the
entire surface of the ground.

—Genesis 2:4-6

The phrase "this is the story of" occurs ten times in the book
of Genesis.[8] Some have in fact used this phrase to outline the
book, but this division "by the word *tôlĕdôt* [this is the story
of . . .] does not work out on close examination."[9]

---

7 This Hebrew word has been translated variously. The term *story* is excellent,
provided it is understood as a true story and not as a myth or fairy tale. The
term has been translated as "generations of" (KJV, RSV, ESV); "account of"
(NASB); "story of" (NEB); "origins of" (JB); and "births of" (Young's Literal).
8 This is the story of the heavens and the earth (2:4).
This is the *scroll* of the story of Adam (5:1).
This is the story of Noah (6:9).
This is the story of Shem, Ham, and Japheth (10:1).
This is the story of Shem (11:10).
This is the story of Terah (11:27).
This is the story of Ishmael (25:12).
This is the story of Isaac (25:19).
This is the story of Esau (36:1).
This is the story of Jacob (37:2).
   The Hebrew word occurs three additional times in Genesis, but with
different nuances (Gen. 10:32; 25:13; and 36:9).
9 Paul Gilchrist, "*tôlĕdôt*," in *TDOT,* 370. Cf. Jason S. DeRouchie, "The
Blessing-Commission, the Promised Offspring, and the *Todedot* Structure
of Genesis," *Journal of the Evangelical Theological Society,* 56:2 (June
2013): 219-247.

The LXX somewhat inaccurately uses the Greek word *genesis* (beginning) to translate *tôlĕdôt*. However, the transliteration of this Greek word has been used as the title to the book in English—Genesis.

Relationship of Genesis One to Genesis Two

Much ink has been spent in attempts to harmonize Genesis 1 with Genesis 2. A cursory glance seems to indicate that Genesis 2 presents a contrasting creation story, a story that bears little resemblance to Genesis 1. But it becomes quite clear on closer examination that chapter 2 is a retelling and expansion of aspects of chapter 1.

Chapter 2 assumes the chronology of chapter 1 and then presents details from the creation week, without much regard to sequence. In fact, the author uses the term *day* (2:4) to describe the entire six-day period of creation. This would argue that chapter 2 is not concerned with the chronological sequence that is so obvious in chapter 1.

Plant Life on the Early Earth

The picture presented in Genesis 2:5 may be somewhat confusing at first glance. "Now no shrub of the field was yet in the earth and no grass of the field had yet sprouted, for the Lord God had not sent rain upon the earth, and there was no one to work the ground" (2:5).

Were there, in fact, no plants on the earth following the week of creation? Had not God overspread the continent with vegetation on Day Three? Why the emphasis on the absence of plants "of the field"?

The second half of the verse helps clear the picture. The condition in the first half of the verse, whatever it may have been, existed for two reasons. First, God had not yet set up the meteorological conditions that would make rainfall a regular occurrence. The development of the evaporation-transpiration-precipitation cycle occurred many years later. Rain fell for the first time in Genesis 7:11-12, coinciding with the initiation of the flood of Noah's day, when God opened the floodgates of the sky.

The second reason for the absence of plants "of the field" is linked to the lack of human activity. No one was present to "work the ground" (2:5), to help meet the moisture needs of the plants. No one was available to irrigate the plants "of the field." Both phrases—"shrub of the field" and "grass of the field"—indicate that certain sections of the earth may have been barren, not because of unproductive soil, but because of arid conditions.

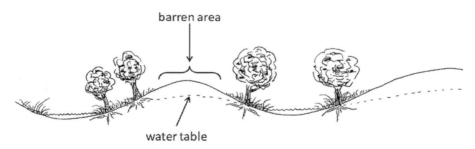

Figure 13: Relationship between the wet and dry regions

The terms used to describe the vegetation created on Day Three in Genesis 1:11-12 are (1) herbaceous plants that produced edible seeds and (2) woody plants (trees) that produced edible fruit containing pits. Genesis 2:5 then names two additional types of vegetation: "shrub of the field" and "grass of the field."

The "shrub of the field" is identified by a rather uncommon Hebrew word used only to describe plants growing in desiccated or wilderness conditions (Gen. 21:15; Job 30:4, 7). This suggests the idea of a desert shrub, which could apparently only be sustained in some areas of the continent.

"Grass of the field" is a more common biblical term and probably refers to prairie or pasture grasses. This type of vegetation requires more water than desert plants, and this plant was evidently absent from drier sections of the earth. These types of plants—"grass of the field" and "plants of the field"—are said to have become more plentiful because of the entrance of sin. A part of the curse on the ground was that "you shall eat 'plants of the field'" (see commentary on 3:18).

A paraphrase of verse 5 might therefore read like this: "Originally neither desert shrubs nor pasture grasses grew in certain areas of the continent, for God had not yet sent rain upon the earth and no one was yet available to irrigate these regions."

In some respects Genesis 2:5-6 reflects 1:2. Neither passage involves creative activity; both are purely descriptive in nature. Genesis 1:2 describes the earth halfway through Day One, and 2:5-6 describes the earth halfway through Day Six, before the creation of Adam.

Water Source on the Early Earth

How was animal and plant life sustained on that early earth if no rain fell? Verse 6 supplies the answer. A huge fountain, whose source was apparently the great deep, welled up from the ground to "water the whole surface of the ground" (2:6).

The connection between the water source ("a huge spring") of Genesis 2:6 and "the fountain of the great deep" in Genesis 7:11 has a very old tradition. The LXX, completed centuries before Christ's birth, used only one Greek word (*pâgâ*)[10] to translate the Hebrew concepts in both passages. The same is true of the Syriac translation[11] (*mbhᶜ*).[12] Good reason therefore exists to understand that both passages speak of the same entity—a huge fountain or spring.

This fountain was the singular source of water for the entire earth. "And it watered the entire surface of the ground" (Gen. 2:6b). It seems reasonable to conclude that the fountain was located at the highest elevation on the continent. The general topography of the landmass was probably rather flat. Low, undulating hills with occasional swells or rises of dry ground were most likely characteristic of the continent.

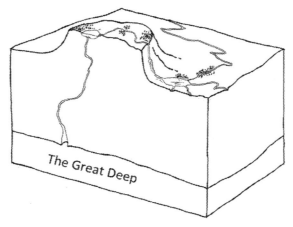

Figure 14: The fountain of the great deep

[10] No alternative readings are listed in either passage (*The Old Testament in Greek According to the Text of Codex Vaticanus, supplemented from other uncial manuscripts, with a critical apparatus containing the variants of the chief ancient authorities for the text of the Septuagint,* eds. A. E. Brooke and N. McLean [Cambridge: Univ. Press, 1906]: 4, 16.)

[11] The Syriac translation is also quite early. Current thought suggests that the translation may have "originated with the early Christians in the first and second century CE" (Emanuel Tov, *Textual Criticism of the Hebrew Bible* [Minneapolis: Fortress, 1992]: 152).

[12] *The Old Testament in Syriac according to the Peshitta Version: Genesis* (Leiden: E. J. Brill, 1977): 3, 12.

— 8 —

Genesis 2: The Early Earth

Now a river flowed out from Eden to water the garden, and from there it was split and became four heads. The name of the first river is Pishon; it meanders through all the land of Havilah, where there was gold, and the gold of that land was good; there was also bdellium and the carnelian stone. And the name of the second river is Gihon; it meanders through all the land of Cush. And the name of the third river is Hiddekel;[1] it travels through the east half of Assyria. And the fourth river is Euphrates.

—Genesis 2:10-14

The Meaning of Eden

That a river flowed out of Eden clearly indicates that the fountainhead was located within the geographic boundary of the region called Eden. The meaning of the Hebrew name *Eden* is not given in the text. Scholars think that the term *eden* means "the area of abundance."[2] This definition is borne out

---

[1] Modern day *Hiddekel* is better known in English under its Old Persian name, *Tigris*.

[2] Magnus Ottosson, "Eden and the Land of Promise," in *Congress Volume: Jerusalem 1986*, ed. J. A. Emerton, in *Supplements to Vetus Testamentum,*

in a ninth century BC Aramaic inscription in which the verbal form (*ᶜdn*) is used in the phrase "who *enriches* all lands."[3] The cognate Hebrew verb occurs only once in the Old Testament: "And they captured fortified cities and a rich land. They took possession of houses full of all sorts of good things, hewn cisterns, vineyards, olive groves, fruit trees in abundance. So they ate, and were filled, and grew fat, and *luxuriated* in your great goodness" (Neh. 9:25). Thus, the etymology suggests that Eden was a rich and luxurious land.

The Function of the River

The function of the river was to water the garden located in Eden's eastern section. That the garden was well watered can be deduced from later scriptural references to the garden of Eden. In Isaiah 51:3 the Lord was coming to "comfort" his people, so he made her wilderness like "Eden, and her desert like the garden of the Lord." This can only be accomplished with an abundance of water.

The description of the district of Jordan in the days of Abraham, before the destruction by the Lord, includes this phrase: "It was well watered everywhere . . . like the garden of the Lord, like the land of Egypt as you go to Zoar" (Gen. 13:10). Zoar was located in the delta of the Nile, where water was abundant. Hence the garden of Eden was probably comprised of islands of lush greenery, landscaped personally by the Lord to please the eye, and surrounded by brooks flowing with an abundance of fresh water. It sounds like paradise.

---

vol. 40 (London: E. J. Brill, 1988): 178; A. R. Millard, "The Etymology of Eden," *Vetus Testamentum,* 34:1 (1984): 103-105.

[3] Alan R. Millard and Pierre Bordreuil, "A Statue from Syria with Assyrian and Aramaic Inscriptions," *Biblical Archaeologist,* 45 (Summer 1982): 137, 140.

The Topography of Eden

Having watered the garden, the river collected itself at the eastern edge of Eden and split into four major rivers. The reason for this breakup of the river is not given. It seems reasonable to suggest that Eden was situated at the highest elevation on the continent. Some type of interruption or descent—perhaps a rapids or waterfall—then triggered the separation of the river into four heads.

Eden may also have been an elevated area because of its significance. Eden was apparently the place that God had chosen as his personal residence. The Bible refers to this garden as belonging to the Lord: "the garden of God" (Ezek. 28:13; 31:8, 9), "the garden of the Lord" (Gen. 13:10; Isa. 51:3). These phrases suggest that God lived in the garden of Eden. According to Ezekiel 28, "the anointed cherub who covers" apparently did his work in "Eden, the garden of God" (v. 13), and, after he sinned, was cast down "from the mountain of God" (v. 16). The association of God with Eden coupled with the association of God with heights (Ps. 78:69; 102:9; Isa. 2:2) could lead to the conclusion that Eden was elevated.

The close of Genesis 3 may also indicate that Eden may have been an elevated region. When Adam and Eve were driven from Eden, cherubim were stationed to "keep *the way* of the Tree of Life" (Gen. 3:24). Notice that only one path led back into Eden. It seems legitimate to suggest, therefore, that the garden of Eden was located on an elevated region of the continent, perhaps similar to the modern day mesa.

Figure 15: Eden in the early earth

Once the river cascaded down from the garden of Eden, it divided into four major rivers. These rivers are then used in the biblical text to mark off the geographic sections of that early continent. The first river was the Pishon, and it meandered through the country of Havilah. Gold and precious stones were found there. The second river was called the Gihon, and it flowed leisurely through the land of Cush. The third river, the Hiddekel, ran through the eastern part of Assyria, whereas the last river, the Euphrates, apparently passed through the western half of Assyria.

Eden and the Four Rivers

These five verses (2:10-14) are essentially the only reference available today describing the geography of the pre-flood earth. With the coming of the worldwide deluge described in

Genesis 6-9, the topography of the early earth was completely reworked. One should not rely on surveys or satellite imagery of the present world to reconstruct the ancient world.[4] "The world at that time was destroyed, being flooded with water" (2 Peter 3:6b NASB).

To ignore this worldwide catastrophe or to suggest that Genesis 2:10-14 "was apparently intended to be meaningful in terms of a post-flood landscape"[5] guarantees that conclusions drawn about today's geography from this section of the Bible will be flawed. The biblical presentation is that of a global adjustment to most aspects of that early earth. Consequently, the only source for pre-flood geography is this ancient text. There is no other resource for a description of the earth between the days of Adam and the days of Noah.

Clues to early-earth geography are sparse. The only available information consists of the names of the four rivers, the lands through which they flowed, and the relative order of the rivers. Etymology of names is certainly not definitive in establishing geography. For example, if *Pishon* means "gusher," *Gihon* means "bubbler,"[6] or *Hiddekel* means "swiftness,"[7] such knowledge cannot help reconstruct the geography. How is a gushing river different from a swift river? There is certainly no clear distinction.

---

[4] An attempt to recover the elusive Pishon was made by James A. Sauer ("The River Runs Dry," *Biblical Archaeology Review*, 22:4 [July 1996]: 52-57, 64). The problems with this attempt are that (1) the rivers (Pishon, Euphrates, and Hiddekel) flow in the wrong direction—not *from* a common source, but *to* a common point, (2) these rivers do not cover or water the entire landmass, and (3) the author has not considered the effects of the global deluge in Noah's day.

[5] John C. Munday, Jr., "Eden's Geography Erodes Flood Geology," *Westminster Theological Journal*, 58 (1996): 127.

[6] Speiser, *Genesis*, 20.

[7] Munday, "Eden," 142.

The participles used to describe the flow of the rivers are not unique. The Pishon and Gihon are said to "meander"[8] (*sôbêb*) through their respective lands, whereas the Hiddekel "goes" (*holêk*) throughout its land. The only suggestion here is that the early earth was quite flat, with little topographic relief. As a result, the rivers probably divided and meandered rather aimlessly, much as rivers flow today in the major delta regions or in areas like the Florida everglades. After all, the function of these rivers was "to water the entire surface of the ground," not to drain off excess rainfall, as today.

Figure 16: Possible scene of plant and animal life on the early earth

The names of the regions appear to relate to the individual river courses. For instance, the land of Havilah is defined as the region through which the river Pishon flowed, Cush is that land through which the Gihon meandered, and so on. The only region for which additional information is given is the land of

---

[8] "Flow around" (HALOT, 739).

Havilah. Havilah had gold, a mineral that resembled manna,[9] and a red stone, carnelian.[10]

The only other geographical notation in the Bible about the early earth is in Genesis 4:16, which indicates that Cain "dwelt in the land of Nod, east of Eden." Since the curse of Cain affected the production of the ground, Nod may very well have been an arid region, located between two river systems.

In summary, these bits of information can be collected from Genesis 2 to help reconstruct the geography of that early earth:

- The landmass was one continuous region;
- The continent overlay a large body of fresh water;
- This body of water vented at the highest area of the continent;
- The elevated region was probably central to the continent;
- Four river systems, separated by four low ridges, constituted the bulk of the continent;
- The continent had rather insignificant topographical relief, except for Eden. A low, undulating landscape characterized the continent;
- The rivers meandered throughout their respective regions and watered most of the landscape;
- Human effort was necessary to make some arid regions productive.

---

[9] The only other occurrence of this word is found in Num. 11:7, where it describes manna. It is difficult to describe the mineral that perhaps lined the riverbed in Havilah. The lexicon identifies this word with "the odoriferous yellowish transparent gum of a South African tree, *Commiphora mukul Engler*" (HALOT, 110).

[10] Positive identification of this stone has been established through the Akkadian language (HALOT, 1424).

These deductions were used to construct the model of the early earth illustrated below. To locate the four rivers, the following question was answered arbitrarily: standing at the eastern edge of Eden, should the first river lay on the right or on the left? It seemed reasonable to locate it on the right. That Cush, in later biblical times, represented extreme south, while Assyria was considered north and east is another consideration. The land of Nod, lying eastward from Eden, was probably situated between the river systems of Gihon and Hiddekel. Here Cain built the first city—the only city mentioned before the flood.

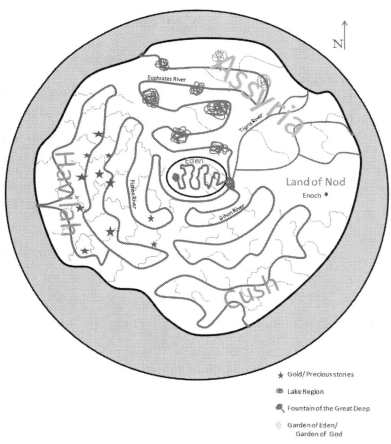

Figure 17: Reconstruction of the geography of the early earth

River Names, Both Then and Now

Can the names of the rivers referred to in Genesis 2:10-14 be used to locate the land of Eden today? Does a relationship exist between the geographic names preserved in the second chapter of Genesis and those found in the Near East today? The answer is no, because the earth was destroyed by the flood and no topographic features remain. The flood totally reworked the original continent. Current estimates suggest that, on average, the top mile of the earth's crust was disturbed by the flood of Genesis 6-9.[11]

The reason the names of the Tigris and the Euphrates Rivers are identical to the names of rivers in the Near East today is doubtless because of the resemblance that Noah and his sons saw between the pre-flood rivers and the post-flood rivers. The flood's destruction was so thorough that any organic union based on modern geography blatantly ignores the biblical claim of global catastrophe. It is not possible to find the location of Eden on this reconstituted earth.[12] Eden was destroyed. The earth was destroyed.

---

[11] This assumes that the sedimentary layers of the earth's crust are the result of the deluge. Estimates by geologists for the volume of sedimentary rock run from five to fifteen percent of the earth's outer ten-mile shell (James Gilluly, et al., *Principles of Geology* [San Francisco: W. H. Freeman, 1960]: 326).

[12] In spite of this, theologically conservative cartographers still attempt to locate Eden on present-day Near Eastern maps (Berry J. Beitzel, *The Moody Atlas of Bible Lands* [Chicago: Moody Press, 1985]: 74-75, map 20).

– 9 –

Genesis 2: God's Special Creation

> Then the Lord God formed the man of dust from the
> ground and breathed into his nostrils the breath of
> life, and Adam became alive.
>
> —Genesis 2:7

God created man in a two-step process. First, he formed Adam's material body out of dust from the ground. Then he animated the body by placing into it a person created in his image and likeness. The result of the union of body and soul produced a man. The method God used to create Adam strongly suggests that the nature of human beings is dichotomistic. We are constituted of a material part and an immaterial part.

Interestingly, the Holy Spirit later used the same procedure to produce the incarnate Christ. When speaking of his incarnation, Jesus said, "a body you have prepared for me" (Heb. 10:5b). The Holy Spirit (Luke 1:35; Matt. 1:20) formed a body out of Mary's flesh and placed therein the *emptied* Son of God (Phil. 2:7).

In Psalm 8, King David was impressed with the importance of the manner of man's creation. He almost appears to have been surprised at the significance of what it means to be a man made in God's image. When compared to the grandeur of the celestial universe, David notes that God *takes thought of him*. He "cares for him" (8:4), "he has set him a bit lower than God himself," and has "crowned him with glory and majesty" (8:5). Finally, God had put man in charge of his created order (8:6-8). Making man was not an afterthought; he was the goal of God's creation.

God Landscapes a Home for Adam

> The Lord God then planted a garden in the eastern part of Eden, and there he set the man that he had formed. And the Lord God caused to grow from the ground every kind of tree that is pleasant to the sight and good for food, as well as the Tree of Life in the midst of the garden and the Tree of the Knowledge of Good and Evil.
>
> —Genesis 2:8-9

Everything that God had created was "good," but to envision a garden that the Lord landscaped with special effort defies human imagination. The garden was aesthetically beautiful, as well as functionally useful. God combined both criteria into one lovely showpiece. The vegetation was pleasant to the eyes and provided an ample source of nourishment. The combination of leaf texture, plant shape, blossom color, and aroma was integrated with varieties of fruits, nuts, and grains, resulting in an exquisite horticultural delight.

Not only is Christ a master gardener, he is doubtless a skilled interior decorator.

> In My Father's house are many dwelling places; if it were not so, I would have told you; for I go to prepare

> a place for you. If I go and prepare a place for you,
> I will come again, and receive you to Myself, that
> where I am, there you may be also.
>
> —John 14:2, 3 NASB

What a glorious future awaits the believer!

As mentioned previously, the garden of Eden was probably also the earthly abode of God himself. This conclusion is based on the following evidence:

- The garden of Eden is also called the garden of God (Ezek. 28:13; 31:8-9; Gen. 13:10; Isa. 51:3).
- "The anointed cherub that covers" was presumably the being most closely associated with God's presence. This cherub was also in the garden of Eden (Ezek. 28:13-16).
- The "mountain of God" is associated with the garden of Eden (Ezek. 28:16).
- The Tree of Life is always mentioned in conjunction with God's presence (Ezek. 47:12; Rev. 2:7; 22:1-2).
- When Adam sinned, he was driven from God's presence and from the garden of Eden (Gen. 3:22-24).

God's First and Only Command

> Then the Lord God took Adam and led[1] him into the
> garden of Eden to cultivate it and tend it. And the Lord
> God commanded Adam, saying, "From any tree of the
> garden you may eat freely, but from the Tree of the
> Knowledge of Good and Evil you shall not eat from it,
> for in the day that you eat from it, you shall surely die."
>
> —Genesis 2:15-17

---

[1] A cognate root (*nḥh*) has the sense of "lead, guide" (HALOT, 685).

Adam was apparently not created of soil from the garden of Eden; otherwise, the Lord would not have needed to bring him to the garden. But after his creation, God led Adam into the garden of Eden to till the ground and to keep the garden. The original design of God was that mankind should have responsibilities that involved work. This did not include the intense struggle that resulted from the curse. Instead, it was therapeutic work that benefited the body and brought a sense of accomplishment.

Adam could certainly have employed animals in keeping the garden. With the full control expressed in Genesis 1:26 and 28, he could have involved various species to perform the tasks necessary in keeping the garden in tip-top shape. Elephants might have carried water, and various species may have helped collect fruit.

After giving Adam the prerogative to indulge in and enjoy any fruit of his choosing, the Lord gave command regarding the Tree of the Knowledge of Good and Evil. The directive was simple and clear: "Do not eat." The Tree of the Knowledge of Good and Evil was not so named because its fruit was unique. This tree was unique because of the command God gave regarding it. Adam's response to the command would determine whether he would become *good* or *evil*. The tree itself may not have been distinctive, but God had selected it to be the moral proving ground for the man he had made in his image and likeness.

As Adam came from God's hand, he had the potential to become an evil person. It is also true that the newly created Adam had the potential to become a righteous person. His original state was that of *blamelessness*—neither righteous nor evil. "God made men upright (*yāshār*)" (Eccl. 7:29b). Man was innocent, completely inexperienced in the exercise of that unique quality defined as the image and likeness of God. Adam's moral state would not be confirmed until he had made a considered decision regarding this command of God—whether to obey or disobey. In that moment, Adam would *become* either good or evil. He would become knowledgeable through experience; hence the name of this tree.

The statement—"in the day that you eat from it you shall die"—should not be considered a threat in which God hoped to prevent Adam from eating of the tree. It should rather be treated as information, defining the results of such an action. Adam could now make an informed moral choice regarding his future. His decision would determine whether he would become good or evil, whether his nature would be righteous or evil.

The Setup

> Then the Lord God said, "It is not good for Adam to be alone; I will make for him a partner that corresponds to his opposite." Now the Lord God had formed from the ground every beast of the field and every bird of the heavens, and he brought them to Adam to see what he would name them, and whatever Adam named these living creatures, it described their nature. So Adam gave appropriate names to all the domesticated animals, and to all the birds of the heaven, and to all the beasts of the field. But Adam did not find a partner corresponding to his opposite.
>
> —Genesis 2:18-20

God did not come to Adam and *command* that he name the animals. Had God done so, Adam would have suddenly been confronted with a moral decision—to obey or disobey the Lord. Such an order would have preempted the function of the Tree of the Knowledge of Good and Evil. Instead, the Lord likely approached Adam with questions like these: "Adam, what name describes the nature of this creature?" or "What word best depicts this animal?" In this way the interaction between

God and man would have stayed purely on the intellectual level, not on the moral level. Most of our decisions during the course of a day are intellectual choices, but the less frequent moral decisions that we are confronted with—often unexpectedly—are profoundly significant.

Adam's intellectual capacity was staggering. The Hebrew conveys the idea that he gave a descriptive title to each living creature. Each name reflected the animal's nature or perhaps the ecological niche it inhabited.

Adam named all of the living creatures that God brought before him, but not one of them was designed for him. Not one could provide the companionship he desired. No animal could satisfy the "not good" (2:18) analysis of the Lord, nor could any beast fill the void that Adam apparently felt. The archaic term *helpmeet* (KJV) comes from a compound Hebrew term that literally means "like his opposite" or "his counterpart."

God's Masterpiece

So the Lord God caused a deep sleep to fall on Adam, and he slept. Then he took one piece from his side and closed up the flesh in its place. And the Lord God built of the piece that he had taken from Adam a woman, and he brought her to Adam. And Adam said,

"Here at last is now bone of my bone,
And flesh of my flesh;
On account of this, she shall be called woman,
Because from man this one was taken."

Because of this, a man shall forsake his father and his mother and shall cling to his wife. And they shall become one unit. Now the two of them—Adam and his wife—were naked, and were not ashamed.

—Genesis 2:21-25

So it was that God created Eve from a portion taken from Adam's side. This could certainly have included the bone of a rib, but the Hebrew phrase is not definitive. The portion taken from Adam apparently also contained immaterial qualities so that Eve shared both flesh and soul with her husband. Eve was not a separate creation from Adam, a completely new creation; she was rather an extension of him. God did not create two humans, separate from each other; instead, he constructed one person and then, by creative action, extended that person to include a second. "He created them male and female and blessed them and called their name Man at the time of their creation" (Gen. 5:2).

There is but one human race.[2] It is composed of two genders, but they share equally in the basic substance of humanness. Both the man and the woman are *ādām*. Both share in the image of God.

God then brought the two of them together. This should be understood as an action of significance on God's part. God not only designed the concept of gender differences; he also intended the two genders to live together, mutually satisfying each other's needs. Marriage is explicit in this statement: ". . . and he brought her to the man."

Adam could hardly believe his eyes. His exclamation— "Here at last!"[3]—does not necessarily imply the passage of an extended period of time; instead, the meaning suggests that Eve was distinctive from all the other creations of God. "This time [I have found] bone of my bones."[4] Adam recognized that standing before him was someone who could be his companion, someone who was made like himself, someone who shared his nature . . . and she was beautiful. But her beauty is not the

---

[2] Paul, speaking in Athens, said, "He made from one blood, every nation of mankind to live on all the face of the earth" (Acts 17:26a NASB margin).

[3] "Finally" (HALOT, 952).

[4] Waltke and O'Connor, *Syntax*, 310.

emphasis of the text. Rather, the emphasis is that the woman was like him. She was someone who could understand him; she was someone who could be his friend.[5]

Verse 24 speaks of leaving father and mother and cleaving to one's wife in marriage.[6] This could be an extension of Adam's comments in verse 23, though it is difficult to comprehend how Adam could know so much about "father," "mother," and marriage. Perhaps this verse should be read as "a parenthetical remark of the author's,"[7] reflecting a later understanding of the issues involved. But the preferred understanding is to see these comments as spoken by the Lord himself. He was giving the couple instruction for their children's later use.

When Christ was confronted with the issue of divorce, he said, "Have you not read, that He who created them from the beginning made them male and female, and said, 'For this reason a man shall leave his father and mother, and be joined to his wife, and the two shall become one flesh'?" (Matt. 19:4b-5 NASB; see also Mark 10:6-8). Jesus understood that this verse had been spoken by God himself and had been part of what appears to have been a marriage ceremony. "So they are no longer two, but one flesh. What therefore God has joined together let no man separate" (Matt. 19:6 NASB; Mark 10:8b-9).

The Lord himself invented the concept of sexual differences. He created us "male and female." He implanted human bodies with drives and responses that ensure the continuation of the human race. God also personally brought the first couple together and pronounced that these two "shall be one." Marriage was instituted by the Lord and should be held in honor by all (Heb. 13:4).

---

5   "She is depicted as the physical counterpart of man, deserving of his unswerving loyalty" (Thomas McComiskey, "*ishshâ*," TWOT, 59).

6   Modern Hebrew uses the verb translated "cleave" to describe the action of gluing two things together.

7   Leupold, *Genesis*, 137.

What was the Lord's meaning when he stated that the two of them "shall be one flesh"? Here the term *one* speaks of companionship, union, closeness, wholeness, and completion rather than of number. John 17 uses the term *one* in a similar way: "That they may all be one; even as You, Father, are in Me, and I in You, that they also may be in Us" (John 17:21a NASB; see also vv. 11, 22-23). Adam and Eve were now a unit. Together they formed a single entity. God's creation was now complete, and everything that he had created was good.

The man and his wife were together. The Lord himself had in fact brought them together—and they wore no clothing. This was not a source of embarrassment, for "they were not ashamed." They were completely comfortable in each other's presence. It was not until the entrance of sin that shame and guilt were equated with nakedness (Gen. 3:7-10). God himself produced the first clothing and dressed Adam and Eve personally (Gen. 3:21). Would they have continued in their naked state had they chosen not to sin? It is not possible to be certain. Clothing might have been worn simply as adornment. Every notation regarding the appearance of angelic beings indicates that even they, though without sin, were clothed. So it is possible that clothing might have become a common commodity of the human race, though for reasons other than modesty.

– 10 –

Genesis 3: The Fall into Sin

> Now the serpent was more crafty than any other
> animal that the Lord God had made. And he said to
> the woman, "Did God really say that you shall not eat
> from any tree of the garden?" So the woman said to
> the serpent, "From the fruit of the trees of the garden
> we may eat. But from the fruit of the tree that is in
> the midst of the garden, God said, 'Do not eat from it
> and do not touch it, lest you die.'"
>
> —Genesis 3:1-3

Enter the serpent. Without explanation or warning, Genesis
3 opens with the comments of a serpent. The text seems to
require that this creature simply be a snake. The body of the
serpent was apparently altered by the curse in verse 14, but all
indications point to this creature being the familiar snake.

The description of the serpent as "crafty" or "cunning"[1]
probably speaks of his intellectual abilities as an animal.
This same Hebrew word ($^c\bar{a}r\hat{u}m$) is used to designate human
beings with attributes that stand in opposition to those of
fools (Prov. 12:16, 23; 13:16; 14:8, 15, 18; 22:3; 27:12). King
Saul acknowledged that fugitive David was "very cunning" (1

---

[1] HALOT, 883.

Sam. 23:22). The word *smart* describes the Hebrew word much better than the term *subtle* (KJV).

The Hebrew word translated "crafty" or "cunning" was carried over into the New Testament as well. Christ admonished his disciples to be "shrewd as serpents and innocent as doves" (Matt. 10:16b). The Greek word here translated *shrewd* is the same word used in the LXX to describe the serpent in Genesis 3:1. It should be obvious to students of herpetology that snakes do not survive because of their great athletic ability but must rely on cunning, bluff, and an uncanny awareness of their prey.

How was it that Eve was not surprised at the ability of this animal to converse? "Only man, of earthly creatures, possesses the ability to speak. Yet the serpent acts as a man. It raises itself above the beasts of the field which the Lord God had made, and it elevates itself to an equality with man."[2] It is not uncommon for man to speak to animals, but it is never true that animals, of their own devices, reply with human language. Perhaps Eve herself understood that she was not speaking merely to a serpent, but rather to someone using the serpent's body.

That "someone" is not mentioned in this text. But the person speaking, the one using the snake's body, was a moral being. He knew the difference between right and wrong. The snake, being an animal, did not have the capacity for such moral distinctions. Yet this moral being is not identified in the narrative of Genesis 3. It is not until the New Testament that positive identification occurs. Twice in the book of Revelation, the Devil is identified as "that old serpent" (Rev. 12:9; 20:2). Furthermore, Satan is called the "father of lies" in John 8:44, and since Eve was about to be confronted with the first lie, it would seem that the identification of the one who interacted with the woman was Satan himself.

---

[2]   Young, *Genesis 3*, 18-19.

The timing of this event is not given in the text. The temptation of Eve probably did not occur on Day Seven—the day on which God proclaimed that all that he had made was very good (1:31). On the other hand, there is no indication that this event happened days, months, or years into earth history. It is generally assumed that the encounter with the serpent occurred soon after Eve's creation.

The dialogue began with a conversational opener that was actually not in interrogative form. "God did indeed say that you shall not eat from any tree of the garden (didn't he?)." The cunning element of this statement is that it directed the conversation, started an inquiry into what God had said, and raised a slight doubt regarding the goodness of God. The entire statement was cast in the negative and drew an immediate response from Eve.

Eve's reply might be paraphrased like this: "Of course, we can eat from any tree in the garden. That's the reason God planted them! Oh, there is one exception—that tree in the middle of the garden. We are not to eat from it—no, not even touch it—lest we die."

It appears from Genesis 2 that God commanded Adam regarding the Tree of the Knowledge of Good and Evil before Eve's creation. So Adam himself must have communicated the restriction to Eve. Eve's additional comment about not touching the tree should not be seen as wrong or evil, or the whole point of the chapter is destroyed, for then Eve would have sinned—by lying—before she ate of the fruit. The text is quite clear that the entrance of sin occurred with *eating* the forbidden fruit, not with false comment about touching it.[3]

---

[3] The source of this comment—"do not touch"—may have originated with Eve herself. It could also have developed as a precautionary measure after conversation between Adam and Eve, or Adam may have suggested it originally. We cannot know the source with certainty.

The woman deviated from the original instruction given by God in two ways. First, she heightened the prohibition with the addition of the comment that they were not to touch the tree. Secondly, she reduced the strength of the consequences of eating from the tree. Instead of saying, "You shall surely die," she simply said, "You shall die." It should be understood that this initial interchange between the woman and the serpent is not viewed in the Bible as the point at which sin entered the human race. The fall occurred the instant God's command was violated.

The Lie Wrapped in Truth

> But the serpent said to the woman, "You will surely not die, because God knows that whenever you eat from it, then your eyes will be opened and you will become like God, knowing good and evil."
>
> —Genesis 3:4-5

Satan then contradicted God by saying that Adam and Eve would "surely *not* die." This was a lie. The implication was that it would be acceptable to eat of the Tree of the Knowledge of Good and Evil. The lie was then encapsulated in this truth: "Because God knows that whenever you eat from it, then your eyes will be opened and you will become like God, knowing good and evil." This candy coating of truth around the lie constituted the temptation.

This is how temptation usually operates. Something potentially good or satisfying is offered, while at the heart of the matter lies something evil. Partaking in the gratifying aspects of such a tempting offer always includes partaking of the evil as well. It is the evil that we are instructed to be on the lookout for. "Do not let yourselves be tricked, my dear brothers" (James 1:16).

That verse 5 is true can be seen by comparing it with the words of God in verse 22—they are identical. Through this incident, by experiencing evil, Adam and Eve *knew* about good and evil. They could also have *known* about good and evil by choosing good. This initial exercise of moral choice caused them to become "experienced"[4] in good and evil.

The KJV uses the plural "gods" to translate 'elohîm. "Ye shall be as gods."[5] This, however, blunts the point of the comment. The woman knew who 'Elohîm was and to become like him would have certainly been an attractive feature. It seems compelling, therefore, that the word 'elohîm be understood by the woman as a personal reference to God himself. The Lord understood it this way, as evidenced by the comment "the humans have become like one of us" (v. 22).

The Rationalization Process

> And the woman saw that good was the tree for food,
> that it was appealing to the eyes, and that the tree
> was desirable to make one wise, so she took from its
> fruit and ate, and she gave some also to her husband
> who was with her, and he ate.
>
> —Genesis 3:6

Following Satan's contradiction, Eve contemplated three issues. First, she observed that the fruit was good for food. The nutritional value of the fruit had nothing to do with whether or not she should eat of it. God had not cautioned Adam against eating from the tree because of a nutritional deficiency in the fruit.

---

4   HALOT, 391.

5   The *New English Bible* (1976) and *The Jerusalem Bible* (1968) have reverted to the understanding of the KJV (1611). Perhaps the translators of the Authorized Version were influenced by the use of the plural in the LXX.

Indeed, the fruit gave every appearance of being an excellent source for nutrition—packed with vitamins, minerals, and fiber; low in fat; and no cholesterol. But all of that was irrelevant.

Eve also observed that the fruit was appealing to the eye. It was apparently in prime condition, completely ripe, and doubtless having the feel and aroma of produce at the peak of perfection. Again, this appeal was irrelevant to whether or not she should eat it. Eve was using rational processes to make a moral decision. This is known as rationalization. It is not wrong to use logical arguments to debate moral issues, but logical arguments are *irrelevant* when making moral decisions. Moral issues are grounded in revelation from God regarding what is good and what is evil.

The command of God was not based on the nutritional excellence of the fruit, nor was it based on how attractively the tree presented its produce. No, the command could have been placed on any tree in the garden. This particular tree was not inherently good or evil. It became the Tree of the Knowledge of Good and Evil when God gave Adam command to refrain from partaking of its fruit.

Adam and Eve were not morally experienced before they ate of the tree. They were without fault in their moral nature as they came from God's hand. But the opposite is also true; they were without a righteous "bent" or inclination at their creation. They were completely neutral in their moral personas.

If Adam had been created with a righteous nature, no temptation to sin would have held appeal for him. He would have been able to view the temptation through an accurate lens because of his righteous nature and would have withstood any temptation. The probability that either he or Eve could have sinned would have been as likely as the probability that Christ could have sinned during his temptation in the wilderness (Matt. 4:1-11)—none whatsoever.

On the other hand, had Adam been created with a sinful nature, then God would be morally responsible for sin. He would have been directly involved in the production of something evil. Since God is righteous in all that he is and does, such a conclusion is inadmissible. The only conclusion that can be drawn is that Adam (and Eve), as he came from God's hand, was morally neutral, morally innocent, capable of becoming either righteous or evil, but completely free from a bent in either direction.

A corollary that must accompany such a conclusion is that once either Adam or Eve exercised their ability to make a moral choice, that decision determined their nature from that point onward. A second chance would not be available. This single decision was determinative and established whether their nature would become righteous or evil. Furthermore, their nature would be propagated to their descendants (Rom. 5:12). This was therefore a very significant decision.

A third issue Eve considered was that the tree was desirable because it would make her wise. She was unaware that, if she chose *not* to eat of the tree, she would also become wise, experienced in good and evil, experienced in morality. She focused on the true statement of the serpent with which he had encapsulated the lie. As a result, Eve succumbed to the temptation and was unaware that her decision also involved disobeying God. She chose to accept the lie that was wrapped in a veneer of truth.

The rationalization process that Eve had entertained apparently affected her decision, which she had not clearly thought through. But moral decisions are not the result of clear rational processes. Moral decisions are choices that are based on revelation from God regarding what is right and what is wrong. These types of decisions are not rational, nor are they irrational. They are moral decisions. Only persons made in God's image are capable of making decisions based on the concept of right and wrong.

Furthermore, the temptation of Eve illustrates that one's choice in moral matters is critical, even when one does not intend to do wrong. The *reason* for doing right or for refraining from doing wrong is not all-important. It is enough that God has spoken and expressed his will.[6]

Eve was deceived. She did not realize the full import of her actions. She had not determined to violate the command of God. Her choice to eat of the fruit resulted in the unintended consequence of sinning against God. "But I am afraid, lest as the serpent *deceived* Eve by his craftiness, your minds should be led astray from the simplicity and purity of devotion to Christ" (2 Cor. 11:3 NASB). "And it was not Adam who was deceived, but the woman being quite *deceived*, fell into transgression" (1 Tim. 2:14 NASB). "And the woman said, 'The serpent *deceived* me, and I ate'" (Gen. 3:13b).

Sinning is always a process. Contemplation[7] leads to a decision and then actions flow from the decision. In this case, Eve was confronted with temptation; she rationalized away the real issue; chose to sin, based on faulty thinking; committed the act of disobedience; and then turned to Adam with an offer to join her. It is the nature of fallen humanity to share sin with others.

Adam had apparently observed the entire procedure because verse 6 indicates that he was "with her." But the serpent did not deceive Adam. He sinned willfully, deliberately, and purposely—with his eyes wide open. The accusation by God in verse 17 was

---

[6] Goodness is not arbitrary (i.e., something that is good simply because God said it was). Goodness is interaction between two moral persons such that benefits increase to one or both, but not to one at the expense of the other. God does only that which is good because his nature is righteous.

[7] Temptation is often involved, as well as some rationalization processes (see James 1:13-16). A sinner's conscience may also become so hardened that he cannot discern that he is sinning. "This is the way of the adulterous woman: She eats and wipes her mouth, and says, 'I have done no wrong'" (Prov. 30:20 NASB).

that Adam had "obeyed his wife" in his decision to eat from the Tree of the Knowledge of Good and Evil. Eve apparently spoke words that encouraged her husband to join her.

The Entrance of Sin

> And the eyes of both of them were opened, and they realized that they were naked, so they sewed together some leaves and made for themselves loin coverings.
>
> —Genesis 3:7

As soon as Adam and Eve have eaten of the fruit, their natures became evil. The Bible expresses it in terms of their eyes being opened and their knowing that they were naked. Suddenly, they felt guilty. They knew that they were exposed, that their sin had somehow made them vulnerable. They recognized that they were not fit to stand before God.

Man's first response to his sin was to try to cover it, in this instance with leaves—perhaps the large leaves of a fig tree. The process was no doubt woefully humorous as the naked couple struggled to attach leaves to their bodies. Bickering may have even ensued over the "best" leaves. Sin is never a pretty thing.

The question might be raised: did God speak the truth when he said "in the day you eat from it, you will surely die"? Were not Adam and Eve both still alive after their sin? But, no, they were no longer alive. It is true, they were still physically in their bodies, but because of their sin, they were no longer alive to God. Their sin had brought about an ontological separation between themselves and their righteous Creator. The essence of death is separation, be it separation between body and soul or between God and man. At the fall—that very day—Adam died spiritually. Over nine hundred years later, Adam died physically.[8]

Confrontation and "Confession"

> And they heard the sound of the Lord God walking in the garden in the cool of the day, so Adam and his wife hid themselves from the presence of the Lord God among the trees of the garden. And the Lord God called for Adam, and said to him, "Where are you?" And he said, "Your sound I heard in the garden and I was afraid because I was naked, so I hid myself." And he said, "Who told you that you were naked? Did you eat from the tree that I commanded you not to eat from?" And Adam said, "The wife that you gave to be with me, she gave me of the tree, so I ate." Then the Lord God said to the woman, "What is this you have done?" And the woman said, "The serpent tricked me, and I ate."
>
> —Genesis 3:8-13

It is a bit difficult to reconstruct exactly what the sinful pair heard as the Lord approached them. Woodenly, the Hebrew indicates that they heard the *voice* of the Lord *walking*. Did they hear his footfalls? Or the gentle rustle of grass? Was God humming to himself? Or was he calling out to them as he had done on other occasions?

---

[8] Christ provides salvation for both aspects of human sin. He first endured separation from his Father during the three hours of darkness (Matt. 27:45-46) as he hung on the cross ("And he himself bore our sins while in his body on the cross" [1 Peter 2:24a]); then he experienced physical separation of body from soul ("And Jesus cried out again with a loud voice, and yielded the spirit" [Matt. 27:50]).

Whatever the sound they heard when God approached Adam and Eve, they recognized immediately that their leafy garments were inadequate. They were totally unprepared to meet God, so they hid. But even this added protection did not assuage their guilt. God, feigning ignorance, played their game by calling to them: "Where are you?"

Adam finally responded and, no doubt wanting to justify his actions, inadvertently told God more than he intended. "And he said 'Your sound I heard in the garden and I was afraid because I was naked, so I hid myself.'" Surely, the last thing Adam wanted was to talk about his nakedness. Yet that was exactly where the interrogation turned.

"And he said, 'Who told you that you were naked? Did you eat from the tree that I commanded you not to eat from?'" God graciously supplied the answer to his own question so that Adam had only to acknowledge his sin with a simple yes. How different the outcome might have been for Adam had he been willing to confess his sin to God and ask for mercy. "The wages of sin is death"—that could not change. But the curse upon the earth could certainly have been mollified had he chosen to confess.

Instead of confessing his sin, however, Adam turned on his companion, friend, and partner, attempting to shift the blame away from himself and to his wife, who, incidentally, the *Lord* had given him. "And Adam said, 'The wife that you gave to be with me, she gave me of the tree, so I ate.'" Adam had clearly hoped that it would be obvious that he himself had had little to do with the predicament in which he now found himself. Amazingly, God did not rebuke him immediately. Instead, he temporarily accepted Adam's excuse and turned to address Eve. "Then the Lord God said to the woman, 'What is this that you have done?'"

Now, Eve was a quick learner. Her husband had just shown her how to handle a sticky situation—"pass the buck"—so she in turn blamed the serpent. "And the woman said, 'The serpent tricked me, and I ate.'" Eve implied that she would not have ever done this had not the serpent *deceived* her. The only reason she ate, she believed, was that the serpent had tricked her into it. This encounter with God hardly constituted a confession. One can only wonder how different things might have been had our parents exhibited broken and contrite hearts (Ps. 51:17).

Throughout this interrogation, God asked only objective questions: Where? Who? Did you? and What? We can learn from this. While raising five children, this author was frequently confronted with situations that involved sin. On more than one occasion, I asked the culprit, "*Why* did you do that?" But such a question was rarely helpful. The response was usually a blank stare or a glum "I dunno," and these were proper responses. No rational reasons exist that justify evil actions.

After conversing with Adam and Eve, God addressed the serpent. He did not ask the snake to account for his actions. The reason is obvious: A snake is not a morally responsible being; it is simply an animal. Evidently, the being that had inhabited the serpent and was responsible for the temptation had vanished. Nonetheless, the serpent was subject to a curse from God simply because he had been the vessel used to introduce sin into the human race.

Curse on the Serpent

The Lord God said to the serpent,
"Because you did this,
Cursed are you more than any domesticated animal,
Or than any beast of the field.
Upon your belly you shall go,
And dust you shall eat all the days of your life.
Furthermore, enmity I will place between you and the woman,

And between your seed and her seed.
He will strike you on the head
And you will strike him on the heel."

—Genesis 3:14-15

The curse resulted in the serpent becoming the lowest of all animals. Its anatomy was changed so that it would now move on its belly, and even the snake's physiology was changed so that it would now "eat dust." This does not mean that the snake would literally consume dirt, as does the earthworm. Instead, the phrase refers to that area of the biosphere where the creature would find its sustenance.

The phrases *eat dust* or *lick the dust* speak metaphorically of "deepest degradation."[9] It is said of God's enemies: "They will lick the dust like a serpent, like reptiles of the earth. They will come trembling out of their fortresses; to the LORD our God they will come in dread and they will be afraid before you" (Mic. 7:17 NASB). This same metaphorical use, denoting degradation, can be found in Isaiah 49:23 and Psalm 72:9.

God also placed animosity and hatred between the serpent and Eve. The Hebrew word *enmity* occurs only five times in the Old Testament,[10] but a cognate participle *enemy* ('ôyêv) appears over 280 times. Therefore, this relatively rare word is quite well understood. The serpent and the woman would be at war with each other. This enmity would be transmitted to their offspring as well.

Some have tried to see a foreshadowing of the salvific work of Christ in verse 15. "He shall bruise you on the head, and you shall bruise him on the heel."[11] This does not seem well-advised

9   Young, *Genesis 3*, 98.
10 Gerhard Lisowsky, *Konkordanz zum Hebraischen Alten Testament,* 2d ed. (Stuttgart: Wurttembergische Bibelanstalt, 1958): 54.
11 A primary example of this position is found in the *Westminster Confession.* "Man by his fall having made himself incapable of life by that covenant [the

because, in the first place, Satan had no significant role in the purchase of our salvation. Peter states in Acts 3:14-15 [2:23; 5:30; 10:39] that mankind killed Christ, not Satan. Secondly, if "bruise him on the heel" refers to Christ's work on the cross, this reference would indicate that Christ did not actually die. "Head bruising" speaks of death, while "heel wounding" refers to little more than inconvenience. "Heel wounding" is certainly not imagery depicting crucifixion.

Thirdly, there was no *quid pro quo*, no trade-off at the time of Christ's crucifixion. Where does the crushing of Satan's head fit into the passion narrative? Romans 16:20 states that Satan has not yet been crushed: "And the God of peace will soon crush Satan under your feet" (NASB).

Fourthly, the reason the Hebrew text switched from feminine "her seed" to masculine "he" in the next phrase is that the Hebrew word *seed* is a masculine collective singular noun. Hebrew grammar demands this switch in gender and number. The Hebrew intends the reader to understand that it is *her seed* that will bruise the serpent on the head. The verse is not intended to be a veiled reference to Christ.

Finally, this verse (3:15) is never cited in the New Testament as being fulfilled by the death of Christ. An allusion to the verse may be seen in the pericope in which Christ sent out the seventy disciples: "And he said to them, 'I saw Satan fall like lightning from heaven. Behold, I have given you authority to tread on serpents and scorpions, and over all the power of the enemy, and nothing shall hurt you'" (Luke 10:18-19 ESV). Christ's statement about seeing Satan fall from heaven should

---

covenant of works], the Lord was pleased to make a second, commonly called the covenant of grace. . . ." The footnote then cites Gen. 3:15, along with others (Philip Schaff, *The Creeds of Christendom: With a History and Critical Notes,* vol. 3, *The Creeds of the Evangelical Protestant Churches* [New York: Harper & Brothers, 1919]: 617)

be understood to be a prophetic statement referring to that future event found in Revelation 12:7-10.

Enmity between women and snakes will always exist. At least that is what this text says. The introduction of our salvation is not bound up in this curse.

Changes to the Woman

> To the woman he said:
>> "I will greatly increase your labor pains and your conceptions,[12]
>> In great pain you shall bear children,
>> Yet for your husband shall be your desire,
>> And he shall rule over you."
>
> —Genesis 3:16

The changes to Eve were three-fold, as was the curse on the serpent. First, her anatomy was changed so that childbearing would now involve considerable pain. As Eve originally came from God's hand, the process of giving birth would have apparently involved labor and work, but the expulsion of new life would not have involved significant pain. It is not clear why the Lord chose to curse the woman in this manner. Eve's sin was certainly not sexual. It was an act of disobedience.

Paul also connected the fall into sin with bearing children. "For Adam was formed first, then Eve; and Adam was not deceived, but the woman was deceived and became a transgressor; yet she will be saved through childbearing—if

---

[12] Both the NASB and the ESV blend these two concepts of "labor pains" and "conceptions" into a single phrase—"your pain in childbirth." This is curious since both words are participles, both have the feminine singular pronoun *you* attached, and they are separated by a conjunctive. They are clearly grammatically distinct concepts.

they continue in faith and love and holiness, with self-control" (1 Tim. 2:13-15 ESV). A woman's "salvation" (KJV) is, in fact, through this means, through childbearing. Was not the incarnate Christ brought into the world through the woman? The context of the Timothy passage argues that the woman's purpose in life, after being told to refrain from leadership in the church, is in bearing children. It is there that she will find fulfillment.

There is a suggestion that God, at the start of the millennium, will mollify the painful physiology of childbirth. "And it will be in that day [i.e., the day of Christ's second coming] when the Lord gives you rest from your pain (*'etzev*) and turmoil and harsh service in which you have been enslaved" (Isa. 14:3). The same root word used to describe the increase of childbirth pain in Genesis 3:16 (*'etzev*) is here spoken of as being reduced significantly. Since a host of other biological changes occur at this time,[13] it is reasonable to find the process of childbirth being altered as well.

God also changed Eve's physiology so that her ability to conceive was greatly multiplied. We cannot know how often Eve would have been able to conceive before this event. Perhaps each reproductive cycle would have been separated by years. "Greatly increase" sounds as though the cycle of the menses was shortened substantially. The long-reaching effect of this curse was that it significantly accelerated the program of God.

Finally, Eve was altered psychologically so that her husband would now rule over her. The first line of this section uses a word that only occurs three times in the Old Testament.[14] It is usually translated *desire*. But it is disputed whether the woman's desire is to have control over her husband[15] or to desire

---

[13] So Isa. 11:6-9; Mic. 4:1-3; Ezek. 47:1-12; Zech. 14:4-8; *passim*.

[14] Gen. 3:16; 4:7; Song 7:10 [Heb. 11].

[15] Susan T. Foh, "What is the Woman's Desire?" *Westminster Theological Journal* 37 (1975): 382.

her husband's control.[16] This issue is somewhat academic, for all agree that the second line means "he will rule over you."

Perhaps the original arrangement between Adam and Eve more closely resembled a partnership. But even then Adam seemed to have a modicum of authority because he was created first and was allowed by God to name his new partner (2:23). "Naming is sometimes an assertion of sovereignty over the thing named."[17] But now, with this curse, God granted more control to the husband. Was this a factor that led Paul to repeatedly say, "Husbands, love your wives"?

Curse on the Ground

> And to Adam, he said, "Because you obeyed your wife and ate of the tree that I had commanded you, saying, 'Do not eat from it!'
>
> Cursed is the ground because of you;
> Through great toil you shall eat from it all the days of your life.
> Now useless plants shall grow for you,
> And you shall eat plants of the field.
> By the sweat of your face you shall eat them,
> Until you return to the ground,
> Because from it you were taken,
> For you are dust and to dust you will return."
> —Genesis 3:17-19

God was very explicit in verse 17. The reason for the impending pronouncement is stated clearly: It was because Adam obeyed

---

[16] Irvin A. Busenitz, "Woman's Desire for Man: Genesis 3:16 Reconsidered," *Grace Theological Journal* 7 (1986): 212.

[17] Leonard J. Coppes, "*qārā'*" in *TDOT*, 810, no. 2063.

his wife in her sin and ate, thereby disobeying God. Again, Eve had not fully understood the scope of her actions, but Adam had been fully cognizant that his actions constituted disobedience. It might seem that Adam should have borne the greater judgment, but the fact that Eve was the first to sin seems to be the reason for this differential (1 Tim. 2:13-14).

For a second time, God used the word *cursed*. In the first case, the serpent was cursed. In this instance, the ground was cursed. It is true that Eve was changed in at least three ways, but those adjustments are not identified as curses. Here Adam's situation was cursed because of his disobedience, but he himself was left untouched.

The same Hebrew root used to describe the pain of childbirth (*'etzev*) is also applied to Adam's toil, by which he would scratch out a living. "Through great toil (*'etzev*) you shall eat of it all the days of your life" (Gen. 3:17b).

It is not suggested here that husbands today can console wives who have just been through the excruciating process of childbirth by suggesting that "I understand, for my work in the field is as hard as your labor pains." This line of reasoning does not stand because the curse placed on the ground was partially alleviated. Note the prophecy given by Lamech at the time of Noah's birth: "Now he called his name Noah, saying, 'This one shall give us rest from our work and from the great toil (*'etzev*) of our hands arising from the ground which the Lord has cursed'" (Gen. 5:29). One of the effects of the global judgment by water in the days of Noah was to change the climate and ecology in such a way that farming is now easier than it was on that early earth. This portion of the Edenic curse has been mollified somewhat, though a complete restoration still lies in the future (see Rev. 22:3—"there will no longer be any curse").

The familiar phrase *thorns and thistles* is a rare combination of two Hebrew words that speaks of non-productive vegetation more than it speaks of hurtful plants. Hosea 10:8 is the only other reference that uses this combination.

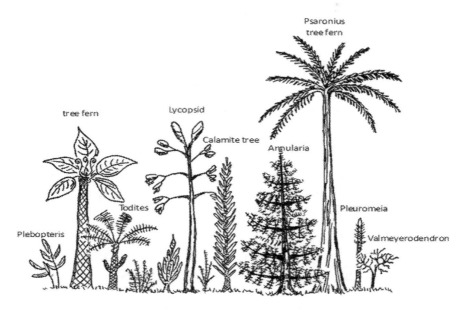

Figure 18: Types of plants found in abundance in coal seams, none of which are useful bearers of edible fruit or seeds

In addition to the ground producing an abundance of useless vegetation such as ferns, cycads, and rushes that are so prevalent in coal seams, the text also states that Adam will "eat the plants of the field." This is at variance with what God had provided for Adam to eat at the close of the creation week. "And God said, 'Behold I have given you every plant yielding seed . . . and every tree yielding fruit'" (1:29). Now Adam's diet would necessarily include "plants of the field" (cf. 2:5). The ground would no longer be a paradise of fruits and seeds. In order to stay alive, Adam's diet would need to include food fit for animals.

From the fall to the flood, this curse on the ground was in full force. The ground would now yield her increase only under man's perpetual, toilsome labor. And, as mentioned, the term *great labor* describes the pain of childbirth inflicted upon Eve's body. Adam's labor would eventually grind him down until he died and returned to dust. In reality, Adam's death would be the result of being denied access to the Tree of Life, not to any part of the curse. In a sense, God was gracious in allowing Adam to terminate his existence on this sin-cursed earth in his fallen condition.

Verse 19 relates to the perpetual nature of this struggle for survival against the elements. "By the sweat of your face you shall eat them, until you return to the dust, because, from it you were taken, for you are dust and to dust you will return." God was not actively instituting a death penalty here. He was merely reiterating that all during the course of his life, Adam would have to work hard in order to eat. He would labor until he died. Death was guaranteed because of the coupling of Adam's mortal body with God's denial of access to the Tree of Life.

Adam Names Eve

> Then Adam named his wife Eve, because she was the mother of all living.
>
> —Genesis 3:20

Our English spelling of the name *Eve* is an anglicized, germanized, latinized, aramaicized form of the Hebrew word that means "to live." To show the same relationship in English that is so obvious in the Hebrew, Adam may have named her Life-y or Lively, built off our verb *to live*, because she was the mother who gave life to all. All other human beings who have ever lived—or will live—are descendants of Eve.

God's Gracious Provision for the Pair

> And the Lord God made garments of skin for Adam
> and his wife, and he clothed them. And the Lord God
> said, "Behold, the man is like one of us, knowing good
> and evil, and now lest he stretch out his hand and
> take repeatedly from the Tree of Life, and eat, and
> live forever. . . ." So the Lord God sent him out from
> the garden of Eden to work the ground from which he
> was taken. And he drove out the pair and he stationed
> the cherubim at the east [entrance] of the garden of
> Eden, along with the flaming sword that spun in all
> directions to guard the path to the Tree of Life.
>
> —Genesis 3:21-24

After pronouncing the curses, God made two gracious adjustments because of Adam and Eve's current sinful condition. First, he made garments of animal skins to clothe the couple. This was God's response to their "having their eyes opened and realizing that they were naked." The skins were obviously derived from an animal. That animal—perhaps a sheep—had to die in order to provide a covering for the naked couple. Typologically, this speaks of the blood of Christ that he shed so that we might be clothed in his righteousness (Gal. 3:27).

Then the Lord took a more drastic step and cast the couple out of his immediate presence. The stated purpose (v. 22) was to deny them access to the Tree of Life. The primary reason we die physically is that we do not have access to the Tree of Life. The primary reason we do not have access to the Tree of Life is sin. To guarantee that Adam and his descendants could do no more than look, wish, and remember, God stationed the cherubim and the flaming sword to challenge anyone who attempted to access the way to the Tree of Life.

It should be understood that Adam was created a mortal being. He was physically capable of dying when he was created. The second law of thermodynamics (the law of entropy) had been in place since Day One.

It is commonly argued that physical death is a result of sin entering the human race and that the second law of thermodynamics was first introduced at the fall of mankind. This position, however, does not address the function of the Tree of Life. What was the purpose of the Tree of Life? It was created and accessible before the fall. It clearly did not have a spiritual function; that was the purpose of the Tree of the Knowledge of Good and Evil.

The Tree of Life was a physical tree whose properties were the perfect antidote for every physical malady. As long as Adam—or any of his descendants, in the event that Adam had not sinned—had access to the fruit or leaves of this tree, he could have overcome the effects of any disease or accident.

Had Adam and Eve chosen to obey when they were tempted, thereby becoming righteous, they would still have needed access to the Tree of Life to physically live forever. In other words, had they obeyed, Adam and Eve would have still been mortal. Mortality was not an effect of the fall, though the inevitability of physical death was. Mortality seems to be a necessary component of procreation.[18]

Because of sin, mankind has been denied access to the paradise of Eden. It is of interest to note that in the new heavens

---

[18] This thought leads to the conclusion that, even in the eternal state, some persons may retain the capacity for procreation. Candidates for this role are probably those who will inhabit the millennium (including resurrected Old Testament saints), who are subsequently purified by the great fire at the close of the millennium, which fire will apparently remove their sinful nature (2 Peter 3:10-13) and who are then allowed to populate the new earth. This situation would then be amazingly similar to that which would have existed had Adam and Eve chosen to reject the temptation, thereby becoming righteous by nature.

and the new earth that the Lord will create,[19] a Tree of Life will again be accessible. "And the leaves of the tree were for the healing of the nations" (Rev. 22:2b NASB; Rev. 2:7; Ezek. 47:12). Here too it is suggested that the life referred to is mortal, physical life[20]—life that stands in need of occasional correction or adjustment. It follows that some[21] people in the eternal state, though righteous, will still possess mortal bodies,[22] like those of Adam and Eve.

---

[19] Isa. 65:17—"For behold, I create new heavens and a new earth; and the former things shall not be remembered or come to mind" (NASB).

[20] The grammar of Rev. 22 does not suggest, as some theologians do, that the benefits of eating from the Tree of Life should be understood as "symbolic of the far-reaching effects of the death of Christ" (Alan Johnson, "Revelation" in *The Expositor's Bible Commentary,* 12 vols. [Grand Rapids, Mich.: Zondervan, 1981]: 12:599).

[21] Members of the body of Christ, the Church, will have been resurrected to an "imperishable" state in a "spiritual body" (1 Cor. 15:42-44).

[22] J. Vernon McGee, *Thru the Bible with J. Vernon McGee,* 5 vols. (Nashville: Nelson, 1983): 5:1076.

– 11 –

A Note on the Fall of Satan

The account of the fall of mankind preserved for us in Genesis does not comment on the being behind the temptation, nor does it refer to his origin or spiritual state. This material comes from other biblical texts.

The consensus among evangelicals is that Eve was interacting with Satan in the events of Genesis 3 and that Satan was evil at the time he indwelt the serpent. A strong case can also be made that Ezekiel 28:11-17a provides a brief exposé of the early history of Satan.

> Moreover, the word of the LORD came to me: "Son of man, raise a lamentation over the king of Tyre, and say to him, Thus says the Lord GOD: 'You were the signet of perfection, full of wisdom and perfect in beauty. You were in Eden, the garden of God: every precious stone was your covering, sardius, topaz, and diamond, beryl, onyx, and jasper, sapphire, emerald, and carbuncle; and crafted in gold were your settings and your engravings. On the day that you were created they were prepared. You were an anointed guardian cherub [or, the anointed cherub who covers the presence]. I placed you; you were on the holy mountain of God; in the midst of the stones

of fire you walked. You were blameless in your ways from the day you were created, until unrighteousness was found in you. In the abundance of your trade you were filled with violence in your midst and you sinned; so I cast you as a profane thing from the mountain of God and I destroyed you, O guardian cherub, from the midst of the stones of fire. Your heart was proud because of your beauty; you corrupted your wisdom for the sake of your splendor. I cast you to the ground.'"

—Ezekiel 28:11-17a ESV

One might object that this passage is addressed to a human king of Tyre and not to Satan. But the attributes attached to this "king of Tyre" go far beyond characteristics of any human king. First, it is stated that this being was "created" (*bārā'*) on a specific day: "On the day that you were created" (v. 13) and "from the day you were created" (v. 15). Adam and his wife were the only humans ever created, so this "king of Tyre" is not a member of the human race.

Secondly, he is identified as "the anointed cherub who covers" (vv. 14, 16 NASB). The Hebrew verb translated *covers* means "to shut off as a protection."[1] This angelic being was apparently more closely associated with the divine presence than any other. This cherub had the most powerful and significant appointment of any of the angelic host. He was more closely aligned to God than any other spiritual being.

Thirdly, the attributes of this cherub were unrivaled. This being had no equal in God's creation.

- You were the signet of perfection (v. 12),
- You were full of wisdom (v. 12),

---

[1]   HALOT, 754.

- You were perfect in beauty[2] (v. 12),
- You had a covering of precious stones . . . in gold settings (v. 13),
- You walked amidst the stones of fire (v. 14),
- You were blameless (v. 15), and
- You were filled with the abundance of your trade.[3]

Finally, the use of the title *king* in referring to angelic beings is not unique to this cherub. In Daniel 10:13, Gabriel spoke of the resistance he encountered in his attempts to deliver the answer to Daniel's prayer.[4] "But the prince of the kingdom of Persia was withstanding me for twenty-one days; then behold, Michael, one of the chief princes, came to help me, for I had been left there with the *kings* of Persia" (NASB, emphasis added). Paul also speaks of rulers, powers, and world forces when referencing the non-material realm (Eph. 6:12). So the title "king of Tyre" has doubtless been used here as a moniker for a spiritual being.

The events surrounding the fall of mankind and its relationship to the fall of Satan may be reconstructed as follows: Satan was created directly by God at the beginning of Day One of the creation week when heaven or the spiritual universe was created (1:1). He was created "blameless" (Ezek. 28:18), free from evil, but capable of great evil. God had endowed him with

---

[2]   While the city of Tyre made this claim for itself (Ezek. 27:3b), this passage, addressed to the "king of Tyre," allows that the untrammeled truth of this phrase does apply to this individual.

[3]   This word is associated with buying, selling, and turning a profit. In this context, it very likely speaks of political clout reflected in granting or refusing to grant others access to the presence of God. Satan would profit from his privileged position.

[4]   Gabriel's name is given in Dan. 9:21.

such great beauty, intelligence, and honor that it was easy for him to be lifted up with pride.[5]

Satan's usual place of operation was in Eden at the throne of God. Eden was designed and designated to be God's dwelling place. This suggests that Satan did not fall until *after* the garden was planted and prepared as a fitting home for both God and man. Satan was still without blame at the close of Day Six. "And God saw all that He had made [including Satan], and behold, it was very good. And there was evening and there was morning, the sixth day" (Gen. 1:31).

The Bible is quite clear that sin is a process (see James 1:13-16). It starts with a thought that evolves into a choice that eventuates in a deed. Satan's mind was apparently filled with pride (the thought), which evolved into a decision (to gain control over Adam), but what did he then *do* to complete the sin? He certainly did not confront God directly in battle, for he would have lost miserably. Instead, it seems reasonable to conclude that the action that resulted from the decision in his heart was seen in his coming in the body of a serpent to tempt Eve. His first sinful act was to lie about the truth of what God had said. Christ himself spoke of Satan, saying that "he is a liar and the father of lies" (John 8:44 NASB).

This was his first act of rebellion. The fall of Satan was intrinsically connected to the fall of mankind. When Satan went back to assume his duty of protecting the Lord, he was doubtless confronted with his sin: "So I have cast you as a profane thing from the mountain of God" (Ezek. 28:16b ESV).

The Lord had doubtless dealt with the sin in his own house before he came to confront the poorly clad, guilty pair. To look for a statement of the condemnation of Satan in the curse of Genesis 3 is futile, for God had already taken care of that.

---

[5]   Perhaps the description in Isa. 14:12ff is also speaking of Satan's fall, though this person is designated as "the man" in verse 16.

− 12 −

Genesis 4: Life on the Early Earth

> Now Adam knew Eve his wife, and she conceived and bore Cain, for she said, "I have gotten a man with the Lord."
>
> —Genesis 4:1

The Bible is interested in expressing more than simple cognition when it says that Adam "knew" Eve. The word *know (yāda^c)* is translated in the NASB with over a hundred distinguishable English words or phrases.[1] In this setting the term clearly has overtones of physical intimacy, for because of this "knowing," Eve became pregnant.

This verse describes the birth of the first baby. It was a boy. Eve marveled at this process of procreation and named her son Cain. The word *Cain* is part of a word play. The word *qayin* [Eng. *Cain*] means *gotten* because Eve said, "I have gotten

---

[1]   *New American Standard: Exhaustive Concordance to the Bible; Hebrew-Aramaic and Greek Dictionaries*, ed., Robert L. Thomas (Nashville: Holman, 1981) 1528, no. 3045.

(*qānîthî*) a man-child with the help[2] of the Lord."[3] An attempt to preserve the word-play in English might read like this: "she bore Gotten because she said, 'I have gotten a man with the help of the Lord.'"

In terms of chronology, Cain's conception is placed subsequent to the curse and man's removal from the garden. The new baby was therefore not innocent in the same way that his parents had been when they came from the Creator's hand. However, Cain shared in the image and likeness of Adam and Eve (see Gen. 5:3), and this image now included a depraved, evil nature.

Cain and Abel

> And again, she gave birth to his brother Abel. And Abel was a keeper of sheep while Cain was a worker of the ground. And it came to pass at the end of certain days[4], that Cain brought, of the fruit of the ground, an offering to the Lord. Likewise Abel also brought from the firstborn of his flock—and the fattest. And the Lord accepted Abel and his offering, but Cain and his offering, he did not accept. So Cain became very angry and his face showed it. And the Lord said to Cain, "Why are you angry, and why has your countenance fallen? If you do what is good, will it [your countenance] not be lifted up? And if you do

---

[2] Waltke and O'Connor, *Syntax*, 195.

[3] The LXX translates the phrase *with the Lord* as *through God* (*dia tou theou*).

[4] The length of time from creation to this incident is not specified. If, however, Seth was conceived soon after the murder of Abel, then Cain was about 125 years old when he killed his brother (see Gen. 4:25). This is deduced from the fact that Adam was 130 years old at the birth of Seth (Gen. 5:3).

> not do what is good, sin crouches at the very door,
> and its desire is for you, but you should overrule it."
>
> —Genesis 4:2-7

A second son was born, named Abel. The Bible does not attach particular significance to his name as Eve had when her firstborn arrived, so it is probably not wise for us to do so.[5] Abel was a herdsman, while Cain was a farmer. Both occupations can be related to the first chapter of Genesis—"rule over the domesticated animals" (v. 26) and "I give to you every kind of plant bearing seeds . . . as food" (v. 29). Farming and ranching were occupations that one would expect to find in this early setting.

Both sons brought offerings appropriate to their occupation. Cain brought of the fruit of the ground, while Abel brought the choicest of the flock. The Bible does not record how these men came to know about offerings. We must assume that God gave instruction to Adam regarding sacrifice. This offering was then brought "to the Lord" (4:3). It was earlier concluded that God lived in Eden. The closest these men could therefore have come "to the Lord" would have been to approach the cherubim that guarded the way to the Tree of Life (3:24).

---

[5] A common Hebrew homonym means "breath" or "nothingness," but this understanding does not add appreciably to the narrative (Richard S. Hess, *Studies in the Personal Names of Genesis 1-11* in *Alter Orient und Altes Testament*, Band 234 [Kevelaer, Germany: Butzin und Bercker, 1993] 27-28).

Figure 19: The acceptance of Abel's sacrifice

God's acceptance or rejection of the sacrifice was immediately obvious. It seems reasonable to conclude that his acceptance involved an outward demonstration, such as the ignition of the sacrifice by the "flaming sword." The subsequent consumption of the offering by fire would have then signaled God's pleasure with the offering. This type of phenomenon is found in other settings in the Old Testament. Manoah's sacrifice was miraculously consumed by the fire of the angel of the Lord (Judg. 13:19-20), as was the offering of Elijah on Mount Carmel (1 Kings 18:38).

The distinction between the sacrifices of Cain and Abel was obviously not simply the difference between a grain offering and an animal offering. If this had been the issue, God could easily have informed Cain that blood was necessary for his sacrifice to be accepted. But God did not make this kind of statement. He simply stated that "sin crouches at the very door, and its desire is for you." In the later Levitical sacrificial system, a grain offering was certainly acceptable as "an offering by fire of a soothing aroma to the LORD" (Lev. 2:2b NASB).

In New Testament passages about Cain and Abel, the emphasis is on Abel's faith, which was mingled with his sacrifice (Heb. 11:4; 4:2). Cain's deeds were evil and Abel's were righteous (1 John 3:12). We do not know what Cain's sin was, but the passage makes it quite clear that the problem was in his heart, not in the type of offering that he brought. "Elsewhere the Lord rejected the gifts of Korah (Num. 16:15), Saul's men (1 Sam. 26:19), and apostate Israel (Isa. 1:13), not because of some blemish in their offerings, but because of their deformed characters."[6]

The Lord, who knows the heart of man, saw that Cain's offering was unacceptable. In his confrontation with Cain, God gave truth regarding sin: one need not submit to the urging of temptation; one can and should override the urge to yield (see 1 Cor. 10:13).[7]

The First Murder

And Cain spoke with Abel his brother, and it came about while they were in the field, that Cain rose up against Abel his brother and slew him.

—Genesis 4:8

---

[6] Bruce K. Waltke, "Cain and His Offering," *Westminster Theological Journal,* 48 (1986): 371.

[7] That the close of verse 7 is similar to the close of 3:16 does not demand that borrowing has occurred (see O. Eissfeldt, *Genesis,* in *Biblia Hebraica Stuttgartensia* [Stuttgart: Wurttenbergische Bibelanstalt, 1969]: 6, n. b-b). The similarity is superficial, incidental, or even "accidental" (Leupold, *Genesis,* 202). "Yet for your husband shall be your desire, and he shall rule over you" (3:16). "And its desire is for you, but you should overrule it" (4:7).

This text does not record the conversation between the two brothers, but a number of Hebrew manuscripts have inserted two words at this point that give the translation: "Let us go to the field."[8] This certainly does not contradict the received text, for the brothers did end up "in the field."

Sin is not rational. Cain, with his evil attitude, apparently reasoned that the murder of his brother would mollify the situation. So he bludgeoned his brother to death. In so doing, Cain became the first murderer, introducing physical death into the human race.

Curse on Cain

Then the Lord said to Cain, "Where is Abel your brother?" And he replied, "I do not know. Am I my brother's keeper?" So he said, "What did you do? The voice of the blood of your brother is crying out to me from the ground. And now you are cursed because of the ground that has opened its mouth to receive the blood of your brother from your hand. Whenever you work the ground, it will no longer yield its strength to you. A vagrant and a vagabond you shall be on the earth." And Cain said to the Lord, "My punishment is greater than I can bear! Behold, today you have driven me from the face of the ground, and from your face I am hidden, and I shall be a vagrant and a vagabond in the earth, and it will happen that anyone who finds me will slay me." And the Lord said to him, "Therefore, whoever kills Cain, sevenfold he will be

---

[8] This insertion is also found in the Samaritan Pentateuch as well as in the LXX, the Syriac Peshiṭta, and the Latin Vulgate.

avenged." So the Lord set upon Cain a sign that he
might not be slain by whoever found him.

—Genesis 4:9-15

In the first eight chapters of Genesis, the Lord gives no
stipulation regarding murder. The law regarding murder and
capital punishment was not established until after the flood
(Gen. 9:6). For this reason, it was necessary for God to intervene and show mankind the heinousness of such action. He did
this by confronting Cain, the first murderer. God first inquired
regarding the whereabouts of his brother. The impudence in
Cain's response is shocking—a bold-faced lie, "I don't know."
The statement that follows seems as though it were designed
to impugn God for even asking such a question of him: "I'm not
the keeper of my brother, am I!"

God then asked a second question, "What have you done?"
Instead of waiting for a response, the Lord revealed to Cain
the source of his information—the voice of his brother's blood.
No indication is given that Cain was even remotely prepared
to confess his sin. His first two responses were insolent lies.
Why should God expect Cain to suddenly change his course of
action? As a result, God proceeded to curse Cain for his evil act.

The curse had a certain ironic appropriateness. Cain was a
farmer; he received his livelihood from the ground. But he had
polluted the ground by shedding on it the blood of his brother,
Abel. God therefore chose to curse him with a corresponding
curse. From now on, Cain would no longer be able to live off his
farming. He was cursed in such a way that he would be forced
to wander from place to place.

This was now the second time that God had spoken curse
concerning the ground. The first curse was global in scope and
occurred when sin was introduced into the human race (3:17-
19). The second curse was personal and occurred the first time
a human being died at the hands of another (4:11). The first

curse involved a change in the botanical structures of the plants so that excessive labor was necessary to achieve a crop. The second curse involved a change in the ground so that a good crop was no longer possible wherever Cain wandered.

Abel was, in all likelihood, the very first human to die. Yet, "through faith, though he is dead, he still speaks" (Heb. 11:4b NASB). Abel's death was premature, Abel's death was unnatural, and Abel's death was caused by an evil brother who was outraged at his righteousness. Nonetheless, Abel's life was of *great value* in the sight of God.[9] Hopefully Abel's example helps free us from the myopic thinking that to be physically alive is of greatest importance. For the evolutionist, this life is all there is, and the greatest contribution one can make is to introduce some useful gene into the pool. But for the Christian, righteous living that flows from a life of faith is of great importance, regardless of its length.

Cain complained about this curse, so the Lord provided him with a mark, a sign to alert others against killing him. Verse 15 contains no hint about the mark, but a violation of it would result in a consequence seven times worse for the offender than the curse upon Cain.[10]

The First City—Enoch

So Cain went out from the presence of the Lord and dwelt in the land of Nod, east of Eden. And Cain knew

---

[9] Homer A. Kent, Jr., *The Epistle to the Hebrews: A Commentary* (Winona Lake, Ind.: BMH, 1972): 220. The entire section on Abel's life (218-220) is cogently argued and highly recommended.

[10] The term *sevenfold* or *seven times* should be understood as conveying a concept of *completeness* similar to that spoken of by Christ when Peter questioned him about forgiveness. "I do not say to you, up to seven times, but up to seventy times seven" (Matt. 18:22 NASB).

his wife and she conceived and bore Enoch, and he was building a city, so he called the name of the city after the name of his son, Enoch.

—Genesis 4:16-17

Cain left the area near Eden and traveled east to the land of Nod. It can be deduced from the terms of his curse that Nod was somewhat arid and not well suited to agriculture. In the region of Nod, Cain's son Enoch was born, and Cain, who was apparently building a city, named it after his son.[11] This notation suggests that Enoch was the name of the first city. One wonders if building a permanent residence was an act of defiance against God's comment that Cain would be a vagrant and a vagabond for life.

Since people had primarily lived out of doors before this, is the notation of a "city" significant? Houses would have been fairly perfunctory—with no rain (2:5); no harmful animals, stinging insects, or poisonous snakes (1:28); a warm, uniform climate throughout the year under the water canopy (1:7); and no need for food storage against the winter. Those kinds of changes had not yet been brought upon the earth (8:22).

Genealogy of Cain

And to Enoch was born Irad, and Irad bore Mehujael, and Mehujael bore Methushael, and Methushael bore Lamech. And Lamech took for himself two wives. The name of the first was Adah, and the name of the second was Zillah. And Adah bore Jabal; he

---

[11] The Hebrew text uses a participle to denote the word *building*. This leads to the conclusion that the birth of Enoch occurred between the time Cain started the building project and the actual naming of the city.

was the father of those who dwell in tents and raise livestock. And the name of his brother was Jubal; he was the father of all who play the lyre and flute. And Zillah herself bore Tubal-cain, the forger of all kinds of implements of bronze and iron, and the sister of Tubal-cain was Naamah.

—Genesis 4:18-22

The descendants of Cain, described in these verses, accomplished many things. Lamech broke with the example established by God in the garden of Eden and initiated the practice of polygamy, taking two wives for himself. His children invented musical instruments and played both the lyre and pipe or flute. They became forgers of all implements[12] of bronze and iron.

Obviously no scientific archaeological dig into this preflood civilization has been undertaken. The flood scattered any and all human artifacts throughout the one-mile deep layer of sedimentary rock in such a haphazard manner that there is no possibility of recovering a grouping of artifacts that can be said to be representative of that time period. With the mining of coal over the last two hundred years or so, reports of serendipitous finds that purport to be of pre-flood origin have been made. Objects found in coal include a bronze bell, an iron bowl, and a ceramic spoon.[13]

---

[12] The syntax of this phrase is quite obtuse. The meaning is generally agreed upon but the construction is unusual. Kenneth A. Mathews provides an excellent discussion of the grammatical issues (*Genesis 1-11*, The New American Commentary, vol. 1A (Nashville: Broadman & Holman, 1995): 287, n. 321).

[13] See John Morris, *The Young Earth*, rev. ed. (Green Forest, Ark.: Master) 2007, especially 74-76.

 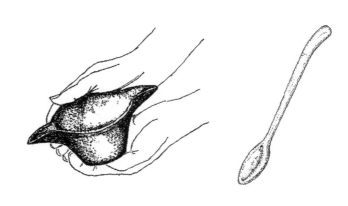

Figure 20: Artifacts purportedly found in chunks of coal or in ash after burning

The least that can be said about these artifacts is that their discovery does not undermine the presentation of that pre-flood civilization found in Genesis 4. An additional piece of information regarding the pre-flood civilization is that the population became very skilled in practicing sin.

Introduction of Polygamy

And Lamech said to his wives,
"Adah and Zillah,
Listen to my voice,
O wives of Lamech,
Give heed to my speech,
For I slew a man for wounding me,
Even a lad for bruising me.
If Cain is avenged sevenfold,
Then Lamech seventy sevenfold!"

—Genesis 4:23-24

This glimpse into the life of Lamech shows the powerful hold that sin had on the civilization at this time. The Bible makes a point that Lamech had two wives. It could be that this was the start of sexual sin. In Genesis 6, sexual exploitation became the rule of the day, and it may very well have had its beginnings in the example of Lamech.

Lamech also boasted of the impunity with which he had murdered a young man.[14] Lamech apparently assumed that since God did not confront him personally regarding his sin, he was somehow justified in seeing himself as very powerful, someone with whom no one dared interfere. If anyone should attempt to curb Lamech, let seventy-times-sevenfold vengeance be upon him.

The Lord had not yet established human government (see Gen. 9:6), so no communal law regulated or controlled actions like Lamech's. By cursing Cain, God had expressed his displeasure with murder, but even so, no mechanism had been established, no law had been given by God to restrain such sinful behavior. This was the "age of conscience" and, as seen in Genesis 6, the unrestrained, hardened human conscience is capable of great evil. Lamech, through unbridled boasting, appears to have been opening the floodgate of human depravity.

A Religious Revival

And Adam again knew his wife, and she bore a son, and she called his name Seth, "for God has set for me another seed in place of Abel, for Cain killed him." And to Seth, even to him, was born a son, and he

---

[14] Perhaps this young man was a "youthful warrior" (Patrick D. Miller, Jr., "*Yeled* in the Song of Lamech," *Journal of Biblical Literature,* 85 [1966]: 477-78). A similar usage may occur in 2 Kings 12:8ff, where Rehoboam consults with the "young men."

called his name Enosh. Then people began to call on
the name of the Lord.

—Genesis 4:25-26

Adam and Eve had another son, and Eve named him Seth
as a memorial to Abel. Seth grew up and had a son named
Enosh. Around this time a significant revival occurred among
the inhabitants of the earth. "Then men began to call upon
the name of the Lord." This revival, of which we know nothing
more, probably occurred about 235 years after the creation
of the earth. Adam was 130 years old at Seth's birth and Seth
was 105 years old when Enosh was born (130 + 105 = 235) (see
Gen 5:6). This notation of revival provides a stark contrast to
the impudent acts of Lamech. But the effects of this religious
renewal obviously did not succeed in stemming the tide of
human decadence. By Noah's time, the earth was "filled with
violence" (6:16) and only Noah and his family were seen by God
as righteous "in that entire generation" (7:1b).

– 13 –

Genesis 5 and 11:10-26: The Genealogies

This is the scroll of the story of Adam. At the time God created Adam, he made him in the likeness of God. He created them male and female and blessed them and called their name Man at the time of their creation.

—Genesis 5:1-2

These two verses reiterate what has already been revealed about mankind's creation. (1) Man was the direct creation of God. (2) Man was created to reflect his Maker in his ability to act from a moral framework, to choose to do something because it was right or because it was wrong. (3) Sexual differences and sexual attractions are the product of the mind of God. And, (4) God understood man's frame and named him "human," which may be a reflection of man's mortality.[1]

---

[1] Agreement on the etymology of 'ādām does not exist. The creation of the first man from "dust" (2:7) and the projected return to the same (3:19) suggests that mortality—biological frailty—lies at the heart of the concept. Note also the similarity of the terms Adam ('ādām) and ground ('adāmāh).

Image and Likeness

> Now Adam lived one hundred thirty years and begot
> a son in his likeness, according to his image, and he
> named him Seth.
>
> —Genesis 5:3

As mentioned, the birth of Seth presumably occurred at about the same time as the murder of Abel (see 4:25). Adam and Eve doubtless had other children both before and after the birth of Seth, but the birth of this child is noted because of the unusual events surrounding his birth.

This verse is theologically significant because it establishes with certainty that, among all God's created beings, only Adam and Eve possessed the attribute of being in the image of God. This attribute was the possession of all their descendants as well. Seth was born bearing the image of God because he was born in the image and likeness of Adam, who in turn had been made in God's image. The clear implication of this verse is that all human beings bear the mark of the image of God. Each of us is related to God in this way. The fact that human beings bear the image of God gives each person intrinsic worth. Each individual is of value to God. In fact, the reason the Lord gives for establishing capital punishment is this: "Because in the image of God he made mankind" (Gen. 9:6b). Capital punishment is not reserved solely for those who take the life of a righteous person, or even an innocent person. If the person killed is a *human*, capital punishment is the just verdict.

More than once in the Old Testament, God considered a sin against an individual made in his image as a personal affront. For example, when Abraham allowed Sarah to be taken into the court of Abimelech, God confronted the king of Gerar in a dream, saying, "I also kept you from sinning against Me; therefore I did not let you touch her" (Gen. 20:6 NASB). God himself would have been violated had Abimelech violated Abraham's wife.

Joseph also recognized this truth. When Potiphar's wife confronted him with an opportunity for sexual dalliance, Joseph's refusal was based on the fact that to sin against his master's wife was an affront to his master and, in fact, not different than sin against God himself. Joseph understood that both Potiphar and his wife were made in God's image and that to sin against one made in God's image was not essentially different than sinning against God. "You are his wife. How then can I do this great evil and sin against God" (Gen. 39:9b NASB).

After Nathan the prophet confronted David about his adultery with Bathsheba and the murder of her husband, Uriah the Hittite, his prayer of repentance was directed to God. "Against You, You only, I have sinned and done what is evil in Your sight" (Ps. 51:4a NASB). David understood that sin against Uriah or Bathsheba, who were made in God's image and likeness, was sin against God himself.

When Christ comes to establish his millennial kingdom and the nations of the world are arrayed for judgment before him, the basis for his decision is linked to how these nations have treated others. "Truly I say to you, to the extent that you did it to one of these brothers of Mine, even the least of them, you did it to Me" (Matt. 25:40 NASB). The same truth is expressed in the negative in verse 45. The reason that treatment of others can be the basis for judgment is grounded in the fact that they bear the image of God. The current policy of our federal government to allow and subsidize the wanton slaughter of millions of unborn children made in the image and likeness of God cannot be a wise position.

The Genealogy of Genesis 5:3-32

The remainder of Genesis 5 is quite stylized. All ten genealogical notations take the following form: *Personal name* lived *X number of years* and begat *descendant's name*. And *personal name* lived *Y number of years* after he begat *descendant's name*, and begat other children. And all the days that *personal name* lived were *X + Y years*, and he died.

Father	Age at birth of son	Son	Additional years		Total life span
Adam	130	Seth	800	=	930
Seth	105	Enosh	807	=	912
Enosh	90	Kenan	815	=	905
Kenan	70	Mahalalel	840	=	910
Mahalalel	65	Jared	830	=	895
Jared	165	Enoch[2]	800	=	962
Enoch	65	Methuselah	300	=	365
Methuselah	187	Lamech	782	=	969
Lamech	182	Noah	595	=	777
Noah	500	Shem, Ham, and Japheth			

It should be obvious that the author of this chapter was quite capable of doing mathematical manipulations. Nine times in this chapter, two rather large numbers are added together to achieve the total span of years for the individual under consideration. Notice though that the years are *not* totaled at the end of the chapter. The author of Genesis does not calculate the

---

[2] "Now Enoch walked with God, and he was not because God took him" (5:24). "By faith Enoch was taken up so that he should not see death; and he was not found because God took him up; for he obtained the witness that before his being taken up he was pleasing to God" (Heb. 11:5 NASB).

collective sum of the years from the birth of the first individual to the time when the last descendant was born. Had he done so, the figure would be a measure of the minimum amount of time from the creation of Adam to the birth of Ham, Shem, and Japheth.

Why did the author of this chapter avoid adding together the ten numbers? Perhaps it was because he knew that such a calculation would have been misleading. Perhaps this was his way of alerting the reader that this genealogy is not without gaps. Its intention is to establish a *genealogy,* not a time line.

A biblical genealogy is sometimes a representative listing of important ancestors that is stylized to aid in memorization.[3] The intention of the author was not to give an all-inclusive listing of the generations, but only a representative sample.

For example, in Matthew's gospel the genealogy of chapter 1 lists forty-one men.[4] These forty-one are then divided into three groups of fourteen each. "Therefore all the generations from Abraham to David are fourteen generations; and from David to the deportation to Babylon fourteen generations; and from the deportation to Babylon to the time of Christ, fourteen generations" (Matt. 1:17 NASB). The mathematically minded reader will notice that 14 x 3 = 42, not 41. To achieve the symmetry stated in Matthew 1:17, Jeconiah must be counted as the last member of the second group *and* the first member of the third group. This illustrates the representative and stylistic nature of these genealogies.

---

[3] For a formal definition and conservative comparison with other ancient genealogies, see Richard S. Hess, "The Genealogies of Genesis 1-11 and Comparative Literature," *Biblica*, 70 (1989): 241-54. He concludes that the biblical genealogies are "distinct" and represent a purpose that differs from that of other extant Ancient Near Eastern literature.

[4] Four women—Tamar, Rahab, Ruth, and Uriah's wife—are also included, but they are not part of the calculation.

The Genealogy of Genesis 11:10-26

Some striking resemblances exist between the genealogies of Genesis 5 and Genesis 11. Both list about ten major men with the last one, in both cases, having three sons. Genesis 5 records Adam to Noah, who begat Shem, Ham, and Japheth, while Genesis 11 registers Shem to Terah, who begat Abram, Nahor, and Haran.

Father	Age at birth of son	Son	Additional years
Shem	100	Arpachshad[5]	500
Arpachshad	35	Shelah[6]	403
Shelah	30	Eber	403
Eber	34	Peleg[7]	430
Peleg	30	Reu	209
Reu	32	Serug	207
Serug	30	Nahor	200
Nahor	29	Terah	119
Terah	70	Abram, Nahor, and Haran	

---

[5] "When Shem was one hundred years old he fathered Arpachshad two years after the flood" (11:10b). According to this verse, Shem was not born when Noah was 500 years old (5:32). Two years after the flood would make Noah 603 years old, and if Shem was then 100, he was born when Noah was 503 years old. Shem was doubtless listed first in verse 32 because of his significance in the genealogy of Christ (Luke 3:36). The particular descendent that was born when Noah was 500 years old was not important to the genealogist (see later discussion of Abram and Terah).

[6] Luke 3:35-36 lists Shelah as the son of Cainan, and Cainan as the son of Arpachshad.

[7] "Now to Eber was born two sons, the name of the first was Peleg because in his days was the earth divided (root *plg*), and the name of his brother was Joktan" (10:25; 1 Chron. 1:19).

Based on the stylized nature of these two genealogical lists, one should consider that they are not designed to be an inclusive list of names but rather a representative list of important men. Notice that in neither chapter does the author total the number of years at the end of the list. The genealogy of Genesis 11 does not include the number of years that each individual lived; Genesis 5 does total the two figures. This difference may suggest that the two chapters were composed at different times by different authors. Moses simply recorded the genealogies in their respective formats.

The precipitous drop in the life span of the men in Genesis 11, along with the decrease in the age at which sexual maturity was achieved, suggests that this genealogy is not closed. If it were strictly closed, Shem, who lived an additional five hundred years after the birth of Arpachshad, would have outlived Abraham by thirty-five years! This is not reasonable. Did Noah's life span likewise overlap Abram's by sixty years (9:28-29)? Probably not.

In this twenty-first century, Americans are concerned with precision when speaking about biological relationships. For example, the terms *great-uncle*, *second cousin*, or *half brother* are clearly understood. Not so for the oriental mind. For example, Ruth 4:17 reads: "A son has been born to Naomi!" In reality, a Moabitess, Naomi's deceased son's wife, and a distant relative of Naomi's deceased husband were the biological parents of the child. Yet it was appropriate in that culture to say that *Naomi* had borne a son.

It is commonly understood that Jacob had twelve sons and one daughter, so it is a bit surprising to read in Genesis 46 that "these are the sons of Leah, whom she bore to Jacob in Paddan-Aram, with his daughter Dinah; all his sons and daughters numbered thirty-three" (Gen. 46:15 NASB). In the same chapter, Zilpah "bore to Jacob these sixteen persons" (v. 18), Rachel "bore to Jacob, fourteen persons in all" (v. 22), and

Bilhah "bore these to Jacob, seven persons in all" (v. 25). The author was obviously counting grandsons as well as sons, while calling them all *sons*.

The genealogy of Moses and Aaron also illustrates that these listings are not designed as strictly closed chronologies. The lineage of Moses, Aaron, and Miriam is given four times in the Bible. Each time the list includes only four generations: (1) Levi, (2) Kohath, (3) Amram and Jochebed, and (4) Moses, Aaron and Miriam.

> Amram married his father's sister Jochebed, and she bore him Aaron and Moses. And the length of Amram's life was one hundred and thirty-seven years.
>
> —Exodus 6:20 NASB

> And the name of Amram's wife was Jochebed, the daughter of Levi, who was born to Levi in Egypt. And she bore to Amram: Aaron and Moses and their sister Miriam.
>
> —Numbers 26:59 NASB

> And the children of Amram were Aaron, Moses, and Miriam.
>
> —1 Chronicles 6:3a NASB

> And the sons of Amram were Aaron and Moses.
>
> —1 Chronicles 23:13a NASB

These verses are so clear that one would not suspect that a gap lies between Jochebed and Aaron. However, if the family of Jacob went down to Egypt four hundred thirty years before the exodus ("Now the time that the sons of Israel lived in Egypt was four hundred and thirty years" [Ex. 12:40]), and Jochebed was born soon after Levi came to Egypt ("And the name of Amram's wife was Jochebed, the daughter of Levi, who was born to Levi in Egypt" [Num. 26:59a]), and Moses was eighty years old at the time of the exodus ("And Moses was eighty years old and Aaron eighty three, when they spoke to Pharaoh" [Ex. 7:7]), then Jochebed would have been between three hundred and three hundred fifty years old when she suddenly gave birth to three children in fairly rapid succession. Remember that her husband lived to only 137 years (Ex. 6:20).

It seems more reasonable to suggest that a gap, not mentioned in the Bible, lies between the couple Amram and Jochebed and their descendants Aaron, Moses, and Miriam. The birth narrative of Moses seems to support this as well, for it fails to provide the name of either parent. "Now a man from the house of Levi went and married a daughter of Levi" (Ex. 2:1 NASB). It is accepted Semitic practice to construct genealogies that give the appearance of being contiguous while actually containing generational gaps. The purpose is to show lineage rather than to construct a time line.

The genealogy of Jesus is given in Matthew 1 and Luke 3. In Luke's account, however, the name Cainan (Kenan) is inserted between Arphaxad and Shelah (Luke 3:36, cf. Gen. 11:12). Which is right, the Luke account or the Genesis record? To the oriental mind, both are correct.

In light of an understanding of the inerrant character of the original autographs, it is not acceptable to posit that Luke correctly handled his material because he recorded the "error" correctly. An error is an error. A better solution is to understand that Genesis 11:12-14 describes ancestry or lineage rather than immediate parentage.

Luke did not merely invent the name Cainan. The name appears in the Septuagint. The source for this Septuaginal addition is not known, but the tradition that Luke used was already over two hundred years old at the time of Christ. So it seems reasonable to conclude that there really was such a man as Cainan and that he was a descendent of Arphaxad.[8]

The Story of Terah

Now this is the story of Terah. Terah was the father of Abram, Nahor, and Haran; and Haran was the father of Lot. Now Haran died in the presence of his father Terah in the land of his birth—in Ur of the Chaldeans. Then Abram and Nahor took wives for themselves. The name of the wife of Abram was Sarai, and the name of the wife of Nahor was Milcah, the daughter of Haran, the father of Milcah and Iscah. Now Sarai was barren; she was unable to bear children.

Then Terah took Abram his son and Lot the son of Haran his grandson, and Sarai his daughter-in-law the wife of Abram his son and they went out together from Ur of the Chaldeans to go to the land of Canaan. And they came to Haran and they dwelled there. And the days of Terah were two hundred and five years, and Terah died in Haran.

—Genesis 11:27-32

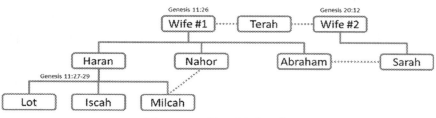

Figure 21: Terah's family

---

8   For a conservative analysis of the differences in the numbers preserved in the Hebrew text with that of the LXX and the Samaritan Pentateuch, see Gerhard F. Hasel, "The Meaning of the Chronogenealogies of Genesis 5 and 11," *Origins*, 7:2 (1980): 53-70.

In those early days, marriage between close relatives was preferred. The gene pool was still quite vibrant and the restrictions later imposed on whom one could or could not marry were not necessary.[9] Genesis 11:26 states that "when Terah had lived seventy years he became the father of Abram, Nahor, and Haran." This verse should not be understood as saying that Terah's three sons were triplets. In fact, the information regarding Haran, his children, and his death suggest that Haran was much older than Abram. Abram is listed first in the genealogy because of his importance to the story, not because of birth order. If Abram left for Canaan at age seventy-five (12:4), and he did this at or soon after Terah's death at two hundred five years of age (Acts 7:4), then Abram was born to Terah when he was one hundred thirty years old, not seventy (205 − 75 = 130 years old). Lot and Abram may therefore have been quite close in age.

For the last one hundred twenty years or so, Ur of the Chaldeans—the place of Abram's birth—has been identified with a tel located near the Persian Gulf. Sir Leonard Woolley conducted an archaeological dig at that site and proclaimed that he had found the city of Abram's birth. A careful reading of the text, however, locates Ur of the Chaldeans in the close vicinity of Haran in northern Mesopotamia, not at Woolley's Ur in southern Mesopotamia. Both cities were named Ur, but the problem with the northern Ur is that its tel has not been located. But notice how the text identifies Ur of the Chaldeans— the *birthplace* of Terah (11:28). Later God told Abram to leave his *birthplace* (12:1), which God understood to be Ur of the Chaldeans (15:7). Finally, when Abraham sent off his servant to find a wife for Isaac, he sent him back to his *birthplace* (24:4, 7). All four verses use the same Hebrew word, though it is

---

[9] The list of sexual restrictions in Leviticus 18 could be construed as a guide to whom one could or could not marry.

common to render this word in a variety of ways in our English translations: "land of my birth," "my relatives," or "land of my kindred." So where did the servant go to secure Rebekah? He did not go to the region of the Persian Gulf. He went to northern Mesopotamia, to the city of Nahor (24:10).

– 14 –

Genesis 6: God Changes His Mind

The Sons of God

And so it was that people began to multiply upon the
face of the land and daughters were born to them.
Then the sons of God saw the daughters of men that
they were beautiful and they took for themselves wives
as many as they chose. And the Lord said, "My Spirit
will not forever tolerate mankind because he is flesh.
Now his days shall be one hundred twenty years."

—Genesis 6:1-3

The sixth chapter of Genesis describes perhaps the lowest
point in the history of mankind. It is a very dismal, somber
section. Evil had become so rampant, so intensely evil that God
determined to destroy his good earth.

The initial statement points out that people—the human
population—were beginning to multiply. These were not some
sort of half-angel hybrids or superhuman freaks. The Hebrew
uses the ordinary word for mankind and notes that daughters
were born to them. Verse 2 mentions two classes of human
beings. The first is male; the second, female. But the men
mentioned here are given a special designation. They were
"sons of God."

In certain contexts the phrase "sons of God" refers to angelic beings.[1] As a result, some have suggested that Genesis 6:1-4 describes the co-mingling of angels with women. The Greek translation could be cited in support of this position. However, the most significant argument against understanding the "sons of God" as referring to angels comes from Christ himself. When asked regarding whose wife the woman would be, who had outlived seven husbands, "Jesus said to them, 'Is this not the reason you are mistaken, that you do not understand the Scriptures or the power of God? For when they rise from the dead, they neither marry nor are given in marriage, but are like the angels in heaven'" (Mark 12:24-25 NASB). Angels, as created by God, are not equipped to produce children—no sperm, no eggs, and no gender.

At other times, people are referred to as being the offspring of God.[2] This is not surprising in light of the fact of our creation is in God's image. So the nature of these beings cannot be determined simply by the use of the phrase "sons of God."

The concept of sonship has a larger usage in the Bible than mere biological descent. For example, the sons of Eli are called "sons of Belial" (1 Sam. 2:12 KJV). They did not have two fathers. Belial was a man known for his laziness or lack of integrity. So for a person to be called a son of Belial meant that that person shared characteristics with the historical, contemptible Belial. "Now the sons of Eli were worthless men" (1 Sam. 2:12 NASB). In the New Testament, some people were called "sons of this age" (Luke 16:8; 20:34), "sons of light" (Luke 16:8; John 12:36), "sons of the resurrection" (Luke 20:36). The phrase "sons of . . ." means "ones characterized by. . . ." Genesis 6:2 therefore speaks of a group of men characterized by the word *'elohîm*.

---

[1] See Job 1:6; 2:1; 38:7.

[2] See Hosea 1:10, "sons of the living God"; John 1:12 and Romans 8:16, "children of God"; Acts 17:28, "we are His offspring."

In a number of places in the Old Testament, *'elohîm* is not translated as "God." For example, Jonah 3:3 describes Nineveh as "an exceeding great city." However, a wooden translation of the phrase is "Nineveh was a great city unto *'elohîm*." The translators were correct in recognizing that this wicked city was being described as an extraordinarily great city by the addition of the phrase "unto *'elohîm*." The words *strong, powerful, mighty,* or *great* are used elsewhere to translate forms of *'elohîm*.[3] So there is good exegetical support for translating "sons of *'elohîm*" in Genesis 6:2 as "men of power"— men characterized by political control. These men were tyrants who domineered others.[4] They saw, they took for themselves whomever they chose, and no one could stand in their way. They exploited the women and no one was able to resist them.

This situation precipitated the judgment of God. The Lord was weary of their excesses and determined that this situation would end in one hundred twenty years. The flow of the narrative suggests that this was the amount of time that would lapse between God's decision to judge the earth and the fulfillment of that judgment. It was during this time that the ark was constructed. To conclude that the construction took the full one hundred twenty years is certainly not demanded by the text, but this notation of time certainly allows for an adequate span of time in which to construct and outfit the ark.

---

3   "*Mighty* prince" (Gen. 23:6), "*great* trembling" (1 Sam. 14:15), "*power* of their hand" (Mic. 2:1), a person of *authority*—"judge," 3 times (Ex. 22:8-9). See also Ezek. 32:21; Ps. 29:1, etc.

4   A particularly helpful article espousing this view is Meredith G. Kline's "Divine kingship and Genesis 6:1-4" (*Westminster Theological Journal,* 24:2 [May 1962]: 187-204).

The Last Generation

> There were giants[5] on the earth in those days. And also afterwards, when the tyrants came in to the exploited women, they bore children for them. These were the ruthless ones, the remarkable ones, men of amazingly [evil] character.
>
> —Genesis 6:4

This verse mentions four categories of people living in the final days of that doomed generation. The first were the giants. These men and women were unusually large, physically large. The text is careful to separate these giants from the rest of the verse. The Hebrew phrase "and also afterwards" functions as a thought divider. The statement about the giants is parenthetical. "Incidentally, there were men of giant stature on the earth in those days." This type of parenthetic construction is common in the Old Testament. It is used to insert additional, relevant information that is contemporaneous but not consecutive.

The story of Leah and Rachel is a good example. The narrative progresses along smoothly until Laban asks Jacob about wages. The reader needs to know about Laban's two daughters in order to understand the sequence that follows, so the narrative is interrupted with these two parenthetic verses: "Now Laban had two daughters. The name of the elder was Leah and the younger, Rachel. Now Leah's eyes were weak, but Rachel was beautiful of form and beautiful of sight" (Gen. 29:16-17).

---

5   Recent translations do not translate the Hebrew word as "giants"; instead, the word is transliterated as "Nephilim" (see NASB, ESV, NIV, HCSB, NEB). This is not helpful. Now the question is, who were the "Nephilim"? The term is used exclusively of giants in other places in the Bible and should be translated as such in this verse.

Gigantism is mentioned three times in the Old Testament:

- In the days of Noah (Gen. 6:4),
- In the days of the conquest—"a people great and tall, the sons of Anakim" (Deut. 9:1-2; their demise is recorded in Josh. 11:21-22), and
- In the days of Saul some four hundred years later (1 Sam. 17:4—Goliath's height was measured at "six cubits and a span").

The second group is called "the sons of god"—the tyrants. These were the thugs, the socially powerful men who preyed on the third group, "the daughters of men." These women had no ability to defend themselves against the bullies who assaulted them. This sets the stage for the fourth group: "and children were born to them." These children apparently grew up without restraint. The exploitation of the daughters of men is the reason cited for this evil situation. One group had gained enough power to abuse another segment of humanity. As a result, a generation was born that was completely unbounded in its sinful abilities. This generation grew up in a situation characterized by exploitation and indulgence, and their capacity for evil was apparently unrivaled.

This was the generation that precipitated the judgment of God. The Lord was tired of their excesses and determined that their end would come in one hundred twenty years.

Completely Evil

Then the Lord saw that the wickedness of mankind was great on the earth, and that every thought of the imagination of his heart was only evil continually.

—Genesis 6:5

The Bible struggles to describe the evil nature of the generation that grew up free from restraint in a milieu of exploitation.
Verse 4 uses three idioms to express the ruthlessness of this
generation, their remarkable ability at excesses, and their
amazingly evil character. This group was given wholly to
wickedness.

This verse portrays, from God's vantage point, the
exceedingly wicked nature of this generation. "Every thought
of the imagination of his heart was only evil continually." It
would seem that for someone to be this wicked—"every," "only,"
"always"—he would require demonic assistance. Interestingly
enough, 2 Peter 2:4-5 speaks of angels who sinned and whose
action occurred in the "ancient world" of Noah. In the parallel
passage of the epistle of Jude, the author speaks of angels "who
did not keep their own domain, but abandoned their proper
abode" (Jude 6a NASB). These angels apparently left their
assigned posts and indwelt the bodies of that generation who
in turn became ruthless, remarkable, and amazingly evil. "For
if God did not spare angels when they sinned, but cast them
into hell[6] and committed them to pits of darkness, reserved for
judgment; and did not spare the ancient world, but preserved
Noah, a preacher of righteousness, with seven others, when
He brought a flood upon the world of the ungodly . . ." (2 Peter
2:4-5 NASB).

The Lord's analysis was that his earth had become
exceedingly evil. It was no longer a fit habitation for mankind.
Evil had succeeded in polluting this world. Had this been the
plan of God? Had he created this earth so that it could become
an unfit residence for those he had created to mirror him?

---

[6] *Tartarus* is a special place in the nether world for imprisoning angels (see
BDAG, 991). This place is referred to in Jude as "eternal bonds of darkness"
(Jude 6).

The Lord Changed His Mind

> And the Lord was sorry that he had made man on the earth, and he was grieved in his heart. And the Lord said, "I will blot out man whom I have created from the face of the land, from man to animals to creeping things and to birds of the heavens, for I am sorry that I have made them."
>
> —Genesis 6:6-7

These verses are the source for much controversy because they make God look like a man. He repented of his earlier decision to make mankind and determined to take an opposite course of action and destroy his creation. How can these statements be harmonized with other clear statements in the Bible, such as,

- For I, the LORD, do not change; therefore you, O sons of Jacob, are not consumed (Mal. 3:6 NASB),
- Jesus Christ, the same yesterday, and today, and forever (Heb. 13:8 KJV).

This Jesus, who is the "same . . . forever," is also the one who emptied himself (Phil. 2:7), who became flesh (John 1:14), who grew in wisdom, in stature, and in favor with God and men (Luke 2:52), who died (Matt. 27:50), who was raised from the dead (Mark 16:6), who was exalted to the right hand of God (Acts 2:33), who received all authority in heaven and on earth (Matt. 28:18), and of whom it is said, "and when all things are subjected to him, then the Son himself will be subjected to the One who subjected all things to him, that God may be all in all" (1 Cor. 15:28 NASB).

These are substantial changes to which the Bible witnesses. In what sense, then, does God *not* change? He does not, he cannot change in terms of his righteous moral character. But his situation can change, his status can change, and his response to various human beings can change. Jeremiah 18:5ff makes it crystal clear how and why the changeless God must change his responses to human beings in order to remain changeless in his righteous moral character.

It would not be correct to imply that God was somehow caught off guard by the intensely sinful situation that led to his judgment of the earth in the days of Noah. Nothing surprises God, but the sin of these people made in his image and likeness grieved him to such an extent that he determined to take drastic action on account of their sin.

It is curious that God's planned destruction also specifically included the animals, the creeping things, and the birds of the heavens. This clearly suggests that man was abusing his control over the animal world. This theme continues throughout the narrative.

- The earth also was corrupt before God, and the earth was filled with violence. *All flesh* had corrupted his way upon the earth (6:11).
- *All flesh* had corrupted his way upon the earth (6:12).
- The earth is filled with violence through them (6:13).
- I will . . . destroy *all flesh*, wherein is the breath of life (6:17).
- Thus he blotted out *every living thing* that was upon the face of the land, from man to animals, to creeping things, and to birds of the heavens (7:23).

Additional evidence indicating that man was abusing his control over the animal kingdom is seen in God's action at the close of the year of the flood when he adjusted and reduced man's authority over the animals. Noah and his descendants would now rule by terror. "And the fear of you and the terror of you shall be upon every beast of the earth" (Gen. 9:2).

We are spared the carnal details of what this abuse entailed, but it does appear that man's ability to control the animal kingdom comprised part of his sinful exploits. Wicked man could have perpetuated unbelievable evil had his pet T. rex been available to do his bidding.

God was "grieved in his heart" over this situation. The Hebrew word ['etzev], here translated *grieved,* is a powerful word. No other Hebrew word conveys such a deep emotional response. This word is used to describe God's emotions toward his wayward children during the forty years of wandering. "How often they rebelled against Him in the wilderness and *grieved* Him in the desert. Again and again they tempted God and *pained* the Holy One of Israel" (Ps. 78:40-41 NASB). "They rebelled and *grieved* His Holy Spirit; therefore, He turned Himself to become their enemy. He fought against them" (Isa. 63:10 NASB).

This verb also describes the deep hurt felt by a divorced woman. "For the LORD has called you, like a wife forsaken and *grieved* in spirit, even like a wife of one's youth when she is rejected" (Isa. 54:6 NASB). This is the emotion of Jacob's sons when they discovered that Shechem had violated their sister. "Now the sons of Jacob came in from the field when they heard it; and the men were *grieved* and they were very angry because he had done a disgraceful thing in Israel by lying with Jacob's daughter, for such a thing ought not to be done" (Gen. 34:7 NASB).

God used a noun based on this verb in the account of the fall to describe the pain of childbirth. "I will greatly multiply your *childbirth pain* and your conceptions. In *pain* you shall bear children" (Gen. 3:16a). Adam also shared in this agony. "Cursed is the ground because of you; through *toil* you shall eat of it all the days of your life" (Gen. 3:17b).

So God was deeply stirred by the global, grievous sin that had taken over his exquisite creation. His plan of action was "to annihilate, to wipe clean, to blot out"[7] this beautiful masterwork—except for one simple fact. . . .

The Grace of God

> But Noah found grace in the eyes of the Lord.
>
> —Genesis 6:8

What a fortunate turn of events for us! How important it is for us to live lives that honor God. Who knows what the future will hold? Noah was not apparently an arbitrary choice on God's part, but he does seem to be novel and unique in terms of his moral standing with God. There was no one else whom God saw as righteous. Genesis 7:1 states emphatically that "*you* I have seen to be righteous before me in this generation." The Hebrew language uses the emphatic pronoun here and places it first in the sentence. In a grossly sinful world, Noah was singled out as a righteous man.[8]

The Story of Noah

> This is the story of Noah. Noah was a righteous man. He was perfect among his contemporaries. Noah walked with God. Noah had three sons: Shem, Ham, and Japheth. But the earth had been ruined[9] in God's estimation, and the earth was filled with violence.[10]

---

[7] HALOT, 567-568.

[8] See also Ezek. 14:14-20 in which the righteousness of Noah, Daniel, and Job are spoken of in singular terms.

[9] "To (become) ruined or spoiled" (HALOT, 1470).

[10] This Hebrew word has an Arabic cognate that means "to be persistent in battle and in religion" (HALOT, 329). Hence, the title for the Palestinian

And God examined the earth and, behold, it was corrupt because all flesh had corrupted his path upon the earth.

—Genesis 6:9-12

What a contrast between Noah and the rest of mankind. Righteous Noah had succeeded in bringing up three fine sons who, along with their wives, would be saved (Heb. 11:7) from the impending destruction. The rest of the earth was rotten to the core.

The Verdict

Then God said to Noah, "The end of all flesh has come up before me for the earth is full of violence [*hāmās*] because of them, and behold, I am going to cause the destruction of the earth."

—Genesis 6:13

The end of the world was at hand but God was not without recourse. Out of destruction he was going to bring forth something new.

The Blueprint

"Make for yourself an ark of gopher[11] wood. You shall make the ark with rooms and you shall cover it inside

---

Islamic organization Hamas.

[11] This is called *gopher* wood because that is how the Hebrew word sounds. Gen. 6:14 is the only place in which the word appears. The least that can be said is that gopher wood refers to a tree whose trunk is constituted of xylem rather than the softer, undifferentiated parenchyma cells. In that

and outside with pitch. And these are the dimensions
that you shall use: three hundred cubits [four hundred
fifty feet[12]] shall be the length of the ark, fifty cubits
[seventy-five feet] its width, and thirty cubits [forty-
five feet] its height. You shall make a roof for the ark
and finish it to one cubit [eighteen inches] above. Set
a door in the side of the ark. You shall make it with
lower, second, and third stories."

—Genesis 6:14-16

These instructions are all that are recorded in the Bible for
building this tremendous structure. Noah may have been
allowed some latitude in the design of the ark. Had he needed
more detail, he certainly could have gone to Eden and made his
request, but God evidently felt that this was enough instruction.
Where was the ark to be built? At the edge of the ocean? It is
more likely that the ark was built near the garden of Eden, far
from the sea.

And what was this "roof," this covering that was to be
"finished to a cubit above"? A gap of eighteen inches was
evidently to be allowed for ventilation. It was not, however,
to serve as a gallery from which to watch the spectacle of
destruction. Noah and his sons were to concern themselves
with the animals on the inside, not with the cataclysm that was
going on outside the ark. In fact, the first time that the account
mentions any observation of the outside occurs at the close of

---

early ecosystem, large vascular plants such as ferns and reeds rivaled hard
wood trees in size. But these were not suited to give support to the type of
structure that God envisioned.

[12] The 450-foot calculation assumes that each cubit represents approximately
18 inches (17.5 inches, to be precise). If the royal or long cubit is intended,
which is 21.4 inches, then the ark would have measured 510 feet in length
(D. H. Wheaton, "Weights and Measures," *The Illustrated Bible Dictionary*
[Westmont, Ill.: InterVarsity, 1980] 1635f). Either cubit results in a vessel
of formidable size.

the year of the flood. "And Noah removed the covering of the ark *and he looked out*, and behold, the surface of the ground looked dry" (Gen. 8:13).

The same was true when God destroyed Sodom and Gomorrah. He made it very clear to Lot when he spoke through the angels: "Do not look back!" These episodes of destruction were not designed for the viewing pleasure of the righteous but were instead recorded for our "instruction" (1 Cor. 10:11).

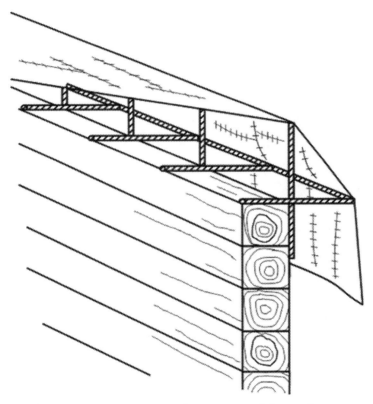

Figure 22: Proposed structure of the roof

The Hebrew word translated *roof* occurs in no other place in the Old Testament. But the only part of the ark that was left for God to define was the top. So this rare word is obviously speaking of the roof. The Hebrew word later used in Genesis

8:13, when speaking of the removal of the *covering* of the ark, seems to be speaking of the same structure as that found in the building instructions of Genesis 6:16. The word used in Genesis 8:13 also describes the covering made of skins that overlay the Tabernacle (Ex. 26:14; 35:11, etc.). It is therefore assumed that the ark also had a covering of skins that shed water and still allowed for some air circulation. Depending on how the skins were treated, they may have had a somewhat translucent quality that suffused light into the ark as well.

The ark was most likely designed as a barge[13] rather than as a seagoing vessel. Its function was not ocean travel. No mention is made of a keel or rudder or of a destination. The flood was not directional in its destructive force, nor did a significant wind pattern displace the ark. It is probable that the ark did not move far from its original location. It was borne up and raised high above the earth (7:17). Then, one hundred fifty days later, the ark came to rest on Mount Ararat (8:4). The ark's salvific property lay not in its ability to escape the flood but rather in its design to endure the flood (1 Peter 3:20).

God's Instrument of Destruction

> "And I, even I, am bringing the *Mabbûl* of water upon the earth to destroy all flesh that has the breath of life in it from under heaven. Everything that is on the earth will perish."
>
> —Genesis 6:17

Here the reader is introduced to the destructive force that God was going to use to rid the earth of its pervasive evil: "the *Mabbûl* of water." The word *Mabbûl* has no equivalent in the

---

[13] "Chest" or "casket" (HALOT, 1678).

English language. It is translated "flood" or "deluge." The Greek translation uses a recognizable word—"cataclysm." The word *Mabbûl* always refers only to this destructive event, when water held sway over the earth.[14]

The function of this destructive force was to bring about the demise of every air-breathing animal that lived on the earth. One and all, they would perish. Peter also references this watery cataclysm: "For when they maintain this, it escapes their notice that by the word of God the heavens existed long ago and the earth was formed out of water and by water, through which the world at that time was destroyed, being flooded with water" (2 Peter 3:5-6 NASB). But good news was coming.

The Promise and the Provision

"And I will establish my covenant with you. And you shall come into the ark: you and your sons and your wife and the wives of your sons with you. And of all the living things—from all flesh—by twos—of all these, you shall bring them to the ark to preserve life with you. They shall be male and female—of the birds by their species, of livestock by their species, of all that creeps on the ground by their species. By twos from all of these, they shall come to you to preserve life. And you shall take to yourself of all kinds of food that may be eaten and you shall gather it to yourself and it shall be food for you and for them." And Noah did everything that God commanded him, so he did.

—Genesis 6:18-22

---

[14] Gen. 6:17; 7:6, 7, 10, 17; 9:11 (2x), 15, 28; 10:1, 32; 11:10; Ps. 29:10.

One consequence of Noah's righteousness was that he did everything that God commanded him to do! We may not know the significance of our obedience in the lives of others.

These added instructions make it much clearer why God wanted Noah to construct such a monstrous ark. The ark needed to house two of each kind of air-breathing animal, plus enough food to keep them alive for a considerable length of time. Noah was given no timetable, nor did he know the nature of God's covenant mentioned in 6:18. He simply moved ahead by faith, trusting that God knew the future. "By faith Noah, being warned by God concerning events as yet unseen, in reverent fear constructed an ark for the saving of his household" (Heb. 11:7a ESV).

The covenant mentioned in 6:18 is understood as God's promise to rescue all who entered the ark from the impending destruction. This passage repeats the phrase *to preserve life* (6:19, 20; 7:3). God covenanted that all who entered would be saved from the Mabbûl.

Between the sixth and seventh chapters of Genesis lies a one-hundred-twenty-year gap, during which Noah did all that God had commanded him. Do we use our time as wisely today? Suddenly God spoke again and gave Noah a seven-day warning.

– 15 –

Genesis 7: The Mabbûl

The Invitation of God

Then the Lord said to Noah: "Come, you and your entire household, to the ark because you I have seen to be righteous before me in this generation. Of all the clean animals,[1] take to yourself by sevens, a male and its female, and from the animals that are not clean only a pair, a male and its female. Also bring in, of the birds of heaven, by sevens, male and female, so as to preserve alive offspring upon the surface of the earth. Because in seven additional days I am bringing rain upon the earth, forty days and forty nights, and I am going to destroy every living thing that I have made from off the surface of the ground." And Noah did all that the Lord commanded him.

—Genesis 7:1-5

The huge barge was standing at the ready. It had been filled with provisions, just as God had commanded Noah. Then came

---

[1] Information regarding clean and unclean animals must have been given by God soon after the fall so that people could bring acceptable offerings to God (4:3-4).

the order, "Fill the ark with animals!" This raises the question, how did Noah round up all the animals and bring them into the ark in just seven days? But that query is predicated on *our* perspective, which sees most animals as "wild" and afraid of men. From creation to the flood, however, men had much greater control over animals and birds. It seems that Noah could speak commands to the animals and they obeyed him.

God had earlier spoken about keeping "species" alive (6:19-20), and Noah understood that term when he began collecting the animals. Precisely what constituted a "species" or "kind" is unclear. But Noah understood what God had said and loaded the ark correctly.

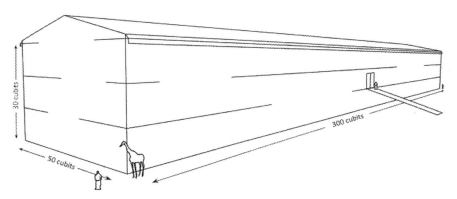

Figure 23: The ark is completed.

The reader of Genesis should recall that the geography of the earth was quite different before the flood. Animals need not have crossed great oceans to reach the ark on the earth's single landmass. Neither did geographical barriers, such as high mountain ranges, deserts, or significant climate variations, exist to obstruct the animals from coming to the ark. It would follow, therefore, that less speciation had occurred due to the lack of physical isolation of the various animal groups. Fish and amphibians were not part of the gathering because they did not share in the "breath of life" (6:17; 7:22). Only air-breathing animals were to be taken. Reptiles, on the other hand, would have been included among the occupants of the ark. Regarding reptiles, the largest specimens need not have been taken into the ark since reptiles continue to grow throughout their lives. A brontosaurus, for example, need not have been one hundred twenty feet long to be classed as mature, though with age it could apparently have achieved that length.

It is very difficult to speculate how many individual animals, birds, and creeping things were housed in the ark. Today an estimated two thousand species of firefly[2] have been identified. Surely not all of them were on the ark. It would seem that one "kind" of firefly was sufficient. Creationists have attempted to determine the number of individuals that inhabited the ark, and estimates run from six thousand "kinds" to fifty thousand.[3]

What *is* known is that the ark was large. It consisted of over one hundred thousand square feet of floor space on its three floors, and each story was about fifteen feet high from floor to ceiling. That height certainly seems adequate for housing a large number of animals.

This was now the second time God mentioned Noah's righteous character (Gen. 6:9; 7:1). His faith in God had been made evident by his work of building the ark. His "faith was active along with his works, and faith was completed by his works" (James 2:22 ESV).

The primary purpose of the ark was to preserve human life on the earth, which is why Noah and his household were invited into the ark first. But animals are also important in God's economy, as seen by the second half of the command. The Hebrew is very clear when God said that Noah was to "take to yourself seven seven, a male and its female." However, the number "seven seven" is not as easily understood. Did God

---

[2] Bethany Brookshire, "An app to track firefly flashings," *Science News Magazine* (August 9, 2014) 28.

[3] John Woodmorappe, *Noah's Ark: A Feasibility Study* (Dallas: Institute for Creation Research, 2009).

intend seven pairs or seven individuals with the extra clean animal included to provide a sacrifice after the flood? Perhaps it is of no consequence, but it seems likely that Noah brought seven pairs of clean animals and birds into the ark.[4]

Noah was given seven days to complete the task of loading the ark. At the close of that week, God promised forty days and forty nights of rain, designed to destroy all the animals that remained on the land.

The Ark Is Loaded

> Noah was six hundred years old at the time the Mabbûl of water came upon the earth. And Noah entered the ark along with his sons and his wife and his sons' wives with them before the water of the Mabbûl. Individuals from the clean animals and from the animals that were not clean and from the birds and all those creatures that creep upon the ground, by twos they came to Noah to the ark, male and female just as God had commanded Noah. All this happened during the seven days before the waters of the Mabbûl came upon the earth.
>
> —Genesis 7:6-10

This passage notes Noah's specific acts of obedience. Because God had given Adam control over all the animals in Genesis 1:26-28 and this control was not rescinded until after the Mabbûl in Genesis 9:2, Noah would not have encountered problems corralling the animals and birds and assigning them their place in the ark. God could certainly have helped Noah with this task, but the passage seems clear that God used Noah to accomplish

---

4 "In groups of seven" HALOT, 1400; "seven pairs," ESV; "take with you seven male-female pairs," Waltke and O'Conner, 660.

these tasks—"just as God had commanded Noah." It is difficult to reconstruct the type of control that man had over the animals, but the Bible makes clear that on that early earth, animals, birds, insects, all kinds of creepers, and even the fish were subject to the human will. Perhaps Noah had the type of control that Jesus had over the fish in the Sea of Galilee when he needed a coin to pay the temple tax (Matt. 17:24-27; see also John 21:4-6).

The Mabbûl

In the six hundredth year of Noah's life, in the second month on the seventeenth day of the month—this very day—the entire fountain of the great deep was broken up and the windows of heaven were opened and a torrent of water fell upon the earth for forty days and forty nights. On this very day, Noah and Shem and Ham and Japheth, the sons of Noah, along with Noah's wife and the three wives of his sons with him, came into the ark. They and all species of beasts and all species of domesticated animals, and all species of creepers that creep on the earth and all species of winged animals, both winged and feathered, came to Noah into the ark in pairs, of all flesh in which is the breath of life. Those coming were male and female of all flesh, just as God had commanded him. Then the Lord closed the door behind him.

—Genesis 7:11-16

The Bible is clear about when and how the great flood occurred. It came when Noah was six hundred years,[5] two months, and

5 The convention of how to understand this chronological notation is not clear. For example, was "*in* the six hundredth year of Noah's life" actually

181

seventeen days old. The source of the water of destruction is also recorded. It came from two places: (1) the huge reservoir of water that underlay the continent and served as the source for the spring that came up in Eden to water the whole surface of the ground (2:6), and (2) the water that had been raised above the atmosphere on the second day of creation (1:6-8). Peter put it this way: "the earth was formed out of water and by water, through which the world at that time was destroyed, being flooded with water" (2 Peter 3:5b-6).

It would be fascinating to know how God accomplished this supernatural feat. Evidence shows that our moon and the earth itself have been struck in the past by meteorites and other astral bodies. Did God use such a barrage to initiate this cataclysm? It is impossible to know. What is known is that this destruction was God's design achieved in God's time. Whatever the method, the author wanted his readers to know that everything was going to be all right. Noah and his family and all the animals were safely enclosed in the ark of God.

All was well. True, the earth was beginning to tremble with the breakup of the continent. And, yes, the canopy of water had begun to pummel the earth below with its liquid barrage, but the chosen ones were safely settled inside the ark, and God had sealed the door "behind him."

To whom does "him" refer? Is this a reference to Noah or to God himself entering the ark. Was not God with Noah and the animals in a special sense? He had invited Noah to "*come into the ark*," implying that this was where God was. The ark was certainly the focus of God's attention, if not actually his dwelling place. Eden had been abandoned. The garden of Eden was being destroyed.

---

a reference to his having celebrated only his 599th birthday? This author attempts to be consistent in the convention used to identify these dates.

The Ark Is Lifted Up

Now the Mabbûl [the cataclysm, the deluge, the flood] came for forty days upon the earth and the waters kept increasing and lifted up the ark so that it rose above the earth.

—Genesis 7:17

As God caused the collapse of the continent that overlay the great deep, the trembling earth could no longer support the ark. Water surged upward through fissures in the ground as the ark slowly began to sink into the muck that only the day before had been *terra firma*. Slowly it descended into the mire of the collapsing earth. The ark sank down five feet—ten feet—twenty feet. Would it also be sucked into the chaos? Then slowly the descent into a watery abyss came to a halt and another force took over. The Mabbûl, the water, the agent of destruction, had an alternate effect on the ark. It gave support to the massive barge as it slowly raised the ark above the surrounding maelstrom.

Figure 24: The ark in the Mabbûl

The destructive force of the water was designed to annihilate the entire air-breathing world, but its effect on the ark was salvific. The water of the Mabbûl lifted the ark above the killing field.

The Action of the Water of the Mabbûl

And the water prevailed. . . .

—Genesis 7:18a

This is a very weak translation. The image that the word *prevailed* brings to mind is commonplace, but the Hebrew verb is dramatic. Both the verb and its corresponding noun are used in Isaiah 42:13: "The LORD goes out like a *mighty man*, like a man of war he stirs up his zeal; he cries out, he shouts aloud, *he shows himself mighty* against his foes" (ESV, emphasis added). This was war. The water was doing the work of a warrior. It had been empowered by God to kill, to destroy, and to annihilate. The water was acting as a raging warrior.

As blocks of the overlying continent broke loose and cascaded down through the great deep, hitting the basement rock with crushing force, gigantic shock waves radiated in all directions. The water would have roared with destructive energy. Powerful tsunamis would have rushed throughout the doomed continent, wreaking havoc of immense proportion. This cataclysm was not necessarily directional. A doomed inhabitant outside the ark could not wait, hoping that it would pass. The churning, grinding action of the rock-laden water would have destroyed everything—except the huge barge that had been lifted above its destructive force.

The Annihilation of the Early Earth

And the water raged and increased greatly upon the earth, but the ark floated on the surface of the water. And the water raged so mightily against the earth that even the highest mountains under heaven were covered. The raging water covered the mountains at least fifteen cubits [twenty-two and a half feet].[6] And all flesh that roamed upon the earth perished: birds, livestock, beasts, anything that swarmed on the earth, and every human being. Anything that had in its nostrils the breath of life from anywhere on the dry land died. Thus he annihilated every living thing that was upon the face of the ground, whether human, or livestock, or creepers, or birds of the heavens. They were all annihilated from the earth and there remained only Noah and those with him in the ark. The waters raged against the earth for one hundred fifty days.

—Genesis 7:18-24

These words bring to mind another: *overkill!* How long could a person have survived on a sinking parcel of land that was soon to be overwhelmed with a tsunami? When the Lord sets out to destroy something, he is very deliberate and very thorough.

What was happening beneath the surface during the one-hundred-fifty-day Mabbûl? First, the entire continent that overlay the reservoir of the great deep was broken up (7:11). Today the depth of the sedimentary rock is an estimated six thousand feet—over a mile thick. All of this was involved in a

---

[6] It can be surmised from this statement that this figure also represents the draft of the ark. It floated above the highest mountain.

thick, churning slurry during the flood. Added to this mixture were the life forms that made up the ecosystem on the day that the Mabbûl burst forth. Huge forests were buried, resulting in the coal beds that are mined today.

Millions upon millions of animals were captured and buried in the cataclysm. From huge dinosaurs to single-celled corals, all were trapped and compressed by the overburden of the layers of destruction. Today the byproducts of this capture are collected in the form of natural gas and oil.

The formation of coal and petroleum products cannot be witnessed anywhere on earth today. Their formation requires extreme, cataclysmic conditions such as have only existed during the one hundred fifty days of the Mabbûl. The fossils, enclosed in the sedimentary layers of rock, represent the life forms that were flourishing on the six hundredth year, the second month, and the seventeenth day of Noah's life. They do not represent "pages of history," as evolutionary geologists interpret them. The sedimentary

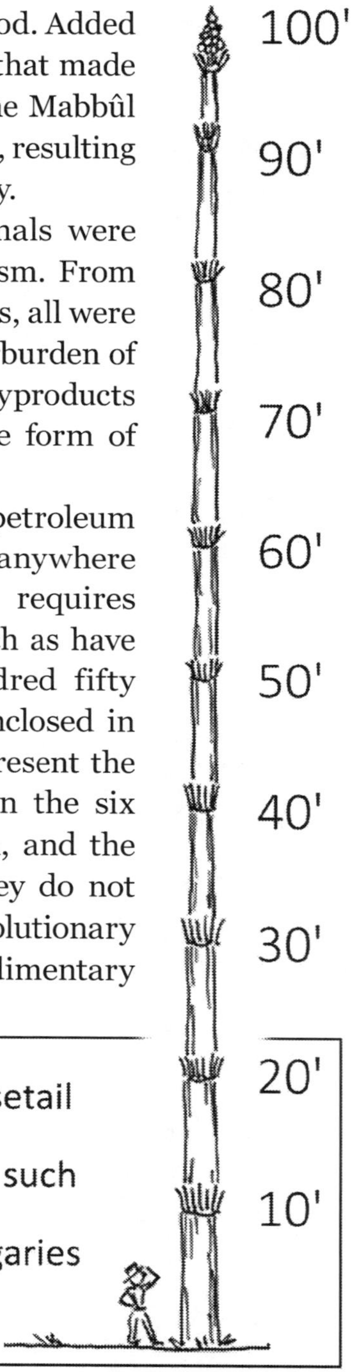

Sample of the common horsetail reed from a coal bed. Such specimens can only grow to such heights under moist, humid conditions free from the vagaries of today's weather pattern.

Figure 25: Pre-flood botanical specimens were uncommonly large.

layers should not be seen as a "video" of evolutionary history. Instead, they comprise a single "snapshot" of that terrible day of destruction.

Nowhere on earth can archaeologists find remains of that early civilization. That generation and their works were destroyed and scattered randomly and ultimately buried within the thousands of feet of sediment. Because of the pervasive nature of this destruction, the science of archaeology cannot contribute to the history of this epoch. Where would one go to unearth Eden? Only a serendipitous scattering of isolated finds that might be credited to the period between Adam and Noah exists today.

The deed was done. God had destroyed the early earth with the waters of the Mabbûl. How would he turn the chaos into something habitable?

– 16 –

Genesis 8: God Rescues Noah

> Then God remembered Noah and all the beasts and
> all the livestock that were with him in the ark. So God
> caused a wind to pass over the earth and the waters
> were subdued.
>
> —Genesis 8:1-3

God not only initiated the Mabbûl, but supernatural action
was also required to suppress this devastation. "Then God
remembered Noah." This clause indicates that God was now
going to intervene on Noah's behalf. God was going to fulfill
his promise of protection to those in the ark (6:18). He did this
by actively restraining the destructive forces that he had set
in motion five months earlier. The Hebrew verb used here to
describe the restraining action of God on the waters is used
twice to describe the quieting of the wrath of the king in Esther
2:1 and 7:10.

In addition to this quieting action, God sent a supernatural
wind that eventually had a tremendous effect on the earth. It
appears that this wind was the mechanism through which God
accomplished continental drift. The crust was quite plastic at
this time, having been newly reworked by the waters of the
Mabbûl. Separating one continent into many would have also
facilitated the removal of the enormous sheet of water.

God also depressed the basin of the Pacific Ocean at this time so that it could serve as a reservoir for the extra water from the great deep and the emptied canopy. The flat-topped seamounts that dot the floor of the Pacific give clear evidence of this change in elevation. At the beginning of the Mabbûl the ocean floor apparently gave birth to hundreds of volcanoes. The tops of these seamounts were then flattened under the action of surface waves during the deluge. These same volcanoes now lie hundreds or even thousands of feet below sea level.[1] Though they vary greatly, the average depth to which these "guyots" have sunk is about five thousand feet or approximately one mile.[2]

Psalm 104 also references this activity on God's part at the close of the Mabbûl. This poetic section further clarifies what occurred.

> He set the earth on its foundations, so that it need
> never stagger.
>
> —Psalm 104:5

God, by supernatural means, constructed the original earth, then destroyed that good earth, and was now about to reshape it into something again suited for habitation. These adjustments to the crust of the earth were not due to an inherent fault in their construction.

---

[1] During World War II, Harry Hammond Hess, captain of an echo-sounding ship, used his many trips across the Pacific Ocean to collect data on seamounts, which he called guyots. He found over 2,000 flat-topped volcanic seamounts. Hess later developed the plate tectonic theory to explain their existence. But, in fact, it is God who takes credit for lowering the basin or valley to contain this water at the close of the flood (see Ps. 104:8). A supernatural explanation is, however, deemed invalid by secular geologists.

[2] Michael J. Oard, *The Missoula Flood Controversy and the Genesis Flood*, Creation Research Society Monograph Series: no. 13, 2004, 73-75.

> You covered it with the deep as with a garment; water
> stood above the mountains.
>
> —Psalm 104:6

This is a clear statement about the flood. The water blanketed the entire earth; even the original mountains were covered.

> At your rebuke they fled; at the sound of your thunder
> they ran in haste. The mountains rose up, the basins
> sank down to the place you appointed for them. You
> set a boundary that they may not pass over, so that
> they may not again inundate the earth.
>
> —Psalm 104:7-9

These three verses refer to the mighty wind God sent in Genesis 8:1, here described as God's "rebuke," his "thunder." The wind drove off the water, but it additionally caused orogeny or mountain building. Mountains were raised on the leading edge of a continent as it glided into its new resting place. Other regions of the globe sank down, while God established boundaries so that a Mabbûl would never again occur. Plate tectonics is not the reason continental drift took place. God is the reason. He was the agent.

The timing of this event is, of course, a curiosity. How long did it take the Americas to break away and migrate to their current location? How long before India came smashing into Asia and raised the mighty Himalayas. How long before Indonesia, the Philippines, Australia, and Antarctica were scattered across the globe? No answer is given to these questions in this account. But it is likely that continental drift occurred in months—not millennia. God was preparing a habitat for Noah and his family, and by the time he gave the command to leave the ark, God had completed his task. From start to finish, the cataclysm and its recovery had taken only a year and a few days.

It is not true that continents today are still sliding along. While changes can certainly be detected in positions between various large and small bodies of land, these changes are not strictly directional. Instead, they are random motions characteristic of a stable earth. Even an earthquake is a notable event today.

The Calming of the Mabbûl

> And the fountain of the deep and the windows of heaven were closed. And rain from heaven was restricted. Then the back and forth motion of the waters upon the earth stopped, so at the close of the one hundred fifty days the water began to recede.
> —Genesis 8:2-3

The concept that the earth was being stabilized after the destruction of the flood continues in verses 2 and 3. The energy flowing from the breakup of the fountain of the deep, as well as the collapse of the canopy of water, was now subdued and restrained. This was a reversal of the action that precipitated the Mabbûl in Genesis 7:11-12. God initiated the flood by supernatural means and ended it by supernatural means. The water was allowed to freely thrash and pummel the earth for one hundred fifty days. Then God placed his hand of restraint on this globe, and the water was subdued. The Hebrew word translated "closed" only occurs twice in the Old Testament.[3] The other occurrence is in Psalm 63:11—"the mouths of liars will be closed." The main idea conveyed by this verb is that the action of the object is forced to discontinue. Whether they are

---

[3] HALOT, 756.

the violent geological actions of water or the lies spoken by men, these activities were or will be forced to cease.

This submission of the raging waters happened at the close of the one-hundred-fifty-day Mabbûl. It was sudden and it was complete. It is reminiscent of Christ's statement to the storm in Mark 4:35-41. "He rebuked the wind and said to the sea, 'Hush, be still.' And the wind died down and it became perfectly calm" (v. 39b NASB).

The Ark Comes to Rest

> And on the seventh month, the seventeenth day of the month, the ark rested on the mountains of Ararat.
> —Genesis 8:4

At the close of the Mabbûl, the ark immediately came to rest on the mountains of Ararat. Noah seemed to give evidence of using a 360-day year, divided into twelve 30-day months. If the destruction took one hundred fifty days (7:24) and it started on the seventeenth day of the second month (7:11) and ended on the seventeenth day of the seventh month (8:4), then the destruction was five months in duration.

$$150 \text{ days} / 5 \text{ months} = 30 \text{ days} / \text{month}$$

This same type of calculation can be deduced from John's recording that 1,260 days is equal to 42 months (Rev. 11:2-3).

$$1{,}260 \text{ days} / 42 \text{ months} = 30 \text{ days} / \text{month}$$

Today a year is based on approximately 365.25 days, but this may not have been the situation in Noah's day. The early earth could easily have resolved a year into twelve 30-day months, resulting in a 360-day year. Caution, however, should be exercised because of the supernatural character of this epic period.[4]

Some inexplicable questions remain. With the descent of forty days of drenching rain from the collapsing canopy, what was the effect on the rotation of the earth? How did the shifting of the landmasses under God's supernatural wind affect the length of the day? Or, for that matter, was this the point at which the axis of the earth was tilted to produce the change of seasons spoken of in Genesis 8:22?

This was certainly an energetic time, filled with unequaled catastrophic occurrences. The biblical text is the major key to interpreting the geography, geology, and climatology of this current earth. The ubiquity and necessity of God's miraculous intervention in this year of earth's history prevents an explanation of these questions with mathematical precision. Our best hope is to model our explanations in harmony with our best interpretation of the Genesis record.

The remaining verses in Genesis 8 focus on the ark and its inhabitants. God had concluded his work of preparing the devastated earth for habitation again. From now on natural law would be the means by which the floodwaters continued to drain and the land continued to dry.

The Tops of the Mountains Appear

And the water continued to retreat and to lessen until the tenth month. On the first day of the tenth month, the tops of the mountains became visible.

—Genesis 8:5

---

[4] Danny R. Faulkner, "Was the year once 360 days long?" *Creation Research Society Quarterly* 49:2 (Fall 2012): 100-108.

God initiated his suppressive activity on the waters at the close of the one hundred fifty days, which was "the six hundredth year of Noah's life, the seventh month, and the seventeenth day of that month." Yet the peaks of the mountains did not begin to protrude above the water until the six hundredth year, the *tenth* month, on the *first* day of that month. Again, assuming a thirty-day month, the math looks like this:

$$\text{10th month: 1st day} - \text{7th month: 17th day}$$
$$= \text{2 months: 13 days} = \text{73 days}$$

Therefore, it took seventy-three days for the water to recede to the level at which mountaintops protruded. Noah and his family had been living in the ark for 223 days—or seven months and thirteen days.

Noah had apparently not been allowed to watch the earth as God judged it, and verse 13 indicates that his first look over the land would not occur for another sixty days. So how did Noah know that the mountaintops were protruding? He may have known by listening. No longer did water lap against the sides of the ark. The ark was now completely out of the water, as was the crown of Mount Ararat.

A Window in the Ark

> And it came about at the end of forty days that Noah opened a window that he had made in the ark.
> —Genesis 8:6

No mention is made in God's instructions in Genesis 6:14-16 of including a window in the ark. The added notation in 8:6, indicating that Noah *had made* a window in the ark that he now opened, suggests that this was not an original feature of the ark but rather a recent construction project on Noah's part. Its intended use was for the release of several birds.

Another forty days was now added to the 223 days since the onset of the Mabbûl. For eight months and twenty-three days, Noah and his family had survived inside the ark with all the animals. The lighting in the ark was subdued. The noise outside the ark had diminished, and the ark lay perfectly still. Daily chores must have become monotonous, though some of the animals may have gone into hibernation or aestivation in response to the ark's low light, tranquil conditions.

Birds Sent from the Ark

> Then he sent out a raven and it went out and flew back and forth until the water was dried up from the earth. He also sent out a dove from him to see if the water was low on the surface of the ground. But the dove could not find a resting place for the sole of her foot, so she returned to him to the ark because the water still covered most of the earth. And he stretched out his hand and took her and brought her to himself inside the ark.
>
> —Genesis 8:7-9

The purpose for sending out the dove is clearly stated. Noah was seeking information about the water level, and he learned that the water still dominated much of the surface of the land. But it is puzzling why Noah first released a raven. The Hebrew word translated "raven" is a general word for members of the crow family. Perhaps this bird had mastered the art of mimicry and become a genuine source of irritation to Noah and his family.[5]

---

[5] This author had the privilege of keeping a pet crow as a child and knows what a nuisance a crow can be.

In any case, these two birds were sent out on the 263rd day and only the dove returned.

Return of Plants to the Earth

> So he waited yet another seven days and again sent out the dove from the ark. And the dove returned to him at evening and behold, a fresh sprig from an olive tree was in her mouth. Then Noah knew that the waters had retreated off the surface of the earth. Then he waited still another seven days after which he sent out the dove, but she did not return to him anymore.
>
> —Genesis 8:10-12

The second release occurred one hundred twenty days or four months after the calming of the flood, which was apparently enough time for a partially buried olive branch to sprout new leaves.[6] Seven days later, the dove was released a third time, and it apparently found enough of the necessities of life to maintain itself outside the ark of safety. It never returned to Noah.

A Peek at the New World

> And it came about in the six hundred and first year, on the first day of the first month,[7] the waters were dried up from off the earth. And Noah removed the

---

[6] Research has been done on the survivability of various types of seed after exposure to water for an extended period. Evidence shows that some plant groups cannot survive, while others clearly can (George F. Howe, "Seed germination, sea water and plant survival in the Great Flood," *Creation Research Society Quarterly* 5:3 [1969]: 105-112).

[7] This calculates to 57 days after the third release of the dove.

covering[8] of the ark and he looked out and, behold, the surface of the ground looked dry. And in the second month on the twenty-seventh day of the month,[9] the ground was dry.

—Genesis 8:13-14

Finally, after 313 days in the ark—ten months and thirteen days—Noah pulled back the skin covering and let the sunshine in. The Bible notes that at this time and apparently for the first time, Noah and his family are allowed to study their new environment. How different it all looked! Gone was the superabundant vegetation that had plagued the earth because of the curse. Perhaps it was at this moment that Noah remembered the prophecy that his father, Lamech, had uttered at his birth: "This one will give us rest from our work and the toil of our hands from the soil that the Lord had cursed" (5:29). Gone were all the useless plants—those that the King James Version refers to as "thorns and thistles." All of that biotic material was buried in the sediment, waiting to be mined as coal.

Gone too was the garden of Eden, as well as the Tree of Life that denoted God's presence. Gone was the canopy of water that had muted the streaming sunlight. The air seemed cooler, drier. The breeze seemed stronger; the sunshine, so bright. It was a new world.

But some things may have also looked familiar. Gazing off to the southeast, the sons of Noah may have thought that they recognized the original Euphrates River. And off to the left was one that reminded them of the Tigris. The topography was completely reworked, but something about those two rivers may have reminded these men of the original rivers. In reality, however, the pre-flood river system was not organically

---

8   See commentary on Gen. 6:16.
9   An additional 36 days are attached.

connected to the post-flood river system. The names, however, were preserved in the minds of the residents of the ark and survive today to remind us of that early earth. The Tigris and Euphrates Rivers of today flow atop thousands of feet of sediment and reworked strata that have scattered within them the shattered debris of that early earth.

Even though the ground *appeared* dry, it apparently was not dry—dry enough for habitation, that is—until another fifty-seven days had passed (1 month + 27 days). One year and ten days had now lapsed since God had sealed up the ark.

Two months of sunlight streaming into the ark had doubtless had a pronounced effect on the biological clocks of the animals. When Noah and the animals left the ark at God's command, they left "by families" (8:19). The ark may have become a veritable beehive of activity in the last two months. The food supply must have been dwindling at an alarming rate, and the animals must have been getting restless.

Leaving the Ark

> Then God spoke to Noah, saying, "Go out of the ark, you and your wife and your sons, and the wives of your sons with you. All the living things that are with you of all flesh, both birds and beasts and everything that creeps on the ground, bring them out with you and let them swarm over the earth and let them be fruitful and multiply upon the earth." So Noah went out and his sons and his wife and the wives of his sons with him. All the beasts and all the creepers and all the birds—anything that moves on the earth— came out by their families from the ark.
>
> —Genesis 8:15-19

It is not likely that it took seven days to unload the ark, as it had to load it. Every creature—both man and beast—was eager to leave. The command of God to leave the ark was as detailed as the command to enter it. No deaths had apparently occurred during the year onboard; each one that went in, came out. In fact, verse 19 indicates that they came out "by families," so more individuals probably came out than went in. Already in verse 17 God expressed interest in their reproduction and multiplication. "Let them swarm over the earth and let them be fruitful and multiply upon the earth."

A Thank Offering

> Then Noah built an altar to the Lord and took from all the clean animals and all the clean birds and offered a whole burnt offering upon the altar. And the Lord smelled the pleasing aroma and the Lord said in his heart, "I will never again curse the ground on account of mankind because the inclination of the heart of mankind is toward evil, even from his youth. I will never again strike down every living creature as I have done.
>
> > As long as the earth remains,
> > Seedtime and harvest,
> > Cold and heat,
> > Summer and winter,
> > Day and night
> > Shall not cease."
>
> —Genesis 8:20-22

Noah's first act upon leaving the ark was to offer a sacrifice to God. God had protected and guarded the ark through the Mabbûl. This thank offering was made to God in gratitude for safety and guidance through this ordeal.

Figure 26: Noah presents a thank-offering to God.

God was pleased with Noah's offering and bound himself never again to curse the ground because of mankind. God essentially repealed the curse he had spoken to Adam at the fall.

- Cursed is the ground because of you (3:17).
- I will no longer curse the ground because of mankind (8:21).

The first result of the original curse was the rapid and unrestrained growth of useless plants. A second was that Adam struggled to grow food for himself and his family (3:17b). But now that the windows of heaven had opened and the canopy of water had collapsed, the climate around the globe changed considerably. The stable, moist, uniform atmosphere that had provided greenhouse conditions for the ferns, cycads, and other useless plants was now defunct. In its place, God instituted the vagaries of weather—the heat, the cold, the dry, the wet, the wind, the rain. It is common to complain about the weather today, but the struggle to farm and to garden under present conditions is much less severe than that which man experienced on the early earth.

Verse 22 initiates the present cycle of seasons. "Seedtime and harvest" often correlate with changes in moisture—the wet and dry seasons. "Cold and heat" correspond with the polar and equatorial regions—changes due to variation in either latitude or altitude. "Summer and winter" are the seasonal variations that result from the tilt of the earth's axis, which likely occurred as the various landmasses shifted. "Day and night"—even these wax and wane as the earth circles the sun. Length of daylight affects many plant species, as well as some animals. Length of sunlight can signal seed setting in some plants and trigger migratory responses in various birds and animals.

All of these dramatic ecological changes were designed by God to fulfill the prophecy given at Noah's birth: "This one shall bring us relief from the work and hard toil of our hands from the ground that the Lord has cursed" (5:29). Great benefit accrued to us in terms of our physical existence. But on the spiritual level, God recognized that his chastening wrath was not the final solution. The Mabbûl had not mollified man's sinful nature. At the heart, everyone was still a sinner. God's wrath is not the source of man's salvation.

– 17 –

Genesis 9: A New Dispensation

The Blessing of God

Then God blessed Noah and his sons and said to
them: "Be fruitful and multiply and fill the earth."
—Genesis 9:1

This blessing from God should again be understood as a
creative endowment. It is identical to the content of the opening
line of Genesis 1:28—"Then God blessed them and God said
to them, 'Be fruitful and multiply and fill the earth.'" This
statement was earlier understood to include the imprinting of
our beings with sexual desires and drives that would ensure
the continuation of the human race. Was God simply repeating
himself here? Perhaps not. This may have been the time when
significant variation was introduced into the human gene pool.
Perhaps those living in the early earth tended to look more
like each other than we do today. Also, no physical boundaries
like oceans, mountain ridges, or deserts divided people into
separate populations in the early earth. Today a plethora of
distinctions in mankind can be appreciated and enjoyed. This

statement appears to speak to the introduction of this great variety that we see today.[1]

The Reign of Terror

> Now the fear of you and the terror of you shall be upon every beast of the earth and upon every bird of the heavens, upon everything that creeps on the ground and upon all the fish of the sea. Into your hand they are given.
>
> —Genesis 9:2

This was a major adjustment. Mankind had previously been in charge of the animal kingdom. He was to rule, to dominate, and to subdue all branches of God's created world (1:26, 28). But now the human form would strike terror into the heart of God's creation. It is not clear from the Bible why God chose to make this adjustment in man's relationship to animals. This change could, however, be linked to comments in Genesis 6 in which "all flesh" was slated for destruction: "God saw the earth and behold, it was corrupt, for all flesh had corrupted their way upon the earth" (6:12; see also 6:17; 7:4, 23). Nor is it clear how mankind had succeeded in polluting the animal kingdom. But it is evident that such subjugation of the animal realm was no longer possible.

A Change in Diet

> Every moving thing that lives shall be food for you.
> Just as I gave you green plants, now I give it all.

---

[1] God even took credit for establishing a system that included people who we might consider disabled. "Then the LORD said to him, 'Who has made man's mouth? Who makes him mute or deaf or seeing or blind? Is it not I, the LORD?" (Ex. 4:11 NASB).

> Except for flesh with its life in it—its blood—do not
> eat that.
>
> —Genesis 9:3-4

God then brought about another major change. He expanded man's diet. Before the flood, man ate fruits, nuts, and seeds. But his diet was now expanded to include chops, steaks, grubs, grasshoppers, and filet of anything that one might like.

Though not specifically mentioned in this passage, it is obvious that a carnivorous diet was now a part of the animal kingdom as well. Before the Mabbûl and during the time that Noah and his family were in the ark, carnivory did not occur. "And to all the beasts of the earth and to all the birds of the heavens, and all that creeps on the earth—anything that has the breath of life—their food shall be the green plants. And so it was" (1:30).

Some creationists argue that carnivorousness was introduced when man fell. But no mention of it is made in the context of the curses on the serpent or the ground for Adam's sake (see 3:14-19). The main body of evidence for pre-flood carnivory is the presence of scratch marks on fossil bones.[2] Is this compelling proof? Given the ferocity of the Mabbûl, there may well be better explanations for this circumstance. In fact, scratch marks can be seen on four *Tyrannosaurus rex* museum specimens, leading some to conclude that T. rex cannibalized its own.[3] In light of the introduction of meat-eating in Genesis 9, it seems more reasonable to conclude that before this change, no carnivorous activity was present.

---

[2] G. M. Erickson and K. H. Olson, "Bite marks attributable to Tyrannosaurus rex: preliminary descriptions and implications," *Journal of Vertebrate Paleontology,* 16 (1996): 175-178.

[3] Nicholas R. Longrich, John R. Horner, Gregory M. Erickson, and Philip J. Currie, "Cannibalism in Tyrannosaurus rex" ("Cannibalism in Tyrannosaurus rex," www.PLONE.org/article, accessed November 2013).

Some might wonder how it is possible to so change the physiology, feeding habits, and diet of an animal—like the lion—so that it becomes an herbivore, or vice versa. Indeed, such a change would require an act of God. And God has promised, through Isaiah the prophet, to again do exactly that at the inauguration of the millennium.

> The wolf will dwell with the lamb, and the leopard will lie down with the young goat, and the calf and the lion and the fattened steer together. And a little boy shall control[4] them. The cow and the bear shall graze. Their young will lie down together and the lion will eat fodder like the ox. The nursing child will play over the hole of the cobra and the young child shall put his hand on the adder's den. They shall not hurt or destroy in all my holy mountain for the earth will be full of the knowledge of the Lord as the water covers the sea.
>
> —Isaiah 11:6-9[5]

In Genesis 9 God issued his first commandment since the fall: "You shall not eat blood." Blood and life are intrinsically connected. They are not identical, but a body without blood is not alive. God has chosen to use blood as a symbol for life. In the Eucharist, the communion celebration, the cup symbolizes the blood of the New Covenant that is poured out for many (Matt. 26:26-28; Mark 14:22-24; Luke 22:19-20; 1 Cor. 11:25-26). Even the Apostle James decreed that we should abstain

---

4   This verb (*nôhêg*) speaks of unquestioned authority. See also Isa. 20:4; 60:11; 63:14.
5   See also Isa. 65:25. Additional passages that may speak to the inauguration of the Lord's peaceable kingdom include Ezek. 34:25ff and Hos. 2:18.

from things polluted by idols, from sexual immorality, from infanticide,[6] and from blood (Acts 15:20).

Capital Punishment Is Introduced

> And especially for your blood, your lifeblood, I will require it from the hand of every beast, I will require it. And from the hand of mankind, from the hand of each his brother, I will require the life of the man.
> Whoever sheds the blood of a man,
> By mankind his blood shall be shed,
> Because in the image of God he made mankind.
> Now you be fruitful and multiply;
> Swarm over the earth and multiply in it.
> —Genesis 9:5-7

God specifically focused his comments here on the untimely death of human beings. Men and women are special because they are made in God's image. For this reason, whoever—beast or man—willfully kills a human, God requires the payment of a death for that death. The Hebrew verb translated "require" is translated "avenge" in Psalm 9:12. "For he who avenges blood is mindful of them; he does not forget the cry of the afflicted" (ESV).

God specified how the "avenging" is to be accomplished. Other men are given the responsibility to shed the blood of the murderer. Capital punishment is the design of God. He is personally offended when evil is perpetrated against a person made in his image and likeness (see also Matt. 25:41-46; Ps. 51:4). God finished this section with a reminder that, instead of

---

6   David Instone-Brewer, "Infanticide and the Apostolic Decree of Acts 15," *Journal of the Evangelical Theological Society* 52:2 (June 2009): 301-321.

killing each other, men should grasp the importance of having children: "Be fruitful and multiply; swarm over the earth and multiply in it" (v. 7).

Summary of Changes

In response to Noah's offering to God, God made three promises.

- I will never again tamper with the ground in response to man's sinfulness.
- I will never again destroy every living thing.
- I will never again alter the earth's ecology.

Then God made three alterations.

- God enhanced the human gene pool.
- God reduced man's control over animals to a reign of terror.
- God introduced carnivorousness.

Finally, God gave mankind three commands.

- Do not eat blood.
- Kill whatever intentionally takes the life of a person made in God's image.
- Have children.

These nine statements from God constitute a very substantial dispensational change. Things were different now. The establishment of human government was incipient in these comments.

God's Covenant with Nature

And God spoke to Noah and his sons with him saying: "Now I—even I—am setting up my covenant with you and your seed after you and with the living creatures that are with you; both birds, cattle, and every beast of the earth with you—everything that came out of the ark. It is for every beast of the earth. I hereby establish my covenant with you that never again will all flesh be cut down by the waters of the Mabbûl. And never again shall there be a Mabbûl to devastate the earth."

Furthermore God said, "This is the sign of the covenant that I am making between me and you, and all the living beings that are with you for all future generations. I hereby place my rainbow in the cloud and it shall be the sign of the covenant between me and the earth. And it shall be whenever I cause a cloud to rise above the earth, then the rainbow will appear in the cloud, and I shall remember my covenant that is between me and you and all living beings of all flesh, and never again shall there come the waters of the Mabbûl to destroy all flesh. And whenever the rainbow is in the storm cloud, then I will see it and be reminded of the everlasting covenant between God and all living beings and all flesh that is on the earth." And God said to Noah, "This is the covenant that I am setting up between myself and all flesh that dwells on the earth."

—Genesis 9:8-17

The most obvious element about God's covenant here is that it was not made with Noah alone. It extended to Noah's sons (v. 8) and to any future generations (v. 12), as well as to every living creature (v. 10), including the birds, the livestock, and the wild animals—every creature that came off the ark (v. 10). Essentially, this covenant was between God and the whole earth (v. 13)—between God and nature.

In this covenant God formally bound himself to never repeat the catastrophe that had been the Mabbûl (vv. 11, 15). Global inundation with water will never again occur. Peter reminds us that there will be a second global destruction, but it will not be achieved with water. The second global cleansing will involve the fire of God's wrath (2 Peter 3:3-13; contrast 2:4-5; for timing see Rev. 20:7-10). Out of this chaos, God will create new heavens and a new earth (Isa. 65:17; 66:22), using fire (Isa. 66:15-16).

The sign of God's covenant with nature is the rainbow that is set in the cloud. Its purpose is to serve as a reminder to God of his promise to this earth (vv. 15, 16). In light of the statement in Genesis 2:5-6 that the early earth was not watered from above by rainfall but rather by the huge spring that rose up from the earth, no rainbow would have been seen before the flood because God was not using clouds to water the continent. It does not seem necessary to suggest that God initiated a spectral scattering property of water droplets at this time. Instead, water had always had this quality, but no pre-flood showers had displayed the beauty of the rainbow.

Figure 27: The rainbow in the cloud

The great flood was ended. It is hard for those of us living in the "now world" to appreciate how much things changed from that early earth. The early earth was watered by a huge spring bubbling up in Eden (2:6). Now the earth is watered by the hydrological cycle of evaporation, transpiration, and precipitation. Then, because of the water canopy, the atmosphere was calm, warm, moist, and uniform, providing the perfect environment for huge masses of vegetative growth that supported large cold-blooded animals, such as the dinosaurs. Now significant seasonal fluctuations in temperature and precipitation are selective for short-seasoned grains, deciduous plants, and warm-blooded animals.

Originally man's dominion bordered on absolute control over all species (1:26, 28). Now man has only partial control, and that is possible only because of the post-flood fear of man instilled in animals. All beasts of the earth, birds of the heaven, and all that crept on the ground were assigned a vegetarian diet in the early earth (1:30). Now a carnivorous menu was introduced to man and to many species (9:3).

The main reason God delivered this deathblow to the early earth was the rampant evil that plagued the whole world. That evil was the outflow of man's depraved heart (6:5). And that—man's heart—has alone remained the same. God recognized that this judgment event did not change the hearts of the eight individuals that left the ark. While Noah's obedience to God was stellar, the Mabbûl had no cleansing effect on his heart (8:21). Only the work of the Spirit, based on the atonement provided by Christ, could ever hope to change that.

An Aside on the Ice Ages

During the flood, the Lord caused the descent of all the waters in the canopy that had overlain the atmosphere of that early earth. With this insulating layer gone, the climate would have changed considerably. Precisely what those changes may have looked like is difficult to imagine. But today ample evidence indicates that since the Mabbûl the earth has experienced major climate changes, one of which is known as the ice age. Evidence of the ice age is found in the existence of remnants of glaciations, rock striations or scratches from glacial movements, and terminal moraines that mark the boundary of this glacial activity.

The data in these next few paragraphs is largely dependent on the writings of creationist Michael Oard. His thoughts, expressed in numerous articles, are collected in his latest book, *Frozen in Time.*[7] Reconstruction of past events is tricky business, but Oard's commitment to the biblical record increases the probability that his proposals are correct, at least in the broad outline.

Two conditions must exist in order for large amounts of snow and ice to accumulate over vast areas of a continent. The first is the presence of warm oceans. The second is the reduction in incoming solar radiation that results in cooler summers.

Warm oceanic water would be expected from the biblical presentation of the climate of the early earth. The evidence of a warm climate from the time of Adam to Noah can be seen in the type of vegetation trapped in coal seams. Even Antarctica has fossil evidence of tropical forestation.[8] The oceanic temperature during the pre-flood period is estimated to have been around eighty-five degrees Fahrenheit—over twenty degrees higher than today. This would have resulted in a greatly increased rate of evaporation that would have pumped huge amounts of water vapor into the post-flood weather pattern.

Secondly, in the sedimentary rock lies evidence of volcanic activity during the year of the flood. The shifting of the continents also suggests that volcanic activity was heightened during this time. The effect of large amounts of ash and aerosols in the upper atmosphere would have been felt in lowered summertime temperatures. These two conditions could result in the accumulation of huge amounts of snow in storm-prone areas of the northern and southern hemispheres. Then, as the oceans cooled and the sky cleared, the conditions necessary to sustain these continental ice sheets would have gradually disappeared.

---

[7]   Michael Oard, *Frozen in Time* (Green Forest, Ark.: Master, 2004).

[8]   "Weird Forests Once Sprouted in Antarctica: *How did tropical-type trees flourish on the South Pole?*" (www.weather.aol.com/2013/11/03/weird-forests-once-sprouted-in-antarctica/, accessed January 12, 2014).

Oard's model suggests that the peak of glacial activity occurred around five hundred years after the flood. The average depth of the continental ice sheet is estimated to have been about one-half mile thick.[9] He further suggests that this condition would have persisted for about two hundred years. Here in the midwestern United States the leading edge of the Laurentide Ice Sheet approximated the current route of the Missouri River. When the ice began to melt, it would have occurred quite rapidly, resulting in major flooding in southern climes and dry, dust-bowl conditions in lands bordering the Arctic Ocean. Oard uses these windy, desiccating conditions to explain the death and entrapment in windblown loess soils of hundreds of woolly mammoths in Alaska, Canada, and Siberia.

Of course, the Plain of Shinar, where the biblical story of Genesis 9-11 took place, was not involved in this type of glaciation, though the landscape even there was doubtless more verdant and lush than it is today. These major phases in the stabilization of the climate after the flood help explain why desert areas were once inhabited and why civilizations like the Chalcolithic culture suddenly ceased to exist, with no evidence of destruction or pillage. Many of these mysteries from the past must inevitably remain just that.

The Dispersion

> Now the sons of Noah who came out of the ark were
> Shem and Ham and Japheth. (Now, Ham was the
> father of Canaan.) These were the three sons of Noah,
> and these were dispersed over the whole earth.
>
> —Genesis 9:18-19

---

[9] Oard, 90; see also Michael Oard, *An Ice Age Caused by the Genesis Flood* (El Cajon Calif.: Institute for Creation Research, 1990).

These verses introduce the next subject—the repopulation of people on the earth. The details are found in Genesis 10 and 11. But before the story continues, an incident must be related, namely, the curse on Canaan. This curse is important because the Canaanites were living in the Promised Land at the time of Joshua's conquest. To understand God's markedly negative attitude toward them, one must see it against the backdrop of the curse on Canaan.

Curse on Canaan

Then Noah became a farmer—a man of the soil—and he planted a vineyard. And he drank too much wine and became drunk and exposed himself inside his tent. And Ham, who was the father of Canaan, noticed that his father was naked and told it to his two brothers outside. Then Shem and Japheth took a garment and set it upon their two shoulders and walked backward and covered the nakedness of their father. Now their faces were turned away and they did not see their naked father. When Noah awoke from his wine, he realized what his youngest son had done to him and he said:
"Cursed be Canaan!
A servant of servants he shall be to his brothers."
He also said:
"Blessed be the Lord, the God of Shem,
And Canaan shall be his servant.
May God expand Japheth and let him dwell
in the tents of Shem,
And Canaan shall be his servant."
—Genesis 9:20-27

This is not a pleasant story. The gist of the event is relayed, but the details are spared the reader. Commentators generally agree that Canaan encouraged his grandfather to get drunk and then took advantage of the situation in a homosexual manner and left. The Hebrew text refers to Canaan as a *son* but it is clear from both verses 18 and 22 that Canaan was Noah's biological *grandson*. In English, this might be considered an error in the text, but the Hebrew concept of *son* can be much broader than a direct biological descendent.[10] So here in Genesis 9 the mention of the "youngest son" is not a reference to Ham, who first noticed his naked father, but to Noah's grandson Canaan. Ham simply stumbled onto the situation and quickly reported what he saw to his brothers. The text does not indict Ham as having sinned.

The Hebrew language has a particular way of expressing sexual intercourse aside from the common *knowing*. That phrase is "to uncover the nakedness" of someone. Leviticus 18 uses this idiom repeatedly in a list of illicit relations. Several modern translations correctly render this phrase with "do not have sexual relations/intercourse with. . . ." This idiomatic phrase is *not* used to describe Ham's actions. He simply looked and saw that his father lay naked inside the tent. Then he went out and reported the situation to his brothers.

Shem and Japheth immediately found a garment and, holding it up to shield their eyes in deference to their father, backed into the tent and covered the sleeping Noah. When he awoke from his stupor, Noah recognized that he had been violated and uttered a curse on the young lad. "Cursed be Canaan!"

The curse on Canaan was a direct result of his immoral actions, and the curse was one of servitude. Canaan was

---

[10] See comments in the genealogical section of Genesis 5 for further explanation (ch. 13).

designated to be a servant to Shem, as well as to Japheth. Genesis 10:15-19 names the exact location of the descendants of Canaan. They inhabited the Promised Land. When God told Abram about his future, he indicated that Abram would encounter a delay before inheriting the land because "the iniquity of the Amorites[11] is not yet complete" (15:16b ESV).

In the Leviticus passage referred to above, which catalogs many illicit sexual liaisons, an extended warning was given to Israel as they were about to enter the Promised Land. They should be careful not to follow the example of the Canaanite nations. "Do not defile yourselves by any of these things, for by all these the nations which I am casting out before you have become defiled. Since the land has become defiled, I have visited punishment upon it, and the land has spewed out its inhabitants" (Lev. 18:24-25 NASB). God is very sensitive about sexual deviance.

The Death of Noah

> And Noah lived after the Mabbûl three hundred fifty years. And all the days of Noah's life were nine hundred fifty years and he died.
>
> —Genesis 9:28-29

Noah was the last of the millennials—those persons whose lifespans approached a thousand years. The ages of other people mentioned later in Genesis drop off precipitously until the last verse of the last chapter of Genesis records that Joseph died in Egypt at one hundred ten years of age (50:26).

---

[11] The term *Amorite* is often used as a general term for the inhabitants of the land of Canaan, as in Josh. 24:15. It is a synonym for Canaanite.

– 18 –

Genesis 10 and 11: The Babel Dispersion

Now this is the story of the sons of Noah: Shem, Ham, and Japheth. And sons were born to them after the flood.

—Genesis 10:1

The Descendants of Noah

To the casual reader of the Bible, Genesis 10 may seem like a conglomerate of peculiar names—a good place to practice speed-reading. Upon closer inspection, however, it becomes apparent that the chapter is composed of three sub-texts—one dedicated to the family of Japheth, one to the family of Ham, and one to the family of Shem.

Genesis 5 begins with "the scroll of the story of Adam" (5:1), and the genealogy in chapter 11 begins with "this is the story of Shem" (11:10). Both of these genealogical listings are of a linear nature. Genesis 10, on the other hand, begins with "this is the story of the sons of Noah: Shem, Ham, and Japheth" and is not linear. Instead, it is a tree with three main limbs and many branches. As a generalization, it may be stated that about two generations of descendants are listed for each of the three sons of Noah. The structure of Genesis 10 follows:

I. The story of the sons of Noah after the flood, v. 1
- A. Genealogical list of the descendants of Japheth, vv. 2-4
- *A.* Statement of separation, v. 5
- B. Genealogical list of the descendants of Ham, vv. 6-19
- *B.* Statement of separation, v. 20
- C. Genealogical list of the descendants of Shem, vv. 21-30
- *C.* Statement of separation, vs. 31

II. The story of the separation after the flood,[1] v. 32

The information concerning each of the three sons of Noah can be diagramed to show the genealogical relationships.

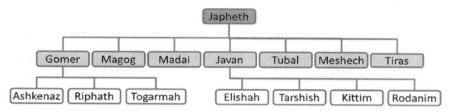

Figure 28: The family of Japheth (10:2-4)

---

[1] The duplication of words and phrases like "these," "account/genealogy," "sons of Noah" and "after the flood" in both verses 1 and 32 serves as bookends, as it were, for the material in chapter 10.

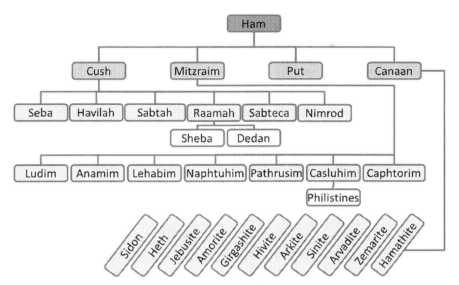

Figure 29: The family of Ham (10:6-19)

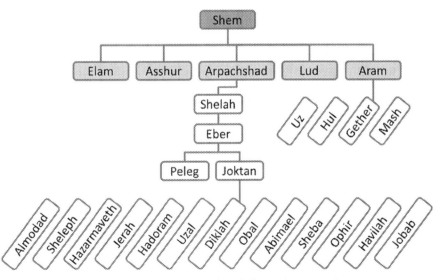

Figure 30: The family of Shem (10:21-29)

Stanley V. Udd

Purpose for the Family Trees

These three family trees are quite stylized. For example, it is not likely that five of Japheth's sons had no children while the remaining two had seven children between them. It seems reasonable to conclude that this listing of descendants is included for reasons other than to serve as a catalog of births. In fact, this chapter spends four verses detailing *why* those that are included are listed.

After the list of Japheth's descendants comes this statement in verse 5: "From *these* the far-flung nations were separated according to their lands, each according to his language, according to their families, according to their nations."

After the list of Ham's descendants comes this statement in verse 20: "*These* are the sons of Ham according to their families, according to their languages, according to their lands, according to their nations."

After the list of Shem's descendants comes this statement in verse 31: "*These* are the sons of Shem according to their families, according to their languages, according to their lands, according to their nations."

The summary verse that closes Genesis 10 states in verse 32 that "*these* are the family units of the sons of Noah according to their genealogy, according to their nations. And *from these* were separated the nations on the earth after the flood."

The repetition of concepts in these verses is striking. These people were separated

- by families—racially,
- by languages—linguistically,
- by lands—geographically, and
- by nations—culturally or socially.

Two notations in Genesis 10 relate to geography. The Canaanites were located within the region bounded by Sidon on the northwest, Gaza on the southwest, the five (four) cities of the plain to the southeast, and Lasha marking the northeast corner (10:19). The descendants of Joktan are said to extend from Mesha "as one goes toward Sephar"[2] (Gen. 10:30) to points east.

The Number of Family Units

How many of *these* family units were involved in the separation, the scattering, or the isolation from one another?[3] It is clear in the case of Japheth that Ashkenas, Riphath, and Togarmah—all sons of Gomar—should be seen as family units. Was Gomar a separate family unit? By extension should Japheth himself constitute a separate unit?

It may not be possible to determine the exact number of family units, but the Bible repeatedly says that the dispersion was from *these* (see vv. 5, 20, 31, 32a, and 32b). In the case of Japheth, fifteen names are mentioned. In the case of Ham, thirty-two names are recorded, while Shem's family tree lists twenty-seven names. If Noah is added from verses 1 and 32, about seventy-five names are mentioned in this chapter.

Seventy-five is therefore the upper limit of family units cataloged in Genesis 10. On the other hand, if the family of Canaan is considered a unit in itself, and if one excludes the immediate family of Noah, then the lower limit comes to about

---

[2] Sephar extends at least to the eastern edge of the Arabian Peninsula (HALOT, 767). The idea of "points east" rises from the wooden translation "mountain of the east."

[3] The Hebrew verbs used to describe this action are *pûtz* and *pārad* (see HALOT, 918-19, 962).

sixty family units. For the purpose of this study, sixty units constitute the number of family groupings in Genesis 10.

Before going further, attention needs to be given to a few side comments inserted into Genesis 10. The following section addresses a notable individual named Nimrod.

Nimrod

> And Cush became the father of Nimrod. He was the first person to become a tyrant[4] on the earth. He himself was a god-awful tyrant;[5] therefore, it became a saying, "like Nimrod, that god-awful tyrant!" And the capital of his kingdom was Babel, then Erech and Accad and Calnah in the land of Shinar. From that land he went out to Assyria and built Nineveh and Rehoboth-Ir and Calah and Resen, that great city between Nineveh and Calah.
>
> —Genesis 10:8-12

The setting for Genesis 11 is found in these comments in Genesis 10 regarding Nimrod. He became the first tyrant on the earth (10:8). He could and would subdue anything and anyone who stood in his way. The Hebrew struggles to express the ferocity of this man. His might is further qualified as being "before the face of the Lord" (10:9, 2 times). This in no way depicts Nimrod as doing exploits to please the Lord. The phrase is rather to be understood as indicating the magnitude of his prominence.

---

4   Nimrod is here called a *gibbôr,* which could be translated "mighty warrior." In Isa. 49:25 this word is parallel to "tyrant" (*'ārîtz*) (HALOT, 172).
5   The phrase *god-awful tyrant* is the author's attempt to render the idiomatic Hebrew that woodenly says that "he himself was a warrior hunter before the face of Yahweh."

The tetragrammaton (Yahweh) is used here as an adjective,[6] much as the word *'elohîm* is used in Jonah 3:3 to describe the significance of Nineveh.[7]

Nimrod had come up with a scheme to localize power in Babylon and to prevent the post-flood population from scattering over the face of the earth (11:4). This he did in defiance of God's command in 9:1 to "fill the earth." Nimrod's power was extraordinary, such that God himself concluded that "this is what they have begun to do and now nothing that they propose to do will be impossible for them" (11:6b). As these verses indicate, Nimrod controlled the plain of Shinar and was expanding his control into the Tigris River Valley (10:11). This important information provides the backdrop for the Babel episode.

The Tower of Babel

> Now the entire population had a single language and used the same words. And it happened as they journeyed eastward that they found a plain in the land of Shinar and settled there. And they said to one another, "Hey,[8] let's make bricks and dry them well." So they had sun-dried bricks[9] for stone and asphalt for mortar. And they said, "Hey, let's build a city for ourselves and a tower whose top will be the seat of power [literally, *heaven*] and we will make a name

---

6   See U. Cassuto, *A Commentary on the Book of Genesis, Part II*, trans. Israel Abrahams (Jerusalem: Magnus, 1992): 201.

7   See also Gen. 30:8; 35:5; 1 Sam. 14:15; Ps. 36:7; 80:10.

8   The word *hey* is not intended simply as an interjection, but as an agreement among themselves regarding a plan of action—a cohortative (HALOT, 236). "The cohortative lays stress on the determination underlying the action, and the personal interest in it" (GKC, §108).

9   HALOT, 518.

> for ourselves, lest we be scattered over the surface of
> the whole earth."
>
> —Genesis 11:1-4

This, then, was the situation: Noah and his family had traveled together as a group to the south and east of Ararat and had come to the fertile plain of Shinar. Two or three generations later an individual from the clan of Cush forced his way into power. Nimrod's[10] plan was to centralize power in his capital city of Babel. More precisely, he constructed a tower—probably a ziggurat—at the top of which was "heaven." The Hebrew text has a *beth* attached to the word *heaven* that could be translated "*in* heaven." But the *beth* often acts as an object marker and in that case remains untranslated.[11] The *beth* simply signals that the following word is the predicate adjective of this nominal sentence. Here the translation should be "let us build a tower whose top *is* heaven." The term *heaven* is being used as a metaphor for the seat of power. No indication in the Hebrew suggests that they intended to invade God's abode. Instead, it was from the pinnacle of this tower that decisions would rain down on the people that would effectively govern and regulate their lives. Nimrod's goal was to control the entire population of the world, and he needed to restrict their travel to accomplish this—"lest we be scattered abroad over the surface of the earth" (11:4b). Genesis 10:11 adds that his control was complete in the plain of Shinar. Nimrod then began expanding his control into the valley of the Tigris River. As masterful as his plan was, Nimrod had forgotten one person—God.

---

[10] Various attempts have been made to identify Nimrod in Ancient Near Eastern literature. See Douglas Petrovich, "Identifying Nimrod of Genesis 10 with Sargon of Akkad by Exegetical and Archaeological Means," *Journal of the Evangelical Theological Society* 56:2 (June 2013): 273-305.

[11] The lexicon lists 23 different ways in which *beth* can function in the Hebrew Old Testament (HALOT, 103-5).

The Inspection Tour

> Then the Lord went down to inspect the city and
> the tower that the sons of men had built. And the
> Lord said, "Behold, the people are united and all
> of them have a single language, and this is only the
> beginning of what they can do. And now nothing that
> they propose to do will be impossible for them."
>
> —Genesis 11:5-6

These two verses give the Lord's analysis of Nimrod's plan. Nimrod had structured a system that was capable of great things. But Nimrod was an evil person and if this program continued, evil would soon rule the world. This had been the precise problem *before* the flood, and now it seemed possible that the same situation would ensue a second time. God did not want that to happen. He needed to break the controlling grip that evil held on the human race.

God's Plan of Action

> "Hey, let's go down and there confuse their language
> such that they will not understand one another." So the
> Lord scattered them from there over the whole surface
> of the earth, and they quit building the city. Therefore
> its name is called Babel because there the Lord babbled
> the language of all the earth and from there the Lord
> scattered them over the surface of the whole earth.
>
> —Genesis 11:7-9

God now had his own plan of action. "Hey, let us go and confuse their tongue." The intervention of the Lord is clear in this passage. In order to prevent these people from understanding each other's speech, God performed a supernatural miracle in their minds. How many languages did God invent on this dreadful day? Here Genesis 10 is helpful. The groups of Genesis 10 apparently represented the sixty or so diverse languages that God implanted in the minds of mankind on the plain of Shinar.

But this was not all that God did. Twice the passage states that the Lord "scattered them over the surface of the whole earth." Does this mean that a worker, unable to understand his fellow worker, simply picked up his tools and went home? The text states otherwise. The Hebrew form of the verb translated "scattered" is, in both cases, the *Hiphil* form, which means that God was "actively causing the action"[12] that was occurring. The Bible could not be more explicit. The author of Genesis 10 and 11 wanted the reader to understand that God supernaturally transported these groups of people, who now shared individual languages that he had imposed on their minds, to their new intended habitat.

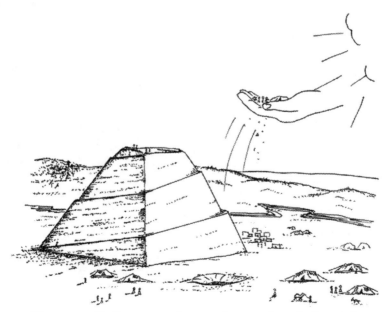

Figure 31: God scatters the people over the whole earth.

---

12 J. Weingreen, *A Practical Grammar for Classical Hebrew,* 2d ed. (Oxford: Clarendon, 1959): 100.

The Hebrew verb used in both chapters 10 and 11 (*putz*) is also used in Isaiah 28:25—"When he has leveled its surface, does he not *scatter* dill, sow cumin, and put in wheat in rows and barley in its proper place, and emmer as the border?" (ESV). The implication is clear that this scattering was not a haphazard event, but a carefully considered process.

These two verses give the solution to a multitude of questions that a student of anthropology might ask. But Christians[13] and secularists alike almost universally ignore this biblical answer. Perhaps it seems too simplistic or even too demeaning to acknowledge that "God did it." The reader will recall that driving off the floodwaters in Genesis 8 furnished the mechanism for both the establishment of the boundaries that God set for the water and the building of the mountains (Ps. 104:5-9). This took place while Noah and the animals were still inside the ark. The continents had already separated before the ark was unloaded.

So, how did the aardvark get to Australia? From the words of the Bible, it is appropriate to deduce that on that day of intervention, God selected an ecologically balanced grouping of plants, animals, and people and placed them in Australia. Animals and plants are necessary to the survival of mankind around the globe, so it seems reasonable that God distributed distinct groupings of ecologically balanced fauna and flora with each people group. He did the same for each of the sixty or so groups identified in Genesis 10. "*These* are the family units of the sons of Noah according to their genealogy, according to

---

[13] Even the *New Living Translation* misrepresents the actions described in the Hebrew text by making the scattering a secondary consequence: "Come, let's go down and confuse the people with different languages. Then they won't be able to understand each other. In that way the LORD scattered them all over the world" (11:7-8a, see also 9).

their nations. And *from these* were separated[14] the nations on the earth after the Mabbûl" (10:32).

Genesis 10 is quite clear that this separation involved four distinct features. The people were separated by race, by language, by geography, and by culture.

The isolation of these sixty family units almost immediately allowed each genetic pool to begin expressing its individuality. This seems to be the concept of separation by families. Supernatural genetic differentiation by God does not need to be invoked at this time. Racial characteristics would naturally have appeared because of this isolation. The development of race would have been the natural outcome of geographic isolation.

The separations by language and land were both supernatural and accomplished by God alone. The separation according to nations appears to be a concomitant development of the linguistic adjustment that God made at this time. Not only did each family unit now speak differently, but they also thought differently, organized themselves differently, and developed unique cultural traits.

Before the flood, everyone had lived on the same continent. No geographic boundaries separated the population naturally into groups. No climatic differences separated those who preferred cold as opposed to those who enjoyed warmer climes. Before the flood, the climate was uniform throughout the earth. Now sharp distinctions existed between cold and warm, wet and dry. Now populations were separated by extreme geographic barriers—mountain ranges, deserts, and oceans.

Diversity was now the dominant characteristic of the human population. This involved variations in thought patterns,

---

[14] Note that in these verses (10:5 and 32) the passive form of the verb is used to describe the action that was done *to* these families. They did not actively scatter themselves (HALOT 962).

climatic preferences, and languages. It is intriguing, even in our global society, that adjustments are required in marketing various products to make them acceptable in another culture. However, no one will succeed in overcoming the effects of Babel through education or commercialization. It will never be possible to have a United Nations that works effectively. It does appear, though, that at the end of the ages, the Beast of Revelation 13 will finally achieve the unification of the entire world. "And it was given to him to make war with the saints and to overcome them, and authority over every tribe and people and tongue and nation [notice the four-fold division] was given to him. And all who dwell on the earth will worship him" (Rev. 13:7-8a NASB).[15]

Is it possible to identify the sixty or so original language groups today? Probably not. Almost immediately after the Babel experience, contact between various groups would have occurred. The borrowing and hybridizing of languages and the conquering and extinction of various ethnic groups would have doubtless taken place. Civilizations have changed to such a degree that it is probably not possible to identify the original groups.

Furthermore, it is not possible to build a "language tree" that could accurately illustrate the relationships and commonalities of the sixty or so original languages. The point of Genesis 10 and 11 is that God created separate language groups at that time. The language of Group A, for instance, was differentiated from the language of Group B by the supernatural action of God at Babel.

The Babel experience is then the source for all racial, linguistic, political, and geographic differences that mark our earth today. Just as God distributed the languages, so apparently he also physically distributed the sixty various family groups onto the seven continents of the world. This "uplift" must have

---

[15] See also Rev. 13:11ff.

included an assortment of fauna and flora so that life could be maintained in these distant lands.

Timing of the Babel Experience

Based on the notation in Genesis 10:25—"for in his [Peleg's] days the earth was divided"—it is possible to chronologically locate this global scattering. Genesis 11:10 states that Shem begat Arphaxad two years after the flood. Arphaxad was thirty-five years old when Shelah was born (11:12). Shelah was thirty years old when Eber was born (11:14). And Eber was thirty-four years old when Peleg was born (11:16). The sum of these figures indicates that the separation into distinct nations occurred a minimum of a hundred years after the great flood (2 + 35 + 30 + 34 = 101).[16]

With the dispersion of peoples around the globe, the science of archaeology could begin. Before this event, evidence of human existence would have been restricted to the Mesopotamian Valley. After Babel, cultures everywhere began generating debris, which is the lifeblood of archaeology.

Hints from Genesis 10 suggest that Japheth was scattered over "distant lands" (10:5). Perhaps this refers to Europe, North America, or South America. Ham seems to have been scattered over Africa and the land of Canaan, while Shem ranged north and east of the Mesopotamian Valley, perhaps toward northern and southern Asia, as well as the continent of Australia. Scholarly attempts have been made to identify each family unit, but most suggestions are simply . . . suggestions.[17]

---

[16] This calculation ignores the possibility of additional generations, so 101 years represents the *minimum* number of years between the flood and Babel.

[17] Nahum M. Sarna, *The JPS Torah Commentary: Genesis* (Philadelphia: Jewish Publication Society, 1989): 70-80.

Summary

The first eleven chapters of Genesis describe some very important events that could not otherwise be known with certainty. And most of the incidents in these chapters had global impact. This information includes the creation of the spiritual world, as well as the material universe. Christ was responsible for it all. "All things were made by him, and without him nothing came into existence that has come into being" (John 1:3).

How would we have known about the capture of that huge body of water, called the great deep, under the continent or the raising of a canopy of water atop the atmosphere had God not revealed it? The disruption of those two bodies of water caused the massive reworking of the continent so that an estimated one-mile layer of sedimentary rock was produced. This layer is filled with plant and animal remains that are still mined today as coal, gas, and oil. This massive sign of God's judgment should serve as a warning that God wants us to live righteously. Most geologists and paleontologists spend their lives working in this flood debris, never recognizing that God left this material as a witness to himself.

We would not know about the entrance of evil into both the spiritual and material universes were it not for Genesis. Why do we have so much trouble living as we know we ought? The first three chapters of Genesis inform us that we have been made in God's image and that sin has marred our nature through the disobedience of Adam and Eve. Murder, demon possession, polygamy, homosexuality, tyranny—all are introduced in these chapters . . . beside men of great faith, men who walked with God, and men who lived righteously.

The shape of our world today cannot be understood correctly apart from a proper understanding of the reshaping that God introduced at the close of the Mabbûl. Why the separate continents? When was the earth tilted on its axis? Why the many unique ecological niches? How were human populations scattered to the four winds? Why so many distinct languages? All of these questions are addressed in the opening chapters of the Bible.

An observation from a study of Genesis 1-11 indicates that God was largely reactive in his interactions with mankind. Adam sinned, so God drove him out of Eden. Cain murdered Abel, so God drove him into desolate country. The human population opened themselves up to every kind of evil, so God brought on a global cataclysm. Nimrod devised a way to control the human population, so God intervened by scattering mankind around the globe. Is God only reactive? Is there no hope for man? Yes, there is hope, and it is found in Genesis 12!

– 19 –

Genesis 12: The Master Plan

The Abrahamic Covenant

Then the Lord spoke to Abram, "Go! Leave your country and your birthplace and the house of your father, to the land that I will show you. And I will make of you a great nation, and I will bless you, and I will magnify your name, so that you will be a blessing.[1] I will bless whoever blesses you and whoever curses you I will curse, and through you all the families of the earth will be blessed."

—Genesis 12:1-3

This is God's plan. This is his covenant. This is the broad outline of what God intended to do, and it is a blessed plan. Reformed theologians have argued that God's command to Adam—"do not eat from this tree"—was a covenant of works. But God's

---

[1] The Hebrew uses the imperative of "to be" followed by the word "blessing." The statement "I will bless you" occurs earlier, so something more was intended with this statement. The consequence or even the original intention of these actions on Abram was to accomplish something special. God intended these actions to be part of his blessed plan. Cassuto states: "it is the imperative that particularly expresses the result of preceding action . . ."(Cassuto, *Genesis,* 2:314; so also the ESV).

command was not a covenant. It was a necessary statement that set the stage for the innocent couple to choose whether to obey God and become righteous or to disobey God and become evil by nature. Some have even tried to squeeze a covenant or proto-covenant out of the curse between women and snakes. But Satan was not and is not involved in our salvation. Even with Noah, God's promise to him was not a promise of eternal salvation. God was simply binding himself in a covenant to never again destroy the earth with a flood.

The Abrahamic covenant is unique. God came to mankind with a promise of blessing. He selected a man through whom he intended to bring great blessing. This covenant was threefold.

- I will take you to a new land.
- I will make of you a great nation.
    I will bless you.
    I will magnify your name.
    I will watch over you.
- I will bring great blessing through you.

Most significantly, Abram heard and obeyed the call of God. "By faith Abraham, when he was called, obeyed by going out to a place which he was to receive for an inheritance, and he went out, not knowing where he was going" (Heb. 11:8 NASB).

It would be difficult to understand the full import of this covenant were it not for additional revelation that God extended to us. Already in Genesis 13:14-17, God repeated to Abram that the land of Canaan was the Promised Land that would someday be his. Then, in Genesis 15, God instructed Abram to set the stage for the establishment of a blood covenant by cutting in half a three-year-old heifer, a three-year-old female goat, a three-year-old ram, along with an uncut turtledove and pigeon. God alone then walked between the carcasses so that "on that day the Lord made a covenant with Abram" (15:18a). Various iterations of this covenant occurred throughout Abraham's life (see Gen. 17, 18, and 22), but they were all based on the three-fold covenant found in 12:1-3.

The Significance of This Covenant for Us

A notable and magnificent expansion flows out of the third promise: "through you all the families of the earth will be blessed." Paul spoke of this enlargement in his letter to the Galatians.

> Know then that it is those of faith who are the sons of Abraham. And the Scripture, foreseeing that God would justify the Gentiles by faith, preached the gospel beforehand to Abraham, saying, 'In you shall all the nations be blessed.' So then, those who are of faith are blessed along with Abraham, the man of faith.
>
> —Galatians 3:7-9 ESV

As believers, we participate in this Abrahamic covenant through the promise of blessing in Genesis 12:3.

Peter also made this connection when he noted in his second sermon that blessing would come through the "seed" of Abraham but would extend to all the families of the world. "It is you who are the sons of the prophets, and of the covenant which God made with your fathers, saying to Abraham, 'And through your seed shall all the families of the earth be blessed'" (Acts 3:25 NASB, quoting Gen. 22:18).

At the close of the epoch of national Israel, when Nebuchadnezzar was bringing in the age of the Gentiles (Luke

21:24), God spoke through Jeremiah about a new covenant that springs out of this aspect of the Abrahamic covenant.

> "Behold, days are coming," declares the LORD, "when I will make a new covenant with the house of Israel and with the house of Judah, not like the covenant which I made with their fathers in the day I took them by the hand to bring them out of the land of Egypt, My covenant which they broke, although I was a husband to them," declares the LORD. "But this is the covenant which I will make with the house of Israel after those days," declares the LORD, "I will put My law within them and on their heart I will write it; and I will be their God, and they shall be My people. They will not teach again, each man his neighbor and each man his brother, saying, 'Know the LORD,' for they will all know Me, from the least of them to the greatest of them," declares the LORD, "for I will forgive their iniquity, and their sin I will remember no more."
>
> —Jeremiah 31:31-34 NASB

This new covenant is the one that Christ spoke of on the evening before his betrayal. "This cup, which is poured out for you, is the new covenant in my blood" (Luke 22:20b NASB; 1 Cor. 11:25). The author of Hebrews, in 8:8-12, quotes Jeremiah 31:31-34, and it is clear that the new covenant has four major provisions.

- I will put my law within them and on their hearts I will write it.
- I will be their God and they shall be my people.
- Everyone will know me, from the least to the greatest of them.

- I will forgive their iniquity and their sin I will remember no more.

These provisions are generally understood as follows.

- The writing on our hearts of God's law is fulfilled in the gift of the indwelling Holy Spirit (John 14:16-17).
- The God-people relationship is a special, elevated status that is unique to his chosen ones (Zech. 8:7-8, cf. 23).
- Evangelism will not be necessary in that day because salvation will belong to every living person.
- Because of the work of Christ on the cross, forgiveness can now be experienced, our consciences can be cleansed (Heb. 9:14).

These four great provisions found in the new covenant have generated a good deal of theological discussion. Does the believer actually participate in each of these? Does he become a member of the house of Judah or the house of Israel? Is there no more need for evangelism? What did Jesus intend when he said that this cup is the blood of the new covenant that is poured out for you?

The book of Hebrews solves this conundrum. Notice carefully how the author put it: "And the Holy Spirit also testifies to us, for after saying, 'This is the covenant that I will make with them after those days, says the LORD: I will put My laws upon their heart and upon their mind I will write them.'" He then says, "And their sins and their lawless deeds I will remember no more" (Heb. 10:15-17 NASB).

The author of Hebrews credited this interpretation of the new covenant to the Holy Spirit. And the Holy Spirit addressed his comments to *us*—not to the house of Israel and the house of Judah. Then he limited the quotation of the new covenant to just two provisions:

- The indwelling of the Holy Spirit, and
- The blessing of realized forgiveness.

The other two aspects of the new covenant will not be realized until Christ returns to set up his glorious kingdom (Matt. 25:31-46). All living unbelievers at that point will be dispatched, and the Old Testament believers will be invited to join in this celebration of life (Dan. 12:1-2). Everyone living on the earth at that time will then be a follower of Christ.

Christ is also going to reestablish his relationship with his people, the Jews. They will be the recipients of special privilege and honor. Zechariah the prophet put it this way: "Thus says the LORD of hosts, 'In those days ten men from all the nations will grasp the garment of a Jew saying, "Let us go with you, for we have heard that God is with you"'" (Zech. 8:23 NASB). These two aspects of the new covenant still await fulfillment.

The other two can, however, be experienced by the believer today. The indwelling of the Holy Spirit—that intimate relationship that we now enjoy with God (Rom. 8:16)—could not happen until Christ had been glorified (John 7:39). On the eve of the resurrection, Christ came to his disciples . . .

> and stood in their midst and said to them, "Peace be yours." And when he had said this, he showed them his two hands and his side and the disciples were glad when they saw the Lord. Jesus furthermore said to them, "Peace be yours; as the Father has sent me, I also send you." And when he had said this, he breathed on them and said unto them "Receive the Holy Spirit. If you forgive the sins of anyone,

they have been forgiven; if you retain any, they are retained."

—John 20:19b-23

Note the inclusion of both aspects of the new covenant that Christ had inaugurated three days earlier—the giving of the indwelling Holy Spirit and the experience of knowing forgiveness. What magnificent blessings we enjoy because of God's gracious covenant extended to Abram first, and by extension to all who believe.

Appendix A

Alternative Views on Genesis 1:1

Dependent Clause View

Though the message of Genesis 1:1 is profound in its simplicity, some readers of the Hebrew text have attempted to modify the translation of this verse so that its meaning is seriously weakened. One such attempt alters the grammar of the verse to the degree that Genesis 1:1 is no longer a complete, independent sentence; it is merely a dependent clause, introducing the main clause, which is verse 2. "In the beginning, *when* God created the heavens and the earth, the earth was. . . ."

The implications of this position are profound. If Genesis 1:1 is not an independent clause—a complete sentence that opens Day One—then the creation narrative does not teach that God is directly responsible for all that is, because when the main clause begins, the earth is already in existence. "Now the earth was . . ." (1:2). "Pre-existing matter was at hand, and, consequently, whatever *bārā'* [to create] may then mean, in the nature of the case it cannot denote absolute creation."[1] This is a serious error.

If one is committed to the evolutionary viewpoint of earth history, then the dependent-clause translation is entirely acceptable. In that case, one is not bound to the biblical text

---

[1]   Young, *Genesis One*, 2.

that teaches that God created all things and that he created them from nothing pre-existing.

To circumvent the clear statement of Genesis 1:1, either an adverb is added: "In the beginning *when* God began to create the heavens and the earth,"[2] or the first phrase is modified with a preposition: "In the beginning *of* creation, when God made heaven and earth (*The New English Bible*, 1972)." In either case, the first verse is subordinated to verse 2: "In the beginning of creation, when God made heaven and earth, the earth was without form and void."

Evidence from the Masoretic Accents

The later Hebrew scribes, called Masoretes, preserved the ancient traditions associated with the Torah by placing small marks around and within the original letters. These "points" were added between the fifth and tenth centuries AD, though the traditions they represent are from a much earlier time.[3] These markings indicate both vowel sounds and accents. The Masoretic accent placed in the first grammatical unit of the Hebrew is designed to show the presence of a thought break

---

[2] "When God began to form the universe" (*The James Moffatt Translation*, 1922);

"When God began to create the heavens and the earth" (*The Bible: An American Translation*, 1931);

"When God began to create the heaven and the earth" (*The New Jewish Version*, 1962);

"In the beginning, when God created the heavens and the earth" (*The New American Bible*, 1970);

"When God began creating the heavens and the earth" (*The Living Bible*, 1971) [not so *New Living Translation*, 1996)];

"In the beginning of creation, when God made heaven and earth" (*The New English Bible*, 1972).

[3] Certain aspects of the system are attributed "to Ezra himself" (Robert Gordis, *The Biblical Text in the Making: a Study of the Kethib-Qere* [New York: KTAV, 1971]: XXI).

between *beginning* and *God*. In English, such a break is often represented with a comma: "In the beginning, God created." If the Hebrew tradition had been otherwise, a continuation accent would have been placed in the word *beginning*. In English, such a continuation accent is often represented by the word *of*: "In the beginning of God's creating."

One of the functions of these accents "is to indicate the interrelationship of the words in the text. The accents are thus a good guide to the syntax of the text."[4] In this instance, it is clear that the oldest known Hebrew tradition understood the first phrase in the Torah to be in the absolute state, which makes the first verse an independent clause.

This precise grammatical phrase occurs nowhere else in the Hebrew Old Testament, but "terms like *reshith*, 'beginning,' *rosh*, 'beginning,' *qedem*, 'olden times,' and *'olam*, 'eternity,' when used in adverbial expressions, occur almost invariably *without* the article, and that in the absolute state."[5] Some examples include Isaiah 46:10; 41:4; and Proverbs 8:23.

The evidence from the received Hebrew text therefore points in only one direction. Genesis 1:1 describes an activity of God at a point in time. It does not allow for the pre-existence of the material (or angelic) realm before "in the beginning."

Evidence from the Septuagint

A second line of evidence in which "in the beginning" is understood to be in the absolute state comes from the third

---

4 Israel Yeivin, *Introduction to the Tiberian Masorah*, trans. and ed. E. J. Revell in *Masoretic Studies*, vol. 5, Harry M. Orlinsky, ed. (Missoula, Mont.: Scholars, 1980): 158. "At present it is best to consider the accents as an early and relatively reliable witness to a correct interpretation of the text" (Waltke and O'Connor, Syntax, 30).

5 Alexander Heidel, *The Babylonian Genesis* (Chicago: Univ. of Chicago Press, 1963): 92.

or early second century BC Greek translation, the Septuagint. It also translates the Hebrew text without the use of the definite article. This Greek phrase perfectly parallels its Hebrew counterpart. Therefore in Genesis 1:1, though it lacks the definite article, this Greek phrase must also be translated "in the beginning." Numerous times in the Septuagint, this anarthrous phrase is used to denote something specific.[6] This Greek phrase "is plainly a reference to the absolute beginning."[7]

Evidence from the New Testament

A third line of evidence for seeing "in the beginning" in the absolute state comes from similar phrases in the New Testament. "*In the beginning* was the Word, and the Word was with God, and the Word was God. He was *in the beginning* with God" (John 1:1-2 NASB).[8] These occurrences do not, strictly speaking, use the definite article; at the same time they bespeak a definite point in time and have led commentators such as Francis Schaeffer to conclude that "'in the beginning' is a technical term meaning 'in the beginning of all that was created.'"[9]

Another New Testament passage that points to this event of creation and uses "definite indications of time: at, on, during . . . 'in the beginning'"[10] is Hebrews 1:10. "You, LORD, in [*kat'*] the beginning laid the foundation of the earth, and the heavens are the works of Your hands" (NASB). The absence of the article in

---

6   See Gen. 10:10; 49:3; Num. 24:20; Deut. 21:17; etc.
7   H. C. Leupold, *Exposition of Genesis*, 2 vols. (Grand Rapids, Mich.: Baker, 1942): 1:39.
8   Robertson cites this passage as "definite," though lacking the article (A. T. Robertson, *A Grammar of the Greek New Testament in the Light of Historical Research* (Nashville: Broadman, 1934): 791-2.
9   Francis Schaeffer, *Genesis in Space and Time* (Downers Grove, Ill.: InterVarsity, 1972): 23.
10 BDAG, 512 B2a.

the Hebrew phrase "in the beginning" should not therefore be viewed as evidence that a specific point in time is not under consideration.

Evidence from the Early Versions

Finally, the early versions of the Bible argue that the Hebrew phrase was understood as definite. As the translator penned his rendition, it was inevitable that he chose between the absolute and construct states. "[W]ith no exceptions the ancient versions construed $b^e r \hat{e} sh \hat{i} th$ as an absolute."[11] Bruce K. Waltke lists the following early versions as evidencing "in the beginning" in the absolute state: "LXX, Vulgate, Aquila, Theodotion, Symmachus, Targum Onkelos."[12] This is also true of the two major Syriac traditions.[13] In none is it rendered as a dependent phrase.

The evidence for seeing "in the beginning" as an independent clause is ancient and widespread.[14] "The use of this root leaves no doubt that Gen[esis] 1:1 opens with the very first and initial act of the creation of the cosmos."[15]

So what is the sense of "in the beginning"? The phrase is a chronological marker; it denotes the opening of Day One of creation week.[16] One would indeed expect a sequential text like Genesis 1 to use a definitive term to indicate the start of

---

[11] Young, *Genesis One*, 5.

[12] Bruce K. Waltke, "The Creation Account in Gen. 1:1-3," *Bibliotheca Sacra* 132 (1975): 223.

[13] J. Payne Smith, *A Compendious Syriac Dictionary* (Oxford: Clarendon, 1903): 540.

[14] The most current biblical Hebrew lexicon states that seeing this phrase as "an independent main clause" is "probably to be preferred" (HALOT, 1169).

[15] William White, *"r'shît,"* in *Theological Wordbook of the Old Testament*, 2 vols. (Chicago: Moody Press, 1980): 2:826.

[16] Though E. J. Young differs on the length of the days of creation, he concurs, "the commencement of the first day, we believe, was at the very beginning" (Young, *Genesis One*, 89).

the sequence of creation, and this is clearly the function of the phrase "in the beginning." Day One had begun.

Summary Statement View

It is common among evangelical commentators to view the first verse of the Bible as nothing more than a summary or introductory statement for the entire chapter. "In recent years it has become commonplace to take this first verse as a title for the whole chapter."[17] This would mean, then, that the creation narrative actually begins with verse 2. Therefore, the first recorded creative act of that six-day period occurred when God called into existence the light of verse 3.

The result of this position is to effectively remove any statement indicating that God created initial matter. Is matter eternal? Has the universe always existed? Those holding the summary statement view could logically answer these questions in the affirmative.

To understand Genesis 1:1 as merely a summary of the first chapter of Genesis is to begin the account of creation with the raw material for the heavens and earth already in existence. Such a position is unfortunate in light of the all-inclusive nature of John 1:3—"All things came into being through Him; and apart from Him nothing came into being that has come into being" (NASB). Notice also the clear statement in Nehemiah.

> You alone are the LORD.
> You have made the heavens,
> The heaven of heavens with all their host,
> The earth and all that is on it,
> The seas and all that is in them.

---

17 Sailhamer, *Genesis Unbounded*, 102.

You give life to all of them
And the heavenly host bows down before you.

—Nehemiah 9:6 NASB

Based on these statements alone, the position that sees Genesis 1:1 as a summary statement should be abandoned.

If the summary statement view is adopted, the Bible opens with "a primeval, dark, watery, and formless state prior to creation."[18] These conditions have been viewed by various commentators as expressions of evil or as the result of some judgmental action.[19] The origin of these sinister concepts then lies quite beyond the pale of inquiry. "The Book of Genesis does not inform us concerning the origin of that which is contrary to the nature of God, neither in the cosmos nor in the world of the spirit."[20] Such a view severely limits the study of the origin of the spirit world. It also forfeits the chronology of God's first creative acts that dovetail so perfectly with other passages in the Bible.

The mere fact that the second verse begins with the word *and* argues strongly that the first verse is not a title that can be viewed separately from the rest of the chapter. The exegetical sacrifice required to designate Genesis 1:1 a chapter title or a summary statement is too great. It shortens the first day, it destroys the concept of initial creation, and it deals improperly with the Hebrew construction of verse 2.

---

[18] Bruce K. Waltke, "The Creation Account in Genesis 1:1-3. Part IV: The Theology of Genesis 1," *Bibliotheca Sacra* 132:528 (October 1975): 329.

[19] See *The New Scofield Reference Bible* (New York: Oxford, 1967): 1, n.5 and 752-3, n. 2.

[20] Waltke, "Creation," 338.

Appendix B

Chart of the Year in the Ark

Noah's call

building the ark during the 120 years
plus loading it with food
Gen. 6:3, 14, 21

Enter!

7 days
loading
animals
Gen 7:1-10

destruction begins

40 days
7:11-12
[600:2:17]

0

Flood crests canopy emptied

40

110 more days
of havoc 7:24

—— Marb bul ——

God remembers Noah

150

1. Ark rests 8:4 [600:7:17]
2. Shut off rain 8:2
3. Stops earthquake activity 8:2
4. Sent wind to
   drive off the water
   separate the continents

mountains become visible

223

water no longer
lapped on side of ark
8:5 [600:10:1]
40 days of drying 8:6

raven and dove sent out

263

dove dove

270 277

7 days 7 days
8:10 8:12

removes top

313

36 days 8:13
[601:1:1]
ground looks dry

57 days

Leave!

370

8:14-19
[601:2:27]
ground is dry!

This chart assumes that a month had 30 days and a year had 360 days. [Compare Genesis 8:3 with 8:4]

Stanley V. Udd

Index

A

Abel 137–143, 147–148, 150, 232
Abraham 92, 150–151, 153, 155, 159, 234–235
Abrahamic covenant 233–236
Abram 154–155, 158–159, 216, 233–235, 239
Altar ix, 199
Annihilation 185
Ararat 174, 192, 194, 224
Ark x, xii, 64, 145, 163–164, 171–185, 188, 190, 192–199, 204, 208–209, 211–213, 227, 248
Assyria 91, 94, 98, 222
Atmosphere 27, 33, 37–46, 57–59, 61, 182, 200, 210–212, 231

B

Babel x, 217, 222–225, 229–230
Barge 174, 177, 183–184
Blessing 56, 64, 68, 70, 84, 86, 202, 233–235, 238–239
Breath of life 45, 71, 100, 168, 174, 178, 181, 185, 204

C

Cain 97–98, 136–147, 232
Canopy 38, 41–45, 57, 144, 182, 189, 191, 193, 197, 200, 210–211, 231
Capital punishment 79, 142, 150, 206
Carnivorousness 72, 204, 207
Carnivory 204
Chaos 31–32, 183, 187, 209
Cherubim 93, 129, 138
Clean animals 177, 180, 199
Coal 62, 127, 145–146, 186, 197, 212, 231
Completed creation view 83–84
Conceptions 123, 137, 169
Continental drift 47, 188, 190
Continuous creation view 83–84
Corrupt 168, 171, 203
Covenant 21, 121–122, 175–176, 205, 208–209, 233–239
Covenant with nature 208–209
Creationism 1, 13–15
Creation of time 18, 22
Creepers 65, 70, 181, 185, 198

Curse 72, 76, 89, 97, 103, 109,
        119–121, 123–129, 135, 137,
        141–144, 197, 199–200, 204,
        214–215, 233–234
Curse on Canaan 214–215
Cush 91, 94, 96, 98, 222, 224

D

Deceive 116
Demonic assistance 166
Dependent clause 241
Die 21, 102, 104, 109, 111–112, 117,
        122, 129, 143
Dinosaurs x, 61–64, 186, 210
Dispersion 213, 217, 221, 230
Door 138–139, 144, 172, 181–182
Dove 110, 195–196

E

Eden 71, 91–95, 97–99, 101–103,
        129–130, 132, 135, 138, 143–
        145, 172, 182, 187, 197, 210, 232
'Elohîm 163, 223
Enoch 143–144, 152
Euphrates 91, 94–95, 99, 197–198
Eve ix, 24, 35, 67–68, 70–71,
        78, 93, 106, 108, 110–117,
        119–121, 123–126, 128–132,
        135–138, 148, 150, 231
Evolutionism 1, 7, 10, 14
Ex nihilo 24, 60
Expanse of the heavens 52, 60

F

Faith xi, 1, 12–13, 24, 35, 48, 57,
        78, 124, 140, 143, 152, 176,
        179, 231, 234–235
Families ix, 64, 70, 148, 156, 159,
        182, 190, 194–200, 204,
        217–222, 224, 227–230,
        233, 235
Firmament 37–38
Flaming sword 129, 139
Forgiveness 143, 237–239
Fossil 2–3, 7, 10–11, 41, 64, 72,
        186, 204, 212
Fountain 39, 47–48, 89–90,
        181, 191

G

Garden of Eden 71, 92–94, 102–
        103, 129, 145, 172, 182, 197
Genealogy x, 80, 144, 149, 152–
        157, 159, 217–218, 220, 227
Geography 94–95, 97–99, 178,
        193, 221, 228
Giants 72, 164
Gihon 91, 94–96, 98
Glory 18, 34, 59, 67, 74–75, 77, 80,
        85, 101
Gopher wood 171
Grace ix, 18, 41, 63, 122, 125, 170
Great deep 39, 47–50, 89–90, 181,
        183–185, 189, 231

H

Ham 86, 152–154, 170, 181, 213–215, 217–221, 230

Havilah 91, 94, 96–97

Heaven ix, x, 13, 16, 18, 21–23, 26–28, 30, 34, 37–39, 42–46, 48–49, 52–53, 59–61, 64, 66–68, 70–71, 73, 82–83, 85–86, 104, 122, 130–131, 134, 162, 167–168, 174–175, 177, 181, 185, 191, 200, 203–204, 209, 211, 223–224, 241–242, 244, 246

Hiddekel 91, 94–96, 98

Holy Spirit 33, 81, 100, 169, 237–239

Horizontality 2, 7, 9, 12

Hosts 13, 28–31, 54, 67, 82, 124, 133, 238, 246–247

I

Ice Ages 211, 213

Image of God 66–67, 74–81, 106, 150–151, 206

J

Japheth 86, 152–154, 170, 181, 213–221, 230

K

King of Tyre 27, 132–134

L

Labor pains 123, 126

Language vii, 16–17, 25, 43, 57, 75, 85, 97, 110, 170, 175, 215, 220, 223, 225–229, 232

Leviathan vii, 61–63, 71

Lie xi, xii, 2, 7–9, 13, 39, 68, 72, 78, 110, 112, 115, 126, 135, 142, 149, 156–157, 176, 189, 192, 205, 212, 247

Likeness 21, 66–67, 75–76, 79–80, 100, 103, 137, 149–151, 168, 206

Living creatures 60, 63, 65, 70, 104–105, 199, 208–209

Loin coverings 117

M

Mabbûl 174–177, 180–181, 183–192, 195, 199, 201, 204, 208–209, 211, 216, 228, 231

Marriage 106–107, 159, 162

Meander 91, 96

Months 39, 52, 55, 57–58, 111, 181–182, 186, 188, 190, 192–198

Moral choice 77–79, 104, 113, 115

Murder 137, 140–142, 147, 150–151, 231

Myth xii, 70, 86

N

Naked 105, 108, 117–119, 129,
    214–215
Nakedness 108, 119, 214–215
Natural gas 186
New covenant 205, 236–239
Nimrod 222–225, 232
Nineveh 31, 163, 222–223
Noah x, xiii, 10, 39, 44, 47, 57,
    63–64, 86, 88, 95, 99, 126,
    148, 152, 154–155, 165–166,
    168, 170–173, 175–182, 185–
    188, 190, 192, 194–202, 204,
    207–208, 211–218, 220–221,
    224, 227, 234

O

Offering 137–140, 177, 199–
    200, 207
Oil 186, 231
Organic succession 3, 10–12
Orogeny 190
Overpopulation 69–70

P

Pacific Ocean 189
Pain 123–124, 126, 128, 169
Peleg 154, 230
Physiology 121, 124, 205

Pishon 91, 94–96
Plain of Shinar 213, 223–224, 226
Polygamy 145–146, 231
Predictability 6
Prevailed 184

R

Raged 185
Rainbow 208–210
Rationalization 113–116
Raven 195
Reign of terror 203, 207
Revival 147–148
River 91–99, 197–198, 213,
    223–224
Roof x, 42, 172–173

S

Satan 28, 110, 112–113, 122, 132–
    135, 234
Scattered vii, x, 145, 187, 190, 198,
    224–227, 230, 232
Scroll xiii, 67, 86, 149, 217
Seamounts 189
Seat of power 223–224
Sedimentary rock 1–3, 7, 10–11,
    99, 145, 185, 212, 231
Separation 93, 117–118, 218, 221,
    228, 230
Sequence 5, 9–10, 17–18, 22, 29,
    87, 164, 246

Serpent 31, 63, 109–112, 115–116, 118–123, 126, 132, 135, 204

Seth 79–80, 137, 147–148, 150, 152

Sevens 177

Shem 86, 152–155, 170, 181, 213–218, 220–221, 230

Shrub of the field 86–88

Signs 52, 54–57, 142–143, 208–209, 231

Sonship 162

Sons of God 29, 33, 77, 80, 100, 161–162, 165

Sorry 167

Stars 27, 29, 38, 52–53, 55–58, 61

Story xiii, 7, 67, 86–87, 149, 158–159, 164, 170, 172, 179, 213–215, 217–218

Superposition 2, 7, 9, 12

T

Terah 86, 154, 158–159

Thorns and thistles 126, 197

Time ix, xiii, 3, 6–7, 9–10, 12–15, 17–23, 28, 33–36, 38–39, 42–44, 47–49, 53–54, 56, 58–59, 63–65, 67, 69, 74, 78, 83, 86, 88, 95, 98, 106, 121–122, 124, 126, 132, 137, 142–145, 147–150, 152–153, 155–157, 162–163, 165, 172, 175–176, 179–180, 182, 188–190, 193, 196–197, 202, 204, 209, 212, 214, 222, 225, 228–229, 238, 242–245

Tree of Life 93, 101–102, 128–131, 138, 197

Tree of the Knowledge of Good and Evil 101–104, 111–112, 114, 117, 130

Tyrants 163–165, 222

U

Uniformitarianism 2–7, 12

Ur 158–159

Useless plants 125, 197, 200

V

Vapor 43–44, 58, 212

Vegetation 24, 50–51, 87–89, 101, 126–127, 197, 212

Violence 133, 148, 168, 171

W

Water cluster ions 40–41

Wind 33, 42, 44, 174, 188, 190, 192–193, 200, 232

Window 7, 39, 181, 191, 194, 200

Windows of heaven 39, 181, 191, 200

Z

Ziggurat 224